D1559521

WITHDRAWN

DANCING ON
COMMON GROUND

DANCING ON COMMON GROUND

Tribal Cultures and Alliances on the Southern Plains

HOWARD MEREDITH

UNIVERSITY PRESS OF KANSAS

© 1995 by the University Press of Kansas
All rights reserved

Published by the University Press of Kansas (Lawrence,
Kansas 66049), which was organized by the Kansas Board of
Regents and is operated and funded by Emporia State
University, Fort Hays State University, Kansas State University,
Pittsburg State University, the University of Kansas, and
Wichita State University

Library of Congress Cataloging-in-Publication Data

Meredith, Howard L.
Dancing on common ground : tribal cultures and alliances on
the southern Plains / Howard Meredith.
p.   cm.
Includes bibliographical references and index.
ISBN 0-7006-0694-7 (cloth : alk. paper)
1. Indians of North America—Great Plains—Politics and
government.   2. Indians of North America—Great Plains—
Social life and customs.
3. Indian dance—Great Plains.   I. Title.
E78.G73M45   1995   94-23557
978'.00497—dc20

British Library Cataloguing in Publication Data is available.

Printed in the United States of America

10 9 8 7 6 5 4 3 2 1

The paper used in this publication meets the minimum requirements
of the American National Standard for Permanence of Paper for
Printed Library Materials Z39.48-1984.

CONTENTS

MAPS

(photo sections follow Chapters 6, 10, and 12)

ACKNOWLEDGMENTS

Although this book is my own responsibility based upon years of experience and research, I am unusually indebted to several gifted people who have inspired and supported me in this effort. I thank the late Vynola Beaver Newkumet (Caddo) and her husband Phil Newkumet for their trust in working with me as to the importance of dance as a metaphor of significance in the Southern Plains life. Much of the thought and feeling in this book has come from my association with tradition bearers, especially Pauline Beaver Harjo (Arapaho); Reatha Cussen (Caddo); Lawrence Hart (Cheyenne); Doc Tate Nevaquaya (Comanche); Linda Poolaw (Delaware); Pat Regan (Fort Sill Apache); Beverly Hicks, Vickie Boettger, and Vanessa Morgan (Kiowa); Gary McAdams, Vanessa Vance, and Wanda Bowman (Wichita). I also thank C. Blue Clark, executive vice-president and professor of American Indian Studies, Oklahoma City University, and Charlotte Heth, associate director for Public Programming, National Museum of the American Indian of the Smithsonian Institution, for reading the manuscript in its entirety. I wish to thank John Feaver, executive vice-president for Academic Affairs, and Roy Trout, president, University of Science and Arts of Oklahoma, for their continuing support of the American Indian Studies degree program. I am grateful to Cynthia Miller, editor-in-chief, University Press of Kansas, for her interest in the manuscript and useful advice. Finally, I thank my wife Mary Ellen Meredith for her involvement in American Indian concerns and her patience.

1

INTRODUCTION

The images and concepts for this book had their beginnings in discussions in American Indian Studies courses at the University of Science and Arts of Oklahoma. Members of the Southern Plains tribes—Apache of Oklahoma, or Plains Apache; Caddo; Cheyenne and Arapaho; Comanche; Delaware of Western Oklahoma; Fort Sill Apache, or Chiricahua; and Warm Springs Apache, Kiowa, and Wichita—enriched these courses. Invited spokespersons such as Mildred Cleghorn, chairperson of the Fort Sill Apache; the late Newton Lamar, chairperson of the Wichita and Affiliated Tribes and chair of the National Tribal Chairmen's Association; Ross Swimmer, then assistant secretary of interior; and others added institutional perspectives to the classroom forum. The discussions made it clear that formal studies of the Southern Plains tribes and their intertribal alliance systems suffered from a lack of attention on the part of scholars.

My own research began with studies of the Caddo or Hasinai traditional perspectives, and my work on traditional tribal approaches to life on the Southern Plains led to the perception of a continuing network of intertribal activities and mutual support among the diverse peoples of the region. I then expanded my work in order to understand the abuse the tribes experienced in the late nineteenth and early twentieth centuries and the crisis that continues in contemporary tribal affairs. I found unexamined archival resources and oral traditions concerning governance and intertribal activity. As my research continued an overarching reality emerged: the United States radically altered tribal affairs, thus damaging traditional relationships, and manipulated decisionmaking processes by enforcing unilateral and secularized relations unsystematically. Factors leading to political and economic destabilization, intervention, and ethnicity paralleled political reform in the United States; intertribal and international systems were distorted so that self-organizing patterns of existence no longer functioned within natural forms.

Peoples of diverse backgrounds found their way to the Southern Plains as the modern era began. Until the nineteenth century the population of the region had consisted primarily of Native American peoples, but by the beginning of the twentieth century the Anglo-American population became dominant both in numbers and in political control of the area.

An understanding of the interaction among these various peoples also has been dominated by Anglo-Americans, who emphasized the conflicts of the various segments of the societies on the Southern Plains. Anglo-American thought depended largely upon intelligent analysis, adequate information, and skilled argument, an approach that relied generally upon Western European adversarial systems of thought in academics, law, and politics. The assumption has been that perceptions and values were common, universal, and permanent, a premise that generally excluded native tribal perceptions and values contained within Southern Plains images and concepts. Much of the documented information available to scholars—military records, Indian service records, legal records—reflected U.S. policy decisions; thus, the truths that were expressed were largely ethnocentric in nature.

Historical studies, in particular, presented arguments based upon popular theoretical frameworks such as Turner's frontier hypothesis, Marxist historical materialism, and the "consensus style" of interpretation. These lines of thought portrayed the Southern Plains Indian presence as little more than a "barrier to civilization." Henrietta Whiteman, a Southern Cheyenne scholar from the Southern Plains, has suggested that "Cheyenne history, and by extension Indian history, in all probability will never be incorporated into American history because it is holistic, human, personal, and sacred. Though it is equally as valid as Anglo-American history it is destined to remain complementary to white secular American History."[1]

Relationships are perceived in different ways by Anglo-American and Native American communities. Cultural assumptions, or conceptual overlays that people may or may not place upon experience, affect values and attitudes. Native cultures indigenous to the

Southern Plains are part of that very experience itself. Conceptual systems are fundamentally metaphorical by nature. Multicultural perceptions of reality thus provide for a truly intellectual vision of the world.

In Anglo-American culture, as in its Western European antecedents, propositions, arguments, and metaphorical systems are grounded in largely adversarial positions. Rational arguments exist as a form of warfare, and strategy and tactics are reasonably assumed to include intimidation, threat, authority, insult, challenge, bargaining, and flattery. In such a system, policy matters are managed in adversarial terms; past examples include the Indian Wars of the 1870s and contemporary ones the War on Poverty of the 1960s and the War on Drugs of the 1980s. No matter the policy focus, with the Anglo-American system of governance the metaphor of war is critical to understanding it. Winning at all costs is paramount.

In the cultural perspectives of the Southern Plains tribes, propositions, arguments, and metaphorical positions are viewed in terms of dance. The participants are perceived as performers; the goal is to perform in a harmonious and aesthetically pleasing way. Arguments and policy formulation are experienced differently, carried out differently, and talked about differently. Metaphorical coherence is grounded in terms of dance.

Anglo-Americans have not viewed the Southern Plains tribes as putting forth arguments at all but have perceived them as simply responding differently. Yet the Southern Plains tribes have expressed their world visions in propositions set forth in the form of dance, for example the Caddo and Wichita Turkey Dance, the Kiowa, Plains Apache, Cheyenne and Arapaho Sun Dance, or the Chiricahua and Warm Springs Apache Fire Dance. Still, Anglo-Americans apparently are unable to perceive the tribal dances as "argument." Even if the words are translated in meaningful form, the interpretive structural differences make successful communication difficult if not impossible in many instances.

A clearer understanding of the tribal peoples of the Southern Plains is buried in endless collections of data. Studies from an ethnological perspective or from the angle of historical materialism attempt to freeze the cultures in the past, and such interpretive findings have been used largely in response to the curiosity of the Anglo-American media and by scholars. In some instances these

collections have served American Indian studies in the investigation of certain problems. But as American Indian people made
increasing demands on these journalistic and academic investigations, the conception of and feeling toward issues began to change
dramatically. In most instances a broader frame of reference than
that offered by the various disciplines is needed.

Eight cultural factors provide a framework through which the
lasting concerns of the Southern Plains tribes can better be examined:

1. Every culture is of critical importance to its possessor.
2. To understand individuals in another culture it is necessary to
   have some appreciation of their worldview.
3. All individuals function in a culture and are a part of it.
4. Every phase of life reflects a cultural frame of reference.
5. A knowledge of the specific environment in which a culture
   exists indicates the relationships among all aspects of that
   community's life.
6. All worldviews are self-complete and self-contained.
7. Cogent analysis must include interactions that are formed
   when tribes and larger systems come together and create
   patterns that either facilitate or impede issue resolution and
   human development.
8. Synthesis must provide an aesthetic response in which judgment always adheres to moral, medical, or logical assess-
   ments rather than separating them out.

Non-Western cultures have not received a significant degree of
attention as functioning elements in the United States. By federal
law, American Indian tribes and individuals have been considered
as wards in a paternalistic system that has existed for more than
160 years. At the core of the U.S. Indian policy is the need for
control, and dependency and dishonesty have resulted from this
policy. Each tribal population has suffered along with the Anglo-
American population because of paternalism. The American Indian
people are critically important to the sense of well-being of all
peoples. They have set aside their own physical, emotional, and
spiritual needs for the sake of others; they come into the present
overburdened and exhausted.

As the Native American societies took part in the destructive relationships with the U.S. government, they have in turn inculcated many of the Western European traits into their own worldviews. These have added to the confusion and multiplied the complexities of issues that native societies continue to confront. In this book I try to look beyond the framework of blame that has emerged in the United States. Although the focus is on tribes and larger systems, many of the principles pertain to individuals as well. The larger systems addressed are primarily public-sector assistance and human services, including spiritual complexes, health-related communities, educational facilities, and institutional governance.

2
SOUTHERN PLAINS
ENVIRONMENTS

Human existence on the Southern Plains began in myth and in the context of the nuclear and extended family. That existence developed from a basis of individuals, families, tribes, and larger sustaining systems including the ecological environment. In traditional thought each feature of the land had its own spiritual being. To live effectively people had to consult and confront the land and the sky. Thus the people and the environment existed and continue to exist in an all-inclusive context that shapes and guides mutual expectations, specific interactions, and outcomes.

Food, water, and shelter remain fundamental to physical, spiritual, social, and material well-being. Each culture has provided for these needs in different ways, using different technologies. The interaction between a society and its physical environment reveals imaginative responses to essentially the same issues basic to existence. The provisions for an adequate environmental infrastructure—water, sanitation, solid-waste management, sustainable development of food resources—in each culture on the Southern Plains have been necessary for environmental protection, increased productivity, better health, and the alleviation of grinding poverty. Sustainable development and efficient use of resources were and continue to be a priority in cultural concerns. These matters were addressed by the Southern Plains peoples in an ecological systems approach that focused on the interactions of the families and tribes with each other and with the environment.

In each of the cultural approaches to the Southern Plains, including the various American Indian cultural expressions as well as the Anglo-American, the imagination served as the authentic voice of the people. It is time to rediscover the imaginative interactions of peoples with each other and with their environment on the plains since our view has become clouded in the contemporary period by the undue sentimentality of individualism, the brutality of efficiency, and the aggrandizement of power.

The systematic approach of the native cultures is reflected in the sense of wholeness in which imagination and perception, thinking and feeling, self and world are one. The tribal imaginations and perceptions responded as a unitary whole; the peoples sensed and responded directly to the world. The tribal peoples, each in their own manner, transfigured matter through wonder within self-organizing systems. This aesthetic perception enhanced the given beyond itself within a cosmic arrangement. The environment was integrated into the very being of the people in an intimate way, and thus did the people face the world. They gained a sense of the Southern Plains expressed in myth and concept: the environment, as image, provided for their sense of the eternal.

The Southern Plains environment bears witness to itself in the image it offers, and its depth lies in the complexities of this image. All things show faces. The earth and its objects are coded signatures to be read for meaning. As the Native American cultures have learned, the objects of the earth are expressive forms that speak and relate their shape. Indeed, these objects regard the people beyond as humans may regard them. This imaginative claim on attention signalizes the spirits in the earth and its objects. The Southern Plains animates its images and thereby affects human imagination. The spirit of the plains corresponds to and coalesces with that of human beings, thus allowing an aesthetic response to the world.

The types of cross-relationships vary in their detail and efficacy. Although they have undergone many modifications over the past several thousand years, in one form or another they are part of the fundamental systems of development that affected the peopling of the Southern Plains and that framed lasting patterns of belief carried by American Indian peoples into the present.

The environment of the Southern Plains is that of a sunbaked landscape; the sun shines as many as 250 days each year. The surface geology of the region was built up as a broad, relatively flat outwash apron or series of alluvial fans extending from the base of the Rocky Mountains. Constant aggradation resulted in raised stream courses, which then overflowed into lower channels. The rolling topography provides a sense of wildness and isolation, a feeling of a land of freedom.[1]

The modern Southern Plains climate is primarily semiarid, with anywhere from fifteen to thirty inches of precipitation a year as lines of average precipitation move east and west in wetter or drier years. Maximum rainfall occurs in spring, primarily from April through June, with a second period of relatively intense rainfall in September. The driest portion of the year is winter, from December through February. Modern extended droughts occurred in the mid-1890s, from 1910 to 1919, the 1930s, and from 1951 to 1957.[2]

Mixed and short grasses dominate the region. The flat to rolling eastern portion of the area is underlain with Permian sandstone. Soils are formed predominantly from sandy and shale bedrock, with alluvium in the river valleys. In the Southern Plains, matured soils are characterized by a dark rich surface layer that varies from dark gray-brown or black in the east to lighter brown in the west. A layer of alkaline slats or caliche has developed below the soil, and valleys exhibit a series of buried soils along the streams and river courses. Major rivers include from north to south the Arkansas, Cimarron, North and South Canadian, Washita, Red, Pease, and Brazos. Native plants include bluestem-gramma prairie in the east and the shorter buffalo grass, needlegrass-gramma plains in the west. On the flood plains cottonwoods and willows grow in small stands, and some isolated groves of postoak, elm, and blackjack cover the uplands. The eastern portion of the Southern Plains is bordered by the Cross Timbers or the oak-hickory savannah that runs north and south through the area that is now Texas and Oklahoma.[3]

Abundant native animals that figure heavily in American mythology have survived the modern changes on the Southern Plains: antelope, coyote, prairie dog, prairie chicken, jackrabbit, quail, and various snakes and other reptiles. Buffalo, bear, beaver, and turkey are gaining numbers after being driven to the point of extinction during the Anglo-American period of dominance. The extensive grasslands originally supported herds of millions of buffalo, with large numbers of deer in the wooded areas along the streambeds.[4]

Surface topography is largely rolling prairie and plains. The greatest relief in the Southern Plains is the Wichita Mountains, which serve as sanctuary for all the peoples of the region. It contains holy ground, including Rainy Mountain and Medicine Bluff Creek. The mountains form a very old uplift of granite. The highest point in the geological past was 10,000 to 15,000 feet above the surrounding surface, but the shallow Permian Sea brought the level of the land to within a few hundred feet of the upper reaches of the mountains. Most of the grasses of the blind savannahs in the mountains are those of the tall-grass prairie, such as big bluestem. Trees include oaks, hackberry, black walnut, elm, and white ash.

The high plains, in the west, are relatively flat and increasingly drier than the rest of the Southern Plains. Because of the higher altitude, this western portion of the region experiences the coldest winters and the greatest snowfall. Buffalo, needle, and gramma grasses dominate the surface and sagebrush and yucca grow on the valley slopes. Scattered cottonwood trees live along the stream margins, with plum thickets and willows on the terraces. Buffalo, antelope, quail, prairie chicken, rabbit, prairie dog, and various snakes remain native to the area.

The Southern Plains grasslands have long been occupied by humans—first by hunters of the great herds of big game, then by the farmers with their crops of cereal grains of amaranth and later corn or maize, and finally by the nomadic peoples of the modern era with the introduction of the horse. The fertile soil has favored all who cared for it, first as pasture and then in intensive forms of agriculture.

The terrestrial biotic regions within the Southern Plains show the effects of gradients that exist in the climate. Complexity appears to be accompanied by stability, however. Human beings among the tribes who occupied the Southern Plains observed and respected this complexity as their aesthetic relationships with the environment has proved to be sustainable over thousands of years. Then within the past 150 years, the Anglo-American population sought to simplify the complex so that it could be managed. Yet such simplification has proved to be dangerous, setting in motion the factors that contribute to instability within the complex communities of this rigorous natural environment.

Change and recurrence in the biotic region or ecosystem occur as part of being alive; the earth shifts continually. The quality of the personal image of space and time is crucial for individual and community well-being. The external physical environment plays a role in building and supporting that sense of place and age among the various peoples who have made this region their home. And the relationship is reciprocal.

Climatic fluctuations have altered the Southern Plains through time, with fossil pollen, animal remains, and soil studies providing a record of the environment through these changes. Dramatic worldwide cooling apparently began 70,000 years ago. The last continental ice sheet began accumulating and spreading when a significant temperature decline occurred approximately 25,000 years ago, theoretically the period in which human beings first appeared on earth. Although ice sheets reached across the Northern Plains of North America, they did not cover the Southern Plains. South of the ice mass was a narrow band of tundra-covered loess and glacial outwash; farther south, pine, fir, and deciduous forest covered the plains.[5]

Core samples taken in present-day Caddo County in southwest Oklahoma indicate the presence of pine forests and parklands about 16,000 years ago, when the climate was cooler and more moist. Bison, camel, small horse, mastodon, and mammoth lived in the region. In nearby Kiowa County the Cooperton site of mammoth remains dates from about 17,000 years ago.[6]

Between 16,000 and 11,500 years ago, all indications point to a slowly warming climate. Ten thousand years ago the glacial retreat was well under way. During this time mastodons, mammoths, horses, camels, ground sloths, and the larger cats became extinct. Dated evidence of human contact with the large game animals exists at the Domebo site in Caddo County, a kill-site with flint blades found beside mammoth remains and dated approximately 10,500 years ago. By this period pollen indicates a grass-dominated landscape, including marshy settings with cottonwood and elm near open grasslands, suggesting that climate was more moist and winters milder than today.[7]

Over 200 years ago, the buffalo ranged over two-thirds of the North American continent from the Appalachian Mountains to the Great Basin of Nevada and from the Gulf of Mexico to Great Slave Lake in Canada. The buffalo trails were innumerable, leading from river crossings and salt supplies into prairies, where grass grew in abundance. Some of the wide trails were imbedded one foot or more into the soil. The buffalo remained central to life on the plains until the latter half of the nineteenth century, and their image remains

Table 1.1. Southern Plains Environments

Date	Climate	Culture
10,500 B.P.	Late glacial stage	Late paleolithic big-game hunting
8,500 B.P.	Retreat of the glaciers	Hunting and gathering cultures
7,000 B.P.	Warm, arid climate	
4,000 B.P.	Warm, moist climate	River valley agriculture
500 B.P.	Warm, semiarid climate	Plains horse culture

important to each of the Southern Plains tribes. The destruction of the buffalo to the point of extinction by the Anglo-American culture marked the end of a 10,000-year period and ruptured the traditional life of the tribes of the Southern Plains. In turn the ecological system was harshly disrupted within a matter of two or three decades.

In the Washita River basin in Grady, Caddo, and Washita counties of Oklahoma the pollen record consisted of zero to eight feet of oak, hickory, cedar, and grass, probably established about 4,000 years ago, and eight to sixteen feet of grass, ragweed, and amaranth, probably bearing witness to vegetation common during the warm, dry interval of 7,000 to 4,000 years ago. Then from sixteen to twenty-four feet oak and hickory pollens peak and decrease, but pine pollen increases.[8]

The Domebo Canyon and Cedar Creek areas reveal evidence of soil development and marshes between 9,000 and 11,000 years ago. Between 5,000 and 4,000 years ago, the Southern Plains climate began to exhibit conditions supporting plant and animal life similar to that known in the contemporary period. People have sustained themselves in the Southern Plains through at least 600 generations and possibly through 1,800.

The extremes of the seasons in today's climate apparently were a less significant factor in the periods from approximately 10,500 to 7,000 years ago and again from about 4,000 to 1,000 years ago. In relation to the earth, specifically the Southern Plains, certain characteristics have framed and continue to frame human existence: the erratic and limited quality of precipitation, the fragile nature of soils and drainage systems, the hardiness and diversity of plants and animals, the extreme and incessant effects of wind and sun, the pronounced seasonal and daily temperature fluctuations.

The Southern Plains manifests a subtle and majestic ecological system; weather systems are dynamic. The indigenous peoples who have lived within this system have found accommodation for long-term sustainable development. Their examples raise many questions about the relationships of systems in general: What methods for understanding relationships between tribes and larger systems allow the recognition of patterns, process, contextual constraints, and themes? How can tribal involvement with larger systems inform current practice? How does a particular larger system interact with tribal affairs for specific outcomes? What are common interactional regularities between tribes and larger systems? What are the effects of actual secrets and presumed secrets in tribal–larger-system relationships? What are the effects of blurred boundaries among various components of a larger system? What are the elements necessary to create beneficial relationships between tribes and larger systems? What are the leadership patterns in tribal–larger-systems relations?

The physical environment of the Southern Plains in its diversity through the past several thousand years has brought forth a variety of social responses. These interactions of cultures with the ecological systems and with other cultures must be seen as living entities. Each of the cultures required the space, time, and spiritual complexities of the plains to sustain itself. These relationships of people to the earth, to the animals, and to the plants exist at the center of the tribal and cultural experiences. An understanding of the chronogeography of the region has brought about the realization of temporal heterogeneity. The peoples of the Southern Plains have learned to recognize in the landscape the memories of the past with which they coexist. They know that they live in a larger system where the different but interlocking times and landscapes of many pasts continue to exist.

N. Scott Momaday, a Kiowa author and poet, built upon his own tribal tradition as it interacts within larger systems in proposing a "land ethic." Thus he wrote about the idea of a Native American attitude toward the ecological system. He saw that it required an act of imagination to bring about an understanding of the physical environment and of the biosystem in which we live. This act of imagination stems directly from cultural experience so that people perceive the landscape in appropriate ways:

My father used to tell me of an old man who has lived a whole life. I have often thought of this image. The old man used to come to my grandfather's house periodically to pay visits, and my father has very vivid recollections of this man whom I never knew. But his name was Chaney. Father says that Chaney would come to the house and he would make himself perfectly at home. He would be passing by going from one place to another, exercising his ethnic prerogative for nomadism. But he would make my grandfather's a kind of resting place. He stayed there on many occasions. My father says that every morning when Chaney was there as a guest he would get up in the first light, paint his face, go outside, face east, and bring the sun out of the horizon. Then he would pray. He would pray aloud to the rising sun. He did that because it was appropriate that he should do that. He understood. Or perhaps I should say that in terms of his own understanding, the sun was the origin of his strength. He understood the sun, within a more formal religious context, similar to the way someone else understands the presence of a deity. And in the face of that recognition, he acted naturally or appropriately. Through the medium of prayer, he returned some of his strength to the sun. He did this everyday. It was part of his daily life. It was as natural and appropriate to him as anything could be.[9]

Like the man in the presence of the sun, the contemporary tribal peoples of the Southern Plains retain a sense of being comfortable with nature and with the responsibility for its well-being. Natural and appropriate action within the ecological and cultural systems has come only with observation and discipline. When this old man prayed, he prayed not just for himself or for the Kiowa people but for the welfare of the entire earth, including every person, creature, and physical feature. He and the peoples of the Southern Plains mean this imaginatively. The old man and others like him feel responsibility for the whole of the earth and for creation.

In this way the tribes and larger systems became engaged with one another in a process that includes the meanings of such engagements for all peoples concerned with initiating and sustaining contact. By attempting congruities between the imagination of the individual human soul and the imaginal patterns that myths call deities, the old man attempted to find the repeated statements of the entire civilization in its root sources.

Changing ecosystems and developing peoples have found and lost and found again the rhythms of life, the movement from season to season, the patterns of the winds, and the flow of the water. The idea of interaction among individuals, tribes, and larger systems dominates the cultural perspectives of the Southern Plains Indian peoples, and this concept is reflected in the symbols that may be taken to represent it. These symbols vary from culture to culture and over time, but a complex of symbols comes to be related one to another in their nature or use.

Native American interaction with the ecosystem was and still is close and intimate, and the ideas and symbols each culture uses reflect each different society. Each of the tribes on the Southern Plains has found a center and extended borders, and it is on the borders where tension is found. Sometimes this tension proves to be creative, sometimes destructive. And as cultural elements transfer back and forth across these boundaries, some exchanges end in refusal, yet others provide for an extension of ideas and technology.

3
ORIGINS

Of the populations that still live on the Southern Plains only the Wichita people, or Kitikit'sh, remain in their place of origin. Their myths, traditions, and history reflect their ability to interact successfully with the ecological system. The mythic images revealing the relationships between the Wichita tribe and the Southern Plains environment remain an integral part of the living Wichita tradition. The elders validate their origins within this region, and material remains signify this sense of location as well as the mythology. Responsive changes in social and economic development and dramatic changes in the climate and topography are reflected in the Wichita tribal memory.

Wichita traditional spirituality focused upon the images of powerful creative forces present in the cosmos that guided tribal and individual destinies. The people obligated themselves to relate to the ecological system and the forces within through meditation, invocation, and ritual. Of the four eras of Wichita mythology, the first encompasses the creation of the earth by Kinnikasus, the Creator; one of his aspects is Nus'-e'cah-oshus, or Man Reflecting Light. During this era of creation the first man and the first woman—Ka-ta-us-t'skis (North Star) and Na-ahsee-ya-sikits (Bright Shining Woman)—were also created. The spirits of the wind took care of the first humans, but the earth was of prime importance to all existence (even today if one wants to be rejuvenated one must lie on the earth). During the second era the peoples scattered over the Southern Plains, named themselves, and became the animal peoples. In this era the great flood occurred, and only a portion of the peoples survived. They depended upon amaranth as the principal grain and used dart throwers and darts for hunting. During the third era, the people settled and acquired maize or corn and bows and arrows and other technologies; they began to live in thatch houses on the plains. The fourth era corresponds to the end period and is considered an era of disaster: Mother-Corn will cease to grow. In this end time a man will be chosen in relationship with a star in the north sky to express clearly every aspect of Wichita tradition as well as the meaning of this cycle of space and time.[1]

Wichita belief and experience have focused upon the tribal community as well as on the larger system of the universe. The Wichita have defined themselves in terms of language, where a person lives, and with whom a person lives and by an acceptance of spiritual and material tradition.[2] In the contemporary era the Wichita recognize the complexities of the brutal uniformity enforced upon them and the degradation of the quality of life. These are realistic criticisms of the external world; in the contemporary world they experience increasing distortions of communication, deprivation of intimacy with the immediate environment, a growing sense of harassment and alienation, and false values and feelings of inner worthlessness, experiences that persist relentlessly in a world dominated by the colonial expansion of Western European cultures. They believe that the world is drawing attention to itself through its breakdown under the pressure of exploitation and that it is entering a new moment of consciousness. To the Wichita all things show faces: the world and the universe are coded signatures to be read for meaning, temperament, and character. As the features of the earth speak, they show their relative shapes, and their souls correspond or coalesce with the tribal community. An object bears witness to itself in the image it offers; its depth lies in the complexity of this image, and any alteration in the tribal culture resonates with a change in the soul of the world and of the universe.

Throughout time it is the responsibility of the Wichita community to enliven all things, to give them their animated faces. The focus of existence is rarely on saving the soul of the individual but is on saving the soul of the world and the universe. The Wichita make a positive effort to return value from the tribal community to the earth, for a world without soul offers no intimacy. All things, whether constructed or natural, carry soul.

The Wichita integrated themselves into the larger ecological system of the Southern Plains with a belief in intimate relationships with each other. Clusters of families formed groups comprising settlements and larger village complexes. These communities repeated patterns of integration throughout the river systems of the plains. A head man assisted by a council of the adults of the village emerged to act as moderator and facilitator and to provide stable governance. Everyone possessed the right to speak in council; issues were discussed, and solutions reached through consensus. These communities ranged from the Arkansas River valley south to the Brazos River valley. Highways connected the riverine settlements north and south, east and west. The most important of the highways, the Wichita Trace, ran north and south immediately west of the Cross Timbers. Communication made possible by these rivers and highways enabled the Wichita to act in concert through a national council when pressured by external forces, and the leader of the council expressed collective-band consensus on issues of broad public concern.[3]

Before the acquisition of horses from the Spanish, the Wichita hunted on foot in venerated fashion that had developed through the centuries. They had learned to use geographic features, such as box canyons and bluffs, to capture and kill the large game animals. In times of drought the Wichita knew that there was always sustenance in the Wichita Mountains. Rich alluvium from the river valleys provided a renewable basis for intensive forms of agriculture that did not destroy the top layers of soil in the process. Bountiful surpluses of maize, amaranth, beans, pumpkins, squash, melons, and tobacco provided for trade and commerce.

Extensive Wichita population centers supported themselves through material means that accommodated changes in the environment and in technology as well as through new plant stock. Hunters switched from darts and throwers to bow and arrows during an extended period over 1,000 years ago; guns, then rifles, largely replaced the bows and arrows in the past 500 years. Within the past 100 years, the integrated market economy has replaced these technologies, and changes in agriculture paralleled and precipitated changes in hunting. Maize or corn replaced amaranth as a principal food grain between 2,000 and 3,000 years ago. Maize was considered to be a spiritual gift to women; it was given along with the knowledge of planting, cultivation, and preparation. Along with beans, squash, pumpkin, and other varieties of cultivated and gathered plants, maize provided for agricultural surpluses that transformed the people's relationships with the environment and the growing populations upon the plains.

The Wichita gave considerable attention to ritual, their principal means of thanksgiving. Concerns for a long life, health, and abundant food were paramount. The Deer Dance was performed by spiritual leaders when the first green grass appeared, when the grain ripened, and when it was harvested. The Calumet Pipe Ceremony involved dances and presentation of pipes to a prominent person. Rain Bundle Ceremonies were performed with rasps and songs on more than one occasion during each annual cycle. The Horn Dance was performed by a society to invoke blessings on those at risk, and the Turkey Dance was performed by the women to celebrate the history of events important to the village communities and to the tribe. Dances such as the Corn Dance celebrated good harvests; others indicated gratefulness for propagation of buffalo and for the health of the community. Each of these dances and ceremonials with their associated songs was an argument for life in community and for harmony with the earth.[4]

Community and the spirits in the earth also were defined in mythic design. The Wichita people of the ancient past (hira:-wis-iha:s) practiced tattooing and painting on their upper bodies. The raccoon-eye design was used by men and women: women applied circles and rays in their designs; men were distinguished by such designs as a bird's foot on the back of the hand, signifying the taking of the first bird as a hunter. Crosses indicated the important symbols of the stars, particularly Flint-Stones-Lying-Down-Above, or Tahanetskihadidia.[5]

As the Wichita established themselves on the Southern Plains, the Gran Quivira as it came to be called in the early modern era, they lived in large grass-thatched houses distinctive in their round configuration. Large villages of 1,200 were noted by the early Spanish explorers. Even as late as the early nineteenth century, Wichita memory indicated that it took three days to travel on horseback from one end of the largest village to the other along the Washita River.[6]

The architecture of the thatch houses reflected the cosmology of the Wichita people. The structure was supported by four large cedar logs with cross supports, put in place by the men to correspond to the four cardinal directions. Upon this structural framework the

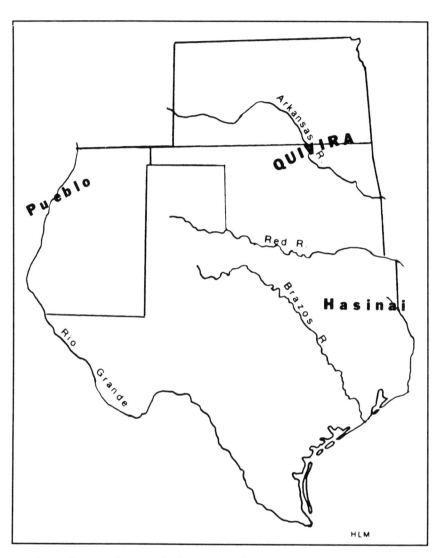

Southern Plains, indicating the location of that portion of the Wichita
Nation referred to as Quivira as well as the general location of the Pueblo
and Hasinai peoples in the sixteenth century. Modern political boundaries
are used for reference purposes only.

women tied willows and then thatch. The ground inside and outside the dwelling was prepared from a mixture of red clay and ash, which was hard and impervious to moisture. A fireplace was situated in the center of the house with a hole in the dome directly overhead. The main entrance opened on the east side of the structure.[7]

Thus did the Wichita community maintain its relationship with the earth and the universe. There were also other systems within which the Wichita lived. The image of the family emerged directly from first man and first woman, and family roles and relationships provide the traditional foundation for existence. Extended relations within families and the tribe are maintained in sophisticated ways and are reinforced through a variety of practices such as game theory. In the origin myth, men were given the shinny game, a team sport to build community: two teams of men use clubs or fieldsticks to get a ball to the goal first. The women were given the double-ball game, emphasizing the same purpose. The double-ball was constructed of two small leather balls tied on a leather thong, which the women tossed using forked sticks; scoring a goal won the game. In both games team movement rather than individual achievement was the basis of performance. The games were things of beauty played within villages and between villages, and bonds fashioned through these games lasted a lifetime.[8]

Humor also served an extremely important role in welding relationships within families and among extended families within the tribe. Joking was clearly defined although different types of humorous relations existed between different kinship categories. For example, joking tempered with respect took place between brothers, brothers and sisters, sisters, and husband and wife. Rougher verbalized humor occurred when sisters-in-law were concerned and between grandparents and grandchildren. Obligatory joking was carried on between a brother-in-law and a sister-in-law as well as between brothers-in-law. These latter relationships permitted rough sexual joking and intense forms of humor. In these relationships that lacked generational difference, conflicts were seen as almost inevitable; thus humor became a socially necessary outlet for such tensions.[9]

Beyond their own internal structure, the Wichita Nation was most closely involved with the Pawnee Tribe, and number of traditions grew from this involvement. Interaction continues today based upon the ceremonial called the Wichita-Pawnee Visitation. Every summer either the Wichita or the Pawnee journey to and stay with the other in their homeland. These visits lasted from three months in the recent past to two weeks in current times.[10] The visitation is always preceded by ceremonials with tobacco and cedar. Alternately, the Head Man of the Wichita or the Pawnee travels ahead, followed in time by the rest of the tribe. They establish camp and a central fire for the stay. During the period of the visitation the campground becomes special holy space, and traditional behavior is mandated. Sharing food is always a principal focus of the visitation, with the admonition that "Food makes for good friends." Every night the Wichita and Pawnee play hand games.[11]

The final day is always the climax of the visit, and the people dance and manifest an expansive spirit. Those people who could not join the others for the entire visitation come at this time. The Wichita and the Pawnee exchange gifts with one another, and the Head Man then ceremonially invites the other tribe to visit the next year.[12]

The Wichita have maintained a variety of relationships with other tribal entities over the centuries, much of it focused upon agricultural enterprise. Although the Wichita regularly used intensive agricultural methods rather than extensive production, they maintained tremendous food surpluses both for protection of themselves and for commerce. Commercial relations existed in the past two millennia between the Wichita and the peoples of the upper Rio Grande. During this period, the principal crops for harvest were maize or corn, beans, squash, and pumpkins; other cultivated or tended plants included sunflowers, marsh elder, and the continuing production of amaranth. Moreover, fruits were collected and processed, including grapes and sand plums.[13]

Through the classical and into the modern era, the Wichita have possessed skills in industries that have served as the basis for their commercial success. Food processing accounted for much of the trade relations to the east, down the Red River into the Caddo Nation, and to the west, into the upper reaches of the Rio Grande among the Tewa and Tiwa Pueblo. Prepared parched corn, dried pumpkin, and cured tobacco continued to be important products into the modern era as trade increased with the horse-culture tribes such as the Comanche, Kiowa, and Plains Apache. The Wichita also processed robes and hides from buffalo, deer, and antelope and served as middlemen in the gun trade as the French ventured into the area in the eighteenth century. These commercial relations actively enhanced cultural interchange and spiritual understandings and were not seen as functions separate and apart from their way of life.[14]

Understanding the Wichita Nation opens the way for understanding the interrelationships among the peoples and between them and the larger ecological system of the Southern Plains. The images of the Wichita associated with the arts, culture, and the heritage contained in their ideas arose from their imagination of primary forms, patterns that appear in their arts, ceremonials, dreams, and social customs. In order to better understand these most fundamental patterns of their existence, one must study Wichita culture and its response to larger systems. These patterns are portrayed in mythology, spirituality, art, architecture, ritual, and grammar. The definition of images for the Wichita—as with other peoples who venture onto the plains—lies in their imagination: their vision-images, dream-images, fantasy-images, and song-images. These serve as the foundation for the interrelationships that have allowed the Wichita to sustain their existence on the Southern Plains. For the Wichita, dreams and reality can exchange places and values; they are not opposed. Dream images are never merely subjective but always enacted and embodied. Whatever is physically or literally "real" is always also an image. The dream-vision focuses upon the soul in the universe and the spirits of the universe. Vision sees through an event to its image.

The Wichita cultural thrust is always to return to the higher principle in order to find a place for and an understanding of the lesser; the mythic image is used to see the event. Imagination is a method for investigating and comprehending existence. The commonplace may be understood as a reduction of the mythic image, and personal feelings and insights are returned to the specific images that hold them.

The world in which the Wichita find themselves is one of intimacy. Throughout the Wichita presence on the Southern Plains, their response has been aesthetic in that they form true notions of things from attentive involvement. This intimacy makes meaning possible because it turns events into experiences, a transformation that is communicated in mythical terms and that has spiritual concerns. Through the imaginative nature of Wichita tradition, people can experience creation through observation, reflective speculations, dreams, and visions in the realization that all realities are primarily metaphorical in nature.

Images, whether in forms of family, architecture, tattoos, or burial, were designed to provide for a more perfect life. Homelife arose from the universal context in which the people lived; intratribal strife was rare. Thus the Wichita served in accord with the stable center of life on the Southern Plains. Exceptional tribes, like the Apache or the Osage, were treated in the enemyway, but the Wichita people found a solid relationship with most tribes on the Southern Plains through commerce and spiritual expression. A sense of the importance of these relations was brought about symbolically in the Ceremony of the Calumet Pipe Sticks, which spread throughout the Great Plains, moving from south to north, during the modern era. The ceremony abounded in ritual and had its origin in one of the earliest myths. Its performance conferred lasting benefit upon the tribe and brought neighboring tribes into close spiritual and commercial relationship with the Wichita.

Primary speech and action among the Wichita come about within the context of myth, growing from mythical accounts in the cultural imagination. The myths themselves are metaphors and thus cannot be taken historically, physically, or literally in the Western European sense. Even if the recollection of mythology is perhaps the single most important path to reality, the myths themselves are understood as metaphors. It is customary before the beginning of a story to offer a sacrifice of smoke to the spiritual entities, addressing them to the effect that the teller is about to relate the story of their life experience; anyone who correctly tells the story of the spiritual lives receives benefit. The general object in relating the mythology is to indicate that the horrible creatures and monsters of the world no longer exist; they were removed from the earth, and their destructive powers were taken from them. The listeners benefit by opening the questions of life to transpersonal and culturally imaginative reflection. Events can be recognized in the context of their mythical background.

The Wichita people functioned in a beautiful, healing world, interacting with a variety of larger systems and using information from these systems, intertribal or universal, for their growth and development. The engagement of the Wichita with the ecological system of the Southern Plains was problematic over many, many centuries. Particular patterns marked the entry and development of Wichita relationships, which must be seen on multiple levels, including individual, couple, extended family, community, and ecological, to acquire the perspective necessary for understanding their life.

4

COMMERCE

Fifteen hundred years ago circumstances began to change on the Southern Plains with increasing rapidity. The Wichita had lived on the plains as no other people had managed to do during the period from 12,000 B.P. to the beginning of the classical Caddoan era; the only people comparable were the Caddo, to their south and east. These people lived along the lower course of the Red River and in the Sabine, Neches, and Angelina river valleys. They comprised several regional alliances, including the Hasinai, Hanai, Kadohadacho, Kiamchi, and Natchitoches, or Adaes.

The traditional expression of Caddo governance and economics comes from the Drum Dance, the ritual that is the primary means of socializing the individual into the tribal community. It is always the initial dance of the night's cycle of dances for the Caddo people and remains as the metaphorical image for their self-defining being. The Drum Dance relates the origin myth and the migration tradition as well as the pattern of governance.

In the Drum Dance the men lead, carrying the drum. They move completely around the danceground, traveling in harmony with the movement of the earth, clockwise. Initially, a sequence of eleven songs relates the origins and early heritage of the Caddo. In these songs, specific events are narrated as the Caddo moved from the preceding world into the Southern Plains. Young boys are allowed to join the lead singers so that they may become familiar with the songs, but they are not allowed to touch the drum. As the dance proceeds around the ground, other men and women join the singers, following their lead. All experience is thereby brought into the image of the tribal narrative.

The second segment of the Drum Dance begins with a faster pace after a short pause. In this portion, the singers are in the middle of the danceground. The drummers rotate, remaining in the center of the dance area, while the dancers continue to move in harmony with the direction of the earth. Personal feelings, including anxiety, desire, confusion, misery, and happiness, are brought into related images that hold them. The face of emotion is individualized, as feelings and concepts are imagined in their details. The tribe returns to the higher principle in order to find a place for and to understand the lesser principles and associated feelings. Myth presents the exceptional to better define the commonplace.[1]

The songs of the Drum Dance reflect the traditional images of Caddo existence. In the earliest space-time context only one man lived as a Caddo; it was a period of relative darkness. Around him, a village emerged. As the people grew in number, they noticed that the man seemed to be everywhere. Then he disappeared for a short period, only to return with different types of food in the form of seeds. The unknown man called the people together and gave the seeds to them, principally corn and pumpkin. He also told the people that the darkness would no longer rule; the Caddo would see with a new sense of vision all that was around them. The unknown man indicated that the people should have a leader in their new existence who should be called the cah-de; he should be the wisest, most able among them and should be obeyed in all things and looked upon as the great father. The people were told to hold council to select a person to serve as cah-de.

When the people came together to select a leader, a man named Ta-sha spoke, saying that the powerful unknown man should be the one called Neesh. After careful consideration, the people decided that Neesh should be the cah-de. He agreed, after some deliberation, to accept this position and selected Ta-sha as his aide. This second man became the tuh-mah, or village crier.

On one memorable occasion, the tuh-mah was sent out to tell the people to assemble; Neesh then gave the gathered Caddo instructions so that they could move from the darkness to the new world of light. The people were to divide into groups; each group should have a head man, who would be given a drum and who would enable the singers and drummers to move to the new world. Upon a signal from the cah-de the people began moving to the west, emerging in established groups, but in the midst of this transition, a disruption divided the people. All the people who had not yet emerged stopped and were trapped in the world of darkness.

The place of emergence became known as the Place of Crying, or Cha-ca-nee-nah, so named because the people who had arrived in the new world sat down and cried over the loss of those who were left behind. Because the Caddo had emerged from the earth, the people call it Enahwahdut, or Mother Earth. The men carried pipes and pieces of flint into the new world, the women seed corn and pumpkin; each meant and continues to mean a great deal to the Caddo people. They have always attempted to hold fast to these objects above all else. There have been difficult times when these things could have been lost, but the Caddo have never thrown them away.

As the Caddo began to live in the river valleys their lives together changed. Agricultural surpluses became available for commerce, and hunting was affected by new technologies. The people adopted bows and arrows to hunt animals, using darts and throwers for protection from men. Caesti, a young man of poor background who grew to be a great leader, is usually credited with the introduction of bows and arrows among the Caddo people. Tradition also holds that Caesti introduced a dualistic code of good and bad.

Even though the Caddo hunted animals, these beings remained on friendly terms with the people. The animals exhibited a wonderful sense of power and at times shared with the people their sense of life and their concerns in visions and dreams. In a real sense these visions of power were used to aid others, to integrate the community with larger systems. Lasting visions were interpreted into the song and dance of the people.

The first major period of difficulty fell upon the Caddo when they lost the first drum and with it all that it symbolized. After a seemingly interminable period of tremendous disruption, a stranger came to four Caddo men who were seated under a box elder tree; he placed a bundle in one fork of the tree and left. Lightning struck the tree; then the drum came out of the bundle. The four men took the restored drum back among the people, and a sense of harmony was restored. Since then the Caddo have kept both flint and coal inside their drums. The drum and its contents are inextricably linked with the images of lightning and thunder in the community life of the Caddo Confereracy.

Thus the origin and collective images of the Caddo are imagined in the Drum Dance cycle. This tradition is complex; it frees the individual within society to reflect on the vision that is found in the universe and singularly within the individual. Such a tradition is not a straitjacket of convention; rather, it provides for a measure of the balance needed for responsible existence.[2]

Cultivation served as a central element within the mythic image of the Caddo and as the basis for commerce. The first among the Caddo to manage this system were the women, who had effected the perennial growth of foodstocks such as amaranth and blackberries. By at least 3,000 B.P. they were raising squash, and corn and pumpkin they had brought with them to their place on the Southern Plains. In all instances the women maintained intensive cropping techniques, and in the long term corn and pumpkin became the basis for sustainable development and commercial exchange.[3]

The Caddo held to a consistent long-range view, looking for images of the future that would serve the community in ever better fashion. One strategy was to find an ethical or an aesthetic basis for accepting present costs to preserve future resources. (This approach was true for the Wichita as well as for the Caddo as their communities spread throughout the Southern Plains river valleys.) Conservation as systematic public effort was inherent in the focal images of the Caddo. Temple precincts and grounds for burial mounds such as Kee-wut, the Davis Site Park on the Neches River, or Dit-teh, the Spiro Mound Complex Park in the Arkansas River valley, served as sanctuaries. There overseers ensured control in the harvesting of plants and water. Conservation served as the means for maintenance of resources that would be important in the long-range, largely unpredictable future. The Caddo prevented soil erosion through intensive agricultural methods so that wind and rain carried away as little of the topsoil as possible. They were concerned with the irreversible pollution of air and water and were particularly careful about the possible defacing of some special quality in a landscape. They were keenly aware of the dangers to other plant and animal species, ensuring that extinction did not result from human activities.

The only resources they destroyed through use were those that could be replaced. Trees, for example, were a renewable resource if their cutting had not caused a loss of soil, and pure water was a continuing resource if pollution was not pushed beyond the sticking point. The basis for action was relatively clear: the first priority was to prevent irreversible change; the second was to reestablish the renewable resource for the generations to come.

The Caddoan tribes shared a culture carefully adapted to the conditions of the river valleys of the Southern Plains. The villages and urban ceremonial complexes were ordered communities located on natural terraces above the rivers, strategic locations that offered extended views along the river valleys. Trees in the bottomlands provided a renewable source of fuel and protection from the wind. In this village context, women owned and maintained the houses, constructed of fire-hardened clay or thatch, owned the fields and agricultural tools, and prepared and stored food. The women's activities served as the foundation of the commercial cycle. Prepared squash, pumpkin, corn, beans, sunflowers, and amaranth were stored and traded in ever-expanding fashion. Large canoes and rafts were capable of transporting large amounts of preserved foods over long distances through the river systems. The Caddoan peoples also traded in nonperishable materials such as manufactured flint points and knives, stone beads, bone pins, copper-coated wooden pins, stone celts, stone ear-spools, incised conch shells, and effigy pipes.[4] Large quantities of buffalo hides and hair and rabbit-fur yarn seem to have served as additional sources of wealth.

Regional and extended trade systems emerged to service not only the Southern Plains but also extended areas to the east and to the north. Between 1,500 to 500 years ago, this integrated system of commerce flourished and expanded. Among the communities, Dit-teh became the most important focus for commerce and for ceremonial activities. It was a cosmopolitan civic-ceremonial center that involved the two large Caddoan nations, the Caddo and the Wichita, as well as the Tunica Tribe to the southeast along the Arkansas and Red river valleys. Dit-teh influenced trade relations far beyond the region, including Cahokia of the Illinois Nation near the confluence of the Mississippi and Missouri rivers, Hiwasee Island on the Tennessee River, Etowah near the Chattahoochee River, and Pawnee villages on the Platte River.[5]

Dit-teh or the Spiro Mound complex, is dominated by two monumental structures and seven smaller mounds. This was a place of sanctuary with no palisades around it for defensive purposes. The riches of burial goods indicate its importance to ceremonialism and commerce throughout the interior of North America.[6] The grave goods reflected the nature of Caddoan commercial relations. Shell cups from conch shells found only along the western coast of present-day Florida and possibly in northeastern Tamaulipas in Mexico were discovered in great number. Copper plates made of raw material from the northwestern Great Lakes region were also found in some quantity. Mica, flints, marble, and greenstone chlorite schist among the burials were from the Southern Appalachian region. Hundreds of thousands of shell beads were found in the burial chambers from a variety of places, from local rivers to the Gulf Coast. Quartz crystals, pigments, and flint came from the Ouchita Mountains, and glena and flints originated in the Ozark Uplift. Prime trade relations during the period from 1,000 to 700 years B.P. were evidenced with the east. Dit-teh served clearly as a concentration point for precious goods. It owed its special character to the mediating control that the Caddoan elite maintained between the primary producers of the hinterland to the west and the cultures to the east.

Integrated with the commerce was the special place of Dit-teh as a spiritual center. It was the home of artisans who influenced the ideas and works of many southeastern peoples. Etched conch shell and embossed copper plates depicted significant images—elaborate scenes of dance, games, and raids as well as creatures of speculation and those commonly recognized—that integrated aspects of life into a unified whole. Among the latter images were winged serpents, spiders and their webs, large cats, images that were important throughout much of the North American continent. Recurring themes were found among the engravings, and one of the most frequent was that of multiple figures in motion, not surprising given the importance of dance as an expression of concepts and feelings among the Caddoan people. The scenes involved elaborately decorated human figures, some of which suggested tattooing but which might have been painted. No two figures were alike, even when only heads were shown. Each figure had a distinct personality. Another important theme was that of paired figures, confronting each other or back-to-back. The paired figures were engaged in ritual activity with vessels of heated liquid, bows, or handheld drums. Chunkee players appeared primarily on gorgets (chunkee was a classic game of skill, involving a hurled stone playing-piece). A recurring theme was that of multiple human figures in boats that had the exact shape of dugout canoes. Standards or sails rose above the boats as the human figures rowed with oars. Birdmen figures were a connecting theme found not only at Dit-teh but also at Etowah. Among the images used most frequently were raccoons, fish with antlers, winged serpents, and spiders, powerful mythic images that were used over much of North America. Other motifs appearing often were crosses, the eye-in-hand symbol, circles, and terraces. These etchings encoded mythic themes that remain important to the existence of the Caddoan people and their understanding of commerce and of spirituality.[7]

For those five centuries Dit-teh and other centers flourished along the Arkansas and Red river systems and along the river courses that flowed directly into the Gulf of Mexico. After 1250 A.D. the Caddoan people began to change their way of life, however. Frontier settlements were abandoned, and by 1450 the structure of society at Dit-teh had changed drastically. Trade with and influence from the Southeast was no longer evident. The oral tradition of the Caddo indicates that at this time the people turned their attention from the east to the west. Monumental mound construction at Dit-teh apparently ceased.

Bison hunting grew in importance. The use of buffalo and the increased use of storage pits indicated that the Caddo people had begun to use their leisure differently. After storing fall harvests, they moved out over the Southern Plains to hunt bison. Travel was made overland on foot and by canoe along the river courses; thus the people could transport meat, hides, and bones back to the villages in early winter. The Caddo shared with the Wichita more than they had in previous centuries. As commerce with the southeastern tribes decreased, trade with the Wichita and the peoples of the upper Rio Grande increased. The burial mound at Dit-teh was ceremonially capped by 1450, and the site was abandoned.

Interaction with the environment has been cited as one reason for the decline of commerce. Material evidence indicates the onset of a drier climate about 1200 A.D., a change that adversely affected the ability of villages to anticipate the production of crops. The movement of people from the western ranges of the Southern Plains river systems placed more demand upon available soils and resources. At the same time, the ideas and images of the western portions of the plains were expressed in a different light. Conservation easily transformed itself into conservatism; keeping things as they were, the landscape, the existing customs, and the ecology, became important because people were used to them. Yet these patterns were the results of previous and ongoing change and would change again. Nevertheless, people hesitated to change patterns because of traditional aesthetic or imaginal reasons or because of the immediate social costs of the change. Conservation may have been used to protect privileges as well. Thus the task at hand was a matter of bringing about social, commercial, and spiritual transition without disaster.

The principles of interaction with the ecology and with other peoples served as a proper guide to environmental decisions. Knowledge about the far-reaching interrelations among living beings and their habitats was of great value in enhancing the Caddo's sensitivity to the unexpected system-wide reactions that accompanied their actions. It was not nature alone but the Caddo interaction with nature that proved to be the foundation of their ethic.

In the long run the proper ethical view saw human beings as part of nature. Human action meant living together with other species in some reciprocal relationship, with concern for them, helping them and the entire ecological system to change and develop in some selective direction. The shift of the Caddoan people's focus from the east to the west was based on selection and on mutually accepted pattern changes; thus the demands of physical nature brought about dramatic changes in human hopes and values.

Environmental adaptability was another way of keeping the future open. Generous communications and facilities that allowed ideas, people, goods, and wastes to be moved about freely provided an adequate means of transition for the Caddoan people, creating space for growth. Temporary or mobile elements, (e.g., dog and horse travois), additive and modular structures (i.e., brush arbors, cave wind breaks), and unspecialized forms (e.g., fire-hardened sticks) were used to advantage.

Although uncertainty and neutrality of form disturbed behavior and environmental images, special measures or arguments in terms of dance and song moderated uneasiness. The ceremonies taught the people how to be comfortable in adapting to a new setting. Stable symbolic focuses—spirituality, river courses, high places— helped to hold a shifting scene in focus. Visible continuity with the relatively certain future conveyed a sense of security; aspiration and continuity were necessities. Continuance and hope were found in the present that was unfolding and in the direction in which it was going. New and old were episodes in the flow of the river courses in the Southern Plains; moving in accord with those streams, the Caddo followed naturally created patterns with anticipation and joy. They responded to the necessity of change not merely by conserving and by adapting but also by creating it. They explained change rather than continuing to hold on to the idealized past and stressed continuity with the near future. Caddo communities internalized conservation and adaptability as contemporary satisfactions, using the spatial and temporal environment to shape attitudes about the future. Primary images and patterns served as precepts by which to measure change.

5

HORSE CULTURE

At the beginning of the modern era in the early sixteenth century, dramatic change began to occur as the Latino people initiated contact with various peoples in North America. Within the first decades of this period, horses were introduced into the Southern Plains, and the Wichita and the Caddo were among the first in the region to obtain them. Communication and transportation were thus enhanced so that the established civilizations were aided in their efforts toward conservation of and adaptation to the plains environment. The Wichita and Caddo increasingly interacted in a significantly interdependent manner with a variety of larger systems in the west, using information from these systems as alternatives for their own growth and development.

In the case of other tribes who lived in the Rocky Mountains, such as the Comanche, the presence of horses revolutionized traditional forms of life. Horses not only drastically altered their ecological and economic interests through new forms of hunting and commerce but also necessitated pastoral concerns that were new to the people. These needs and opportunities brought the Comanche people out of the Rocky Mountains, which had been their traditional home for centuries, onto the Southern Plains.

Particular patterns and themes marked this entry into the plains ecological system as well as the process of relationships between tribes. Venturing south, the Comanche and Soshone peoples left the high country of the upper Missouri River. The Shoshone moved into the Wind River valley, and the Comanche migrated further south along the front range of the Rockies following the valley of the Arkansas River, gathering in the summer months and dispersing in the winter. The movement was slow, and they proceeded in small bands through the mountains.

The Comanche name for themselves is Nim-ma, or people. They share a common language and culture although that culture was in a rapid state of change with the move to the plains. Each of the bands within the tribe worked as a semiautonomous entity within specific areas, children usually belonging to the band of the father. Their identity and the health of the people were closely associated with the landscape. Thus the change from the mountain environment to that of the plains was taken with great care. At first, the Comanche moved from the front range of the mountains to the plains and then back again with the change of seasons.

Once on the Southern Plains the Yapahtukkah band, or Yampa Root Eaters, ranged north of the Arkansas River. The Kwahada, or Antelope Eaters, settled on the High Plains south of the Arkansas where they resisted the Apache peoples who raided in the region. The Comanche people consider the Kwahada the fiercest of all fighters. The Kutsotuckkah, or Buffalo Eaters, settled in the region of the upper Red and Washita river valleys and were the first band among the Comanche to ally with the Wichita Nation in its extensive villages in these valleys. It was through this band that the remainder of the Comanche bands came into relationship with the Wichita. To the far south were the Penatuckka, or Honey Eaters, the largest of the divisions of the Comanche Tribe. Other bands existed on the Southern Plains for various lengths of time, including the Pahahnaxnu (Living Higher), Noyeka (Wanderers), Mu Tsane (Under Cut Bank), Tuttsahkunnahnu (Sewing on the Move), Woah (Maggots), Taninatuckkas (Liver Eaters), and Wieahmu (Hill Wearing Away). The larger bands have been able to sustain themselves into the present.[1]

The Comanche effectively widened their range of operations between the Wichita settlements on the Southern Plains and the Pueblo villages on the upper Rio Grande. The various bands operated from the Arkansas River to the San Antonio River in the south, and Comanche parties moved even further south into New Spain on an irregular basis. The horse increased the range of the contact parties so that totally new relationships developed in the modern era; many of these contacts were commercial in nature, but occasional raids were the focus of Comanche efforts.[2]

The Comanche emphasized hunting bison or buffalo on an ever-increasing scale as they reached out into the Southern Plains. Their

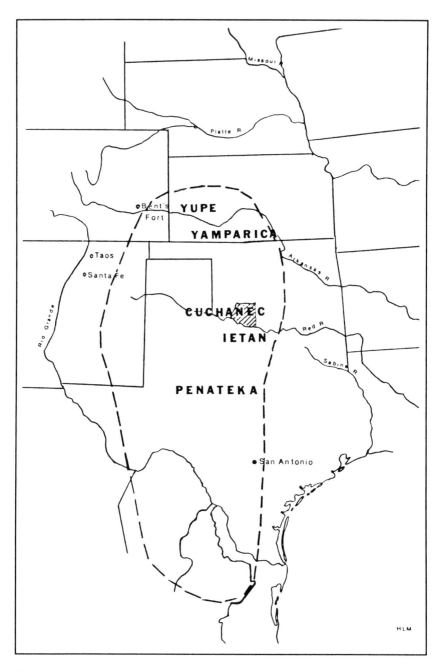

Comanche range in the Southern Plains, indicating the general location of the tribe. The segmented lines enclose the range of the Comanche Tribe as it moved in its seasonal pursuits during the modern era. Small circles indicate significant trade centers and diagonal lines the Comanche reservation, which is shared with the Kiowa and Plains Apache as well as with the Fort Sill Apache.

economy was based in modern times upon the presence of buffalo in great numbers (estimates range from 6 to 10 million buffalo on the Great Plains as a whole during this era). Great communal hunts of buffalo occurred during the late summer or early fall after the seasonal molting when hides were in their prime. The buffalo served as a new foundation for the tribe's economy, supplying the necessities: meat and blood were prepared and preserved for long-term use, hides provided housing and clothing, bones and horns became tools and service instruments, and other parts of the animal were used as containers and for glue and other needs.

The place and time of the hunt were determined in open assembly where everybody was welcome to listen. The date for departure was set; then the young and able-bodied men and women joined together for the organized hunt. Children and elders remained in the camps. The expedition traveled lightly, taking small and undecorated tepees, necessary weapons, and tools. The hunt was orderly and cooperative: recognized leaders directed the party, and scouts returned information to the main party on a regular basis.

Because of the abundant success resulting from the modern hunt on horseback, the Comanche people concerned themselves increasingly with the preservation of food. They preserved buffalo meat as well as antelope and deer in two primary ways. One was jerking—slicing the meat into thin strips and drying it on racks. Jerky weighed only about one-sixth as much as fresh meat, but in rain and dampness it absorbed moisture readily, gained in weight, and molded or decayed. The second method was to create pemmican, a combination of pulverized, dehydrated meat and rendered fat. Pemmican was packed into bags of sewed buffalo rawhide, and hot, liquid marrow fat formed a film around the meat. The bags were then stitched at the mouth and sealed with tallow along the seams. Before the contents had time to harden, each bag was pressed into a flat shape about six or seven inches thick. A single sack weighed about ninety pounds. Properly prepared with only dried lean meat and rendered fat, pemmican would last almost indefinitely.

The most striking element of the Comanche culture in the modern period was their organizational ability. Their life on the plains focused upon hunting, commerce, and raiding, their main objectives being to provide food and shelter and an active social environment. As the population on the Southern Plains grew, protection from enemies became increasingly important. Hunting, commerce, and raiding were very much matters of organizational initiative. Any Comanche male was theoretically eligible to lead a raiding party; no chief or social power existed to prevent him, but a leader could muster followers only through his ability. Dreams about a successful venture were important but not deemed necessary as a sanction for starting any effort. Nevertheless, in most cases such dreams and visions were the effective stimulus.

This important link connecting hunting, commercial, and raiding efforts with universal images through dreams and visions remains critical to understanding the system of Comanche culture. The images in dreams reveal the purposes of instinct within nature; this imagery is the principal means of aligning the community with the truth of reality. For a dream image to work in life it must be experienced as fully real; there is no duplicity in these images. Interpretation arises when people have lost touch with the images, when their reality is derivative, so that this reality must be recovered through conceptual translation. Dream images are never generalities; they are natural and specific. To the Comanche a dream is an exciting mysterious message from the natural, primal source of creation. Individuals often recreated the dream image in song.

The leader of a party was absolute director of all the activities of his party of followers as long as they remained with the organization. The invariable conviction of the Comanche is that they never fail to attempt what the leader asks of them. It was always said that a leader of quality never asked of his people what he himself would not readily do. Each member knew this and also knew that to disobey might bring disaster upon the party.

Some Comanche parties were on their projected course for over a year at a time. During this period the leader had the power to determine the objective of a project, to delegate information gathering and direct scouts, to establish a general strategy, to determine camping places and periods of rest, to appoint the cook and water carriers, to divide the profits, to negotiate truce with possible enemies, and to order cessation of activities and the return home. In conflicts involving larger systems or other community groups, the leader set the example of resolute courage in the face of adversity as well as daring in choosing acceptable risks. Still, each person could act in freedom according to the dictates of his or her own vision and personal inclinations, but community images influenced such individual actions. A reputation for fairness in dividing the spoils enhanced the prestige of a leader and gained followers for him in future projects.

The internal structure of the Comanche bands and tribe was strengthened by the presence of male and female groups, which included dance societies, medicine societies, smoke-lodge societies, and mothers' societies. The Comanche had a clear understanding of status within each element of society, obligations within the hierarchy, and contractual agreements. Hierarchical obligations resulted from duties inherent in relations, which carried on indefinitely. Oral contracts with defined objectives were made for specific periods of time, and the arrangement ended when the stated obligation was fulfilled. Traditional Comanche activities were less political than most. Above all, the Comanche people were practical and businesslike.[3]

As practical as their actions were, their efforts were always undertaken with a clear focus on the importance of the spiritual qualities of the operations. The Comanche relied upon their guardian spirits to lead and protect them, and responsibility for spiritual concerns fell largely upon the individual. Every Comanche had direct relations with the spiritual powers and had to understand the images affecting him or her early in life and observe every activity in relation to those images.

The vision was fundamental to understanding the complexities of the eternal ones, or guardian spirits. A solitary place was selected as a proper space to obtain the visionary images essential to life. High places remained important to the Comanche people even after they left the Rocky Mountains to live in the Southern Plains. For example, Medicine Bluff in the Wichita Mountains was a place where visions might be sought properly. The Wichita Mountains had served as a sanctuary to the Wichita people throughout their existence; the Comanche recognized the importance of the spiritual nature of the place as well. Located at the confluence of Cache and Medicine Bluff creeks in present-day Oklahoma, it is a mile in length, forming a perfect crescent, and rises 310 feet from the bed of

Medicine Bluff Creek. From the south slope three high places can be seen. Most often a place was selected on a south slope so that a person could see east and west; the time allotted there usually was four days and four nights. The visionary power obtained was generally referred to as "making medicine."[4]

To the Comanche, the earth and the features of the land are alive just as plant and animal life are. Certain places such as Medicine Bluff are critically important in the same way that certain people play significant roles in the life of the community. Another important place on the Southern Plains is called Medicine Mounds, a line of hills in present-day Texas between the Red and Pease rivers. Medicine Mounds are conical in shape, rising about 350 feet above the surrounding plain. To the west is a trace from an ancient buffalo trail. On the top of the highest of the four mounds is a flat cap rock, and a gypsum water spring exists at the mound's base. This mound is alive in a spiritual way, powerful and benevolent.

A number of Comanche leaders were killed in the Council House Fight during negotiations with the Texas military in San Antonio in 1840. Po-cha-na-quarhip, or Buffalo Hump, retired to Medicine Mounds to seek a dream vision during this crisis for the Comanche people. "Buffalo Hump's medicine dream promised that the Texans would be driven into the sea if he attacked them."[5] This image of Texans in the waters of the Gulf was so strong that Buffalo Hump was joined by others, including Isimanica, Little Wolf, Santa Anna, and their followers. Their action resulted in a push through Texas ending at Linnville on the Gulf of Mexico, where the Texans were actually driven into the sea. Thus did Buffalo Hump's image carry reality.

Even before the introduction of the horse in North America, interaction between the Caddoan peoples and the Pueblo peoples was increasing measurably. Then the advent of the horse and the resulting cultural changes brought by the Comanche peoples widened this interaction on the Southern Plains to include the Rio Grande villages. A major factor affecting the engagement of tribes and existing systems arose in the wider context of giving and receiving assistance. Most larger systems were embedded in a deficit perspective that implied weakness. Comanche bands successfully incorporated raiding into their strategies among the Wichita villages on the Southern Plains as well as among the Pueblo villages in the Rio Grande valley. But as the Comanche interacted with the settled elements on the Plains and in the mountains, these relatively stable centers became increasingly important to commerce so that they were no longer targets for raids. Alliances were forged among the three—Comanche, Wichita, and Pueblo—in competition against the Lipan and Mescalero Apache and the Ute. The mobile Comanches served as useful trading partners and as a policing unit, a function that became increasingly important as people became more mobile through the use of the horse.

Interaction was mutual, and all three populations benefited from it. It was more efficient for each group to concentrate upon specific tactics. The Comanche served as the most active agent in the larger system of commerce and mutual support since their culture had changed most in reference to the horse and the buffalo. Given the Pueblo peoples' limited transport capabilities and their problems with searching for the buffalo herds, it was more effective for them to trade and to depend upon the Comanche.

Relations between the Pueblo and the Southern Plains peoples were not entirely amicable. But over the seventeenth and eighteenth centuries their relations were dominated by mutual support rather than by hostility. Trade was a primary provisioning strategy for the Wichita, Pueblo, and Comanche populations and served as the main form of interaction. Cotton cloth, feathers, and precious stones were included in the exchanges to the east, and deer or buffalo hides, prepared meat, pigments, and shell moved west. None of these three tribal entities controlled the other two politically.

The importance of the Comanche as intermediaries between the settled villages of the Southern Plains and those of the Rio Grande valley grew for 250 years. Latino sources have stressed the value of this trade in supplying colonial New Mexico. Pueblo and Latino populations used trade as did the Caddoans to support their respective broad-based agrarian-commercial economies and thus extended the range of resources available to them by participating in the interregional commercial system.[6]

As the Comanche people engaged the larger system that had developed on the Southern Plains, the tribe felt the broad and specific mandates, both overt and covert, that were placed upon them. On a broad level, the larger system defined itself and was defined by the Comanche presence. Hunting and raiding had been specific tasks for the extended families who came from the mountains onto the plains. The Comanche's way of life changed on the plains, but they remained a nomadic hunting people, striking compromises with their new environment to create a way of life that combined the old and the new. Despite the interchange, the Comanche still sought freedom. Spirituality continued to reflect this independent aspect of their lives so that there were no great communal dances or seasonal celebrations as existed among the Pueblo peoples in the mountains or among the Wichita people on the plains. Although the Comanche were considered among the most effective fighters in times of war, there were no strictly military societies within the tribal structure.

Horses reinforced the cultural patterns that already existed, providing mobility and speed so that the Comanche people became more effective traders, hunters, and raiders. With the horse and the buffalo the Comanche flourished; better nourishment throughout the year allowed the population to grow in stature and numbers. Moreover, the horses thrived on the grass of the Southern Plains, and because of Comanche mobility no area was overstocked for any extended period. In time the horses were bred carefully so that the Comanche herded extremely fine stock that was useful in trade. The Comanche became excellent riders, and both men and women spent much of their lives on horseback.

While horses provided the mobility necessary to improve Comanche life, buffalo provided food, clothing, shelter, and tools. As the Comanche added value to the buffalo by processing the meat and hides, they enriched themselves and their community in ways acceptable within their traditions. Their nomadic way of life enhanced their existence. They lived in bands and camped beside a source of fresh water, in the modern era living along the tributaries of the Arkansas, the Red, the Pease, and the Brazos rivers above the Caddoan peoples, who lived along the same water courses. Larger camps might stretch for miles along a stream or river. Everything was recycled so that there was never permanent damage to the ecology of the site. Their housing was practical as was their clothing.

Comanche tribal customs engaged the larger systems within the context of social policy, economic decisionmaking, and the law ways that shaped and directed their work. Comanche decisions were never as dependent upon political concerns as they were among the Caddoan peoples; Comanche life was a continuous journey among imaginal essences. The images that had come to them constituted the basis of their nature, where their courage lived. Their thought served to unify their purposes. They perceived that in all events imagination and perception, thinking and feeling, the self and the world were one. Each response to events was aesthetic in form and purpose. All was beauty. Beauty was the very sensibility of the cosmos; it had textures, tones, tastes that were attractive. Comanche thought was innately aesthetic and sensately linked with the world; life was intimate. Comanche people did not need elaborate spiritual or military institutions. They faced the world in a way that enabled them to sense it as expressed in joy. Their aesthetic sense perceived the form of things.

As the Comanche redefined themselves on the Southern Plains they also became part of the redefinition of the larger interregional system. Social and economic policies were developed in relationship to the existing peoples and affected the systems that directly and indirectly guided their lives. Ancient traditions found new images with new technologies and spatial contexts. Homes and multigenerational family systems provided for the necessary concerns of individuals and communities. Larger systems dealt with the frequent shift in policies and circumstances placing demands on the extended organization. Yet these changes occurred without the necessity of political hegemony. Participation in the process of change provided the means to make the shift clearly and with the necessary training for success. Broad-based participation in governance and in economic activity lessened the attendant upheaval when changes in leadership occurred. Such changes did not directly affect specific practices in the interactive services that provided stability. Comanche people were drawn into the bands and the tribe and into the larger systems by their desire to help others, to work with people, and to participate in enhancing life for the larger community.

The great cycle of life linked the Comanche people with the natural world. Kindred beings throughout nature were to be treated with respect; animals and fish, high places, all of creation were viewed as having intelligence and power. These beings could influence the course of events in terms of their interrelationships, system within system. The Comanche knew that human beings could not escape their obligations to ensure the well-being of the land and its inhabitants without suffering dire consequences.

6

RELIGION

Meaningful systems assume different configurations of relationships and beliefs so that any given tribe's concerns and issues make
sense. Interrelationships on the Southern Plains continued to become more complex in the eighteenth century. In addition to increased Wichita and Caddo commercial relationships new elements
appeared, including the introduction of the horse and the development of Comanche horse culture. These developments took place
within the boundaries of tribal spiritual traditions, however. Respect was extended to another tribe's beliefs and frames of reference, engaging tribal and larger systems beyond tribal cultural
boundaries.

In the eighteenth century a new presence arrived as the Kiowa
Tribe and the Plains Apache Tribe entered the Southern Plains.
Intertribal and pan-Indian religious expression accompanied their
arrival as well as different expressions of modern horse culture.
Seemingly angry and/or beneficient relationships with larger systems provided for unexpected adaptations. The Kiowa and Plains
Apache assessed viable points of entry into the complex intertribal
spheres of influence with difficulty. The overall thrust, however,
remained creative, sustaining new and even unanticipated relationships with larger systems. A major issue was how to account
for systemic constraints and still maintain viable relations.

Kiowa tradition located the tribe in the Rocky Mountains in the
upper reaches of the Yellowstone and the Missouri rivers prior to
the modern era. But in the late fifteenth and early sixteenth centuries, the Kiowa began a long-term movement through the Rocky
Mountains to the east. They requested and received permission
from the Crow Tribe to settle in their country for extended periods
of time as they moved among the mountain ranges. Even as they

learned about living in the lower reaches of the mountains and finally in the plains, the Kiowa were still drawn back into the mountains on a cyclical basis. During this transition period, the Kiowa obtained their first horses.[1]

The intertribal alliance with the Crow people remained close even as the Kiowa transformed their culture, a friendship that endured after the Kiowa continued on their way into the Great Plains to the south. This alliance proved to be critically important as they made common cause against the Cheyenne and Lakota Sioux tribes. Just as the Kiowa were entering the plains from the mountains and developing their sense of the horse culture, the Cheyenne and the Lakota Sioux were undergoing parallel transitions in their lives in the region of the Great Lakes.[2]

Once on the plains, the Kiowa continued to travel south to the sacred country of the Black Hills and the Devil's Tower. In the Northern Plains the Kiowa people associated themselves with the Plains Apache, sometimes known as the Kiowa Apache and who referred to themselves as the Nasiisha Dene. They continued in the migration south with the Kiowa, and each developed concerted forms of horse culture and spiritual expression.

The Kiowa perception of space and time as a force that affected their changing environment grew evermore sophisticated. Their calendar histories created related images of movement in space and time, with emphasis upon events that carried the religious nature of civilization through cycles of travel. In the nineteenth century, the Kiowa's selection of significant events can be compared with those of the Anglos and Latinos, yet these choices varied markedly. For example, Anglo historians emphasized the activities of George Armstrong Custer and the Seventh U.S. cavalry in the Southern Plains in 1868. In the record of events in Kiowa histories, however, no mention was made of this military policy. Kiowa concerns focused upon making medicine while the Anglo interpretation of events stressed military and political activities.[3]

Kiowa people sought harmony in their lives as they adapted to new environments. By the late seventeenth century, the Kiowa and their allies, the Plains Apache, had reached the "center of the earth" at Rainy Mountain, or the northwestern extension of the Wichita Mountains, already so important to the existence of the Wichita and the Comanche peoples. For the Kiowa, this holy space was defined by divine order of their religious experience and by their presence there. Order within the tribal structure was imperative. Tribal government was built around a head chief and the chiefs of the several bands within the Kiowa Tribe, together with the war chiefs. Only after internal stability was ensured could intertribal concerns be enjoined. The basic social and economic grouping in Kiowa life was the multigenerational family. Brothers, along with their wives and children, were the elements that tied the family together. The extended family included sisters and their spouses and children, half-brothers, half-sisters, and even pact-brothers (who were created by oral agreement). Residence was usually matrilocal; the head of these family units usually was the eldest brother.[4]

These extended families were the foundations of the primary political unit, the topadoga, or band, headed by one man—the topadok'i, chief or head man. In general the size of the band indicated the leader's ability and resulting prestige. A band was a relatively fluid body in spite of its stable nucleus. When the band was large, it was easier to use the resources of the natural environment and to protect the camp; thus it was desirable to attract people far beyond one's immediate relatives. The most important attracting force was the wisdom and generosity of the band chief, which also created a cohesive bond. He managed the affairs of the group through their voluntary cooperation and their informal acknowledgment of his position. Obedience to his directions was incumbent upon all followers to ensure the relative safety of the community, and it was in their best interests to cooperate. Any dissatisfied member could depart at any time, but the chief would never order a person to leave his band.

The chief's responsibilities were primarily to maintain harmony and order without any police assistance, to direct the movements so that economic needs were satisfied, and to protect the community against external disaster, whether of natural or of human origin. To keep peace, the chief might step in personally to stop any bickering or fighting. In interband affairs, two chiefs more often than not cooperated to stop a fight before either side won, thereby saving face for those involved if possible. Since his own behavior was more or less an example for all, the chief could never quarrel over small matters without risking the loss of his followers' respect and confidence. An awareness of this role was the ultimate reason for the restrained and lofty behavior among leaders of great eminence.[5]

The size of the band in residence varied according to the season. At its maximum in winter, the camp might have 400 people living together; in spring and fall, smaller family groups hunted apart from one another. In summer, a large encampment took place with thousands of Kiowa people living in community, especially at the time of making medicine.

Once a year in summer the entire Kiowa tribe gathered at the Sun Dance site to make medicine. The Sun Dance was celebrated not only by the Kiowa and Plains Apache but also by the Shoshone, Cheyenne, Arapaho, Bannock, and Lakota and Dakota Sioux as well as by other plains peoples. The Kiowa bands encamped around the Sun Dance lodge in a traditional great circle that included the Plains Apache; this was the center of the earth. Thus at Rainy Mountain the symbolism of the mountain and of the tree at the center of the Sun Dance Medicine Lodge was situated in a powerful way. The fourth element critical to the Kiowas, the Tai-me, was then brought to the center to complete the symbolic elements for the Sun Dance. The Tai-me is a partial image nearly two feet long— a sacred image among sacred images. "Harmony rule" was declared so that all quarrels and jealousies were forgotten. No one was to speak out or act in anger for any reason whatsoever. The great chief exerted all civil authority.

Five dance societies helped to ensure order; in increasing order of prestige they were the Adltoyui, Tsetanma, Tonkongya, Daimbega, and Koisenko. Their collective membership included the entire adult male population of the tribe. Each society had two leaders and two whip-bearers, who functioned only during the four or five weeks of the Sun Dance gathering.

Each summer at the time of the solstice, the Kiowa held their Sun Dance, or "Procession entering the lodge." It was a time of thanksgiving for the Tai-me's protection, and thanks was offered in the form of a gift, possibly a blanket, and then by a dance in the lodge. Elaborate rituals governed the entire period of the dance.

The focus of the Sun Dance was directly on the buffalo hunt and on community well-being. Kiowa tradition made this celebration the grandest of all religious ceremonies. The dance was usually centered on the young men who would lead a successful hunt and thus ensure a bountiful supply of buffalo. These men danced for four days and nights to the accompaniment of the singers. The dancers sacrificed for the community in the form of ritual fasting and thirsting. The ceremony was a matter of making medicine for the person and for the earth's communities. The dancers sought power, good health, success on the hunt, and the general welfare of the Kiowa and all peoples.

The Sun Dance brought together the sacred tree at the center of the lodge within the great circle in the presence of Rainy Mountain where the image of the Tai-me was unveiled. The installation and consecration of the sacred tree, a cottonwood, constituted the rite of the center. The Sun Dance was performed for the health of the entire tribal community; it served as the way toward absolute reality. Through sanctity and medicine, or soul-making, human beings passed from the unreal to the real. The place of the Sun Dance Medicine Lodge was a very holy place, a place where the sacred incurred into common space. Imagination and the desire for reality brought the universe and its beings into harmony.

The spiritual life of the Kiowa is bound up in the older tribal tradition of the medicine bundles, symbols that are integral to the spiritual and natural well-being of the entire tribe. These are distinguished from personal bundles or medicine bags used in everyday social and economic activity. The medicine bundles are held in families through the generations and are normally handed down from father to eldest son. Women can be bundle keepers, however. Indeed one woman among the Kiowa in the last decade of the twentieth century holds three bundles. The medicine bundles are given ceremonial sweat baths, have their outer coverings repaired, and are prayed over on behalf of individuals; each bundle is treated in exactly the same way, for they are equal in power. No violence may take place in the presence of a medicine bundle. The place where the medicine bundles are cared for constitutes a sanctuary where individuals may take refuge in time of peril.

A keeper of a medicine bundle has a critical legal function as well as a spiritual one linked with the presentation of a peace pipe in a quarrel. The relatives of anyone who is accused or guilty of an act against the common good or another individual or who is involved in matters of life and death can seek the intervention of a keeper to offer a pipe of peace to the person or persons charging the defendant with wrongdoing. When the pipe is offered it is almost never refused. The use of the peace pipe involves no judgment about who is right and who might be considered to be wrong; consequently there is no loss of face by anyone involved.[6]

Within the past decade, the Kiowa historian Linn Pauahty corrected the misinterpretation by Anglo ethnologists of the nature of the medicine bundles. The term "ten grandmothers" to refer to the ten medicine bundles bearing the spirit of Tah'lee has been misused. Taw-lee is the Kiowa word for paternal grandmother; it has been confused with tah'-lee, or half-boy. When the Kiowa refer to the ten sacred medicine bundles kept among the Kiowa and the Plains Apache tribes, they mean the ten bundles containing the spiritual force in the image of Tah'lee; they are not referring to "ten grandmothers." The error has been perpetuated by Anglo academic publications.[7]

Penal sanctions were used to maintain the institutional integrity of the tribe and its common peace. Offences included scolding and ridiculing, calling names and triggering disruptive incidents in the camp at night, composing ridicule songs, and invoking the male societies during the Sun Dance. In every conflict situation among the Kiowa many forces worked to resolve and pacify tensions. First there were the primary peace-restoring institutions—the medicine bundle pipes and the sanctuary provided by the presence of the bundles themselves. When the whole tribe was together, organizational control was at its maximum strength through the male societies or through settlement at the Tai'meh keeper's request. At other times the band chiefs and war-party leaders devoted themselves to restoring peace, never to aggravating a situation by fighting themselves. Fear of disrupting the religious unity and spiritual sanctity of the tribal order in nature internalized the peacekeeping concerns within all members of the tribe.[8]

As the Kiowa and Plains Apache continued to move south, they came into contact with the Comanche. At first these engagements were hostile. Each of the tribes, however, had mutual contacts in the valley of the Rio Grande at Taos and Picuris Pueblos as well as in the Spanish colony at Santa Fe. It was in Santa Fe, in the large house of a Spanish trader, that a party of Comanche overheard several Kiowa speaking in a nearby room. The Latino host intervened and suggested that this might be an opportunity for peace. He offered to serve as mediator.

The leaders of the two parties, Wolf-lying-down, Kiowa, and Afraid-of-Water, Comanche, saluted each other. Wolf-lying-down decided to return with the Comanche party to their camp on the Double Mountain Fork of the Brazos in the province of Texas and to remain with the Comanche all summer. Consequently, the Nokoni band of Comanche decided to arrange peace with the Kiowa bands. At the end of the summer season, the Comanche and Kiowa met in council, and a treaty resulted, spreading friendship and alliance throughout both tribes. The Plains Apache joined this significant alliance to make it a tripartite agreement. In time, this relationship among the Kiowa, Comanche, and Plains Apache brought them into alignment with the Wichita. The Kiowa also made peace with the Mescalero Apache in the late eighteenth century, an interaction that allowed increased commerce with the Tewa Pueblos in northern New Mexico.[9]

Although the Plains Apache maintained a close alliance with the Kiowa and formed a component in the Kiowa tribal circle, they preserved their own language and cultural integrity. The Plains Apache had followed the Jicarilla Apache from the north and kept in periodic contact with them even after the former had joined in the alliance with the Kiowa. The Plains Apache are traditionally related to the Sarsi, who still live in present-day Saskatchewan.[10]

The Plains Apache religious organization was a sympathetic reflection of the Kiowa ceremonial patterns. Within the tribe the Manatidie and the Klintidae as well as the Izuwe maintained the ceremonial sequence of rites, which, from the seventeenth through the nineteenth century, centered upon the Sun Dance. The most important duty was to stabilize the ceremonial structure of the tribe; each individual had the responsibility to support the tribe's central spiritual nature.[11]

Tradition apart from the Sun Dance focused on the medicine bundles of the Plains Apache, which had been given to the tribe centuries earlier through supernatural events. There are four medicine bundles among the Plains Apache. The custodians of these bundles have the right and the duty to settle disputes among individuals and families in the same manner as the Kiowa.[12]

A more elemental sense of spirituality forms a part of the Plains Apache religious perspective. This understanding is founded upon belief in a class of supernatural beings thought to have lived as people on the earth in a remote time. Because of sickness and death, these beings set out in search of a place without disease. They found it and began to experience eternal life, but the location is uncertain. The special beings may have separated, some finding the place without disease in the mountains, others in underground realms. Each domain belonged exclusively to those who had discovered it. In these migrations of the special beings as well as in their own, the Plains Apache move from north to south.

Plains Apache recognized the supreme being with the power of creation, Nuakolahe, or "earth he made it." The creator was neither benevolent nor punitive but was considered to be the originator of the tribal cultural hero twins, Fireboy and Waterboy. These two removed threats to humans and made the earth safe for them. In this understanding of spirituality there was no sense of thanksgiving or of special rite as in the Sun Dance. Religion at this level for the Plains Apache was a system to fulfill the requirements of living. When death came, men and women became one with the cosmos; it was a normal end of the life cycle.[13]

Songs are critically important to the Plains Apache to reflect the significant images of existence. Any person who wants to can compose a song, but only a few individuals have composed songs for major functions. These are men who are leaders in tribal affairs and active participants in ceremonial observances. Women compose lullabies and household songs.

Blackfeet songs, for example, are regarded as ceremonial because of the performances of the Manatidie, or Blackfeet Dance, which is highly ritualized with spiritual themes. The staffs used in the dance are venerated and handled carefully, with respect. A number of traditions surround the handling and disposition of the staffs; the most important one is that during the Blackfeet Dance no one is allowed to walk between the drum and the staffs. The four staffs are covered with otter fur, but a few Plains Apache people say that buffalo skin could be used as well. The staffs are held through the entire ceremony and never allowed to touch the floor although some participants allow the staffs to be placed in wooden stands. These staffs are symbolic of leadership and are decorated with eagle feathers fastened in pairs at three places.

The Blackfeet Dance area is a square with dancers lined up on the west side facing the drum. The majority of the women are on the north side. At least five men are required to perform the Manatidie, the four staff bearers and the whip. The whip dances on the south side. The singers sit around the drum, which is placed in the center of the dance square. Women singers sit on the east side. The Manatidie is generally divided into four parts: the four opening songs; the dance proper, which is interrupted by the Smoke Song; the Smoke Song; and the four closing songs. Both men and women participate in the singing, but men always begin the songs. The melodic movement of the songs is primarily descending.[14]

The religious symbolism of the Sun Dance, the medicine bundles, and the Blackfeet Dance reinforced Kiowa and Plains Apache well-being. These ceremonials also provided paths to relations with the universe. The great images of the sun, the moon, wood, and water were incorporated in ways that denote power to the people. New intertribal meanings were added to this rich imaginative existence but did not destroy the structure of the symbols; the image of the tree at the center of the earth is preserved in astonishing purity. The images provide openings into a unified world. The people inquired into the world with symbol, myth, and ritual in order to reveal something of the human condition regarded in its own right and as a mode of existence in the Southern Plains and in the universe.

The religious behavior of classical Kiowa and Plains Apache reveals an awakening of human consciousness of the cosmos and of themselves, an awakening expressed by a pattern of symbols seen as an interplay of concepts—a whole and coherent conception of reality. Symbols reflect cosmic rhythms as natural phenomena, but they also reveal something more than the aspects of cosmic life they are thought to represent. Separation of the spiritual and the material is meaningless; the two planes remain complementary in a natural sense. This complementarity is realized in the sense that the Sun Dance Lodge rests at the center of the world. The symbolism is an answer to specific needs and is shaped by the climate, by the economic structure of Kiowa and Plains Apache societies, and by their respective architectural traditions.

Symbolism adds a new value to an object or an activity without any prejudice whatever against its own immediate value; applied to objects or actions, symbolism renders them open. Symbolic thought breaks open the immediate reality without any minimizing or undervaluing of it. From such a perspective the world is not closed. No object exists for itself in isolation; everything is held together by a compact system of correspondences and likenesses. The Kiowa and Plains Apache societies emphasize consciousness of themselves in an open world that is rich in meaning, embracing the possibility of attaining the true reality of the earth and the universe.

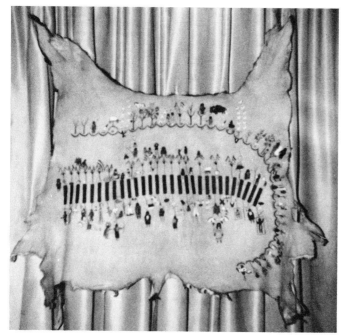

Onuko Calendar, Kiowa. (Western History Collections, University of Oklahoma Library)

Home of Tawakonie Jim, a Wichita Indian chief, northwest of Anadarko, OT, 1901. (Archives and Manuscripts Division of the Oklahoma Historical Society)

Tawakonie Jim, Wichita chief.
(Western History Collections,
University of Oklahoma Library)

Arthur and Bertha Pickard and their
baby. Wichita. (Western History
Collections, University of Oklahoma
Library)

Caddo Indians. Left to right: Julia
Edge, Zachary Taylor, and Pauline
Washington, c. 1908. (Archives and
Manuscripts Division of the
Oklahoma Historical Society)

*"Arapahoe Indian Village. Oklahoma," 1909. Published by H. H. Clarke,
Oklahoma City. (Archives and Manuscripts Division of the Oklahoma
Historical Society)*

*A Comanche Indian village in 1871. (Archives and Manuscripts Division of the
Oklahoma Historical Society)*

Red Bird, a Comanche woman. Postcard printed c. 1918–1922. (Archives and Manuscripts Division of the Oklahoma Historical Society)

A Comanche woman. (Western History Collections, University of Oklahoma Library)

Henry Red Horn and his family. (Western History Collections, University of Oklahoma Library)

Martha Napawat and children in Washita River. (Western History Collections, University of Oklahoma Library)

Mrs. Frances Ross Greeley, as a child, with her father, Walter Ross, and sister, Edna. (Western History Collections, University of Oklahoma Library)

Nancy North and family, Cheyenne-
Arapaho. (Archives and Manuscripts
Division of the Oklahoma Historical
Society)

Left Hand, an Arapaho. Hickox
Collection. (Archives and
Manuscripts Division of the
Oklahoma Historical Society)

Heap-a-Bird, a Cheyenne,
in 1958. (Archives and
Manuscripts Division of
the Oklahoma Historical
Society)

Chief Whirlwind, his daughter and
grandchildren, Cheyenne. Photo by
Christopher C. Stotz, El Reno, OT.
(Archives and Manuscripts Division of
the Oklahoma Historical Society)

"Roman Nose," a Cheyenne chief.
Copy courtesy of the Bureau of
American Ethnology, Smithsonian
Institution. (Archives and
Manuscripts Division of the
Oklahoma Historical Society)

Mary Buffalo, a Kiowa, beside her tipi. (Western History
Collections, University of Oklahoma Library)

Koon-Ka-Zachey, Kiowa-Apache chief. Army scout in 1875. Died 1927. Buried at the post cemetery, Fort Sill, Okla. (Western History Collections, University of Oklahoma Library)

James Takone, Kiowa medicine man. Anadarko, Okla., 1900. (Western History Collections, University of Oklahoma Library)

Kicking Bird, a Kiowa. Photo by William Stinson Soule, Fort Sill, IT. (Archives and Manuscripts Division of the Oklahoma Historical Society)

Lone Wolf, a Kiowa. Photo by William Stinson Soule, Fort Sill, IT. (Archives and Manuscripts Division of the Oklahoma Historical Society)

Satanta, White Bear, a Kiowa. Photo by William Stinson Soule, Fort Sill, IT. (Archives and Manuscripts Division of the Oklahoma Historical Society)

Ni-astor, or Shot-in-the-Foot, a Towakony, age 78, May 12, 1912. (Archives and Manuscripts Division of the Oklahoma Historical Society)

Big Tree (A'do-eette), Kiowa chief. (Western History Collections, University of Oklahoma Library)

Tsa-toke, or Hunting Horse, with a bow and arrows, making a prayer. (Western History Collections, University of Oklahoma Library)

Mrs. Peddlety, a Kiowa. (Western
History Collections, University of
Oklahoma Library)

White Bear, war chief of the Kiowa.
(Western History Collections,
University of Oklahoma Library)

Kiowa man inside tipi. (Western History Collections, University of Oklahoma
Library)

Naiche, c. 1906, an Apache. (Archives and Manuscripts Division of the Oklahoma Historical Society)

Mrs. Julia Hall of Ramona, Okla., a Delaware, pre–April 1930. Photo printed by Bingham, Rogers, Ark. (Archives and Manuscripts Division of the Oklahoma Historical Society)

Geronimo wearing his famous war bonnet. (Archives and Manuscripts Division of the Oklahoma Historical Society)

Plains Apache Indian camp near the Washita River, 1894. Photo by William E. Irwin, Chickasha, IT. (Archives and Manuscripts Division of the Oklahoma Historical Society)

Apache camp. First snow in two years. (Archives and Manuscripts Division of the Oklahoma Historical Society)

"Drying Beef in Camp." Hickox Collection. (Archives and Manuscripts Division of the Oklahoma Historical Society)

Drying corn at Joe Kaulaity's in July 1938. Photo printed by Call's Studio, Lawton, Okla. Kiowa agent's report, 1938. Parker McKenzie Collection. (Archives and Manuscripts Division of the Oklahoma Historical Society)

7

TRADITIONAL ALLIANCES

The growing numbers of tribal peoples on the Southern Plains shared methods through which they invested themselves in the region. Institutionally each tribe found paths by which it engaged larger systems. The earth's ecological system was of paramount importance and always their prime concern as their means of sustainable development. Engagement with other systems in the form of intertribal relations was an issue of great significance also and meant translating institutional and personal associations across cultural boundaries. The order of these engagements stemmed from the creative logic and the patterning abilities of the peoples of the Southern Plains in their changing circumstances.

Each of these tribes—Wichita, Caddo, Comanche, Kiowa, and Plains Apache—that established themselves in the plains on a long-term basis did so by examining images and patterns with intuitive insight. Tribal members shared and continue to share these collective images and patterns as a part of their identity. Deep connections existed not only within a tribe but also among the larger systems of the land and the universe that extended through space and time, systems that drew the collective environment of plants, animals, the physical features of the earth, and other peoples into familiar relationships. The spiritual energies emerging from the whole of creation into collective images are expressed in song, ritual, design, color, and reflective activity. Each tribe with its self-defining symbols engaged in relations that were recognized as a part of the whole.

The tribes of the Southern Plains were traditionally liberating, not in a political sense but in broader terms of living where little is defined as waste or as a deficit. Over the years a number of propensities developed within the institutional systems that predisposed each tribe to assume a creative logic that could accept new ideas and concepts while maintaining defining images and patterns. When transformations did occur, they were so thorough that they conveyed the impression of crossing critical passages, naturally enough within the Southern Plains environment. Each passage offered insights into the circumstances and produced a multiplier effect in active cooperation. Physical manifestations of social and economic change—composition, design, accumulation of material wealth—as well as overarching changes in population growth, human ecology, technology, social solidarity, exchange, conflict, and spiritual expression provided necessary themes in tribal engagement with larger systems.

Southern Plains alliances stemmed from continuing traditions and networks of patterns that focused upon solidarity among peoples and within the ecological system. The invariant pattern was that of the circle. The circle appears through the ages in the various cultures: in the hunting surrounds on the prairie; in housing design, whether the large thatched houses of the Wichita and Caddo or the tepees of the Comanche, Kiowa, and Plains Apache; in the dance patterns of each of the tribes, the ceremonial Drum and Turkey dances, the social Round Dance, the camp circle at the time of the Sun Dance. Southern Plains tribes as well as their commercial trading partners recognized the potential of the circular foundations for collaborative action.

Spirituality in the Southern Plains traditions provided networks of systems and processes that governed the peoples' social and economic behavior. Everyone did not possess all the mental and emotional capacities belonging to all the tribes; individuals developed small sectors, and people used different sectors according to their culture. Customary traditions served as reinforcement for interpersonal and intertribal engagements. Natural forces in the larger ecological system created tacit yet powerful sanctions that contributed to the maintenance of order. Means for identifying peoples' place and frequency on the land as well as for regulating external relationships with other peoples were tested by mutually understood images.

The Wichita and Affiliated Tribes, the Waco, Tawakoni, and Keechi, served as an ancient focus for intertribal relations in the Southern Plains. Because their own mythic tradition reached back to their creation as a people in the region, their primary patterns of society and commerce served as critical elements by which intertribal affairs were perceived and enunciated. Their actions had the freedom of integrated systems until well into the modern era, which brought infectious diseases and increasing turmoil. Pressure for new forms of intertribal action through cooperative and integrated effort then materialized. Leaders such as Kikisee-rookah, Wichita; Acaaquash, Waco; and Sarpouro, Tawakoni, emerged largely because of their abilities to bring about concerted action among the region's tribes.[1]

Wichita, Waco, Tawakoni, and Keechi solidarity has provided a means of mutual support by which their influence far exceeded their numbers. Their names were left on the geography of the Southern Plains, particularly in the river valleys and on the mountain sanctuary. These sites include the city of Waco on the Brazos River, Tawakoni Creek in the Blackland Prairie of present-day Texas, and Wichita Falls on the Red River. The Wichita Mountains and the Washita River were a central focus of the Wichita homeland in present-day Oklahoma. The city of Wichita on the Arkansas River in Kansas marked a northern boundary of the tribe's traditional sense of place.[2]

Alignment among the Wichita bands was grounded largely on elements including a common grammar and logic, parallel kinship systems, interdependency in commerce based upon agrarian surpluses, sympathetic mythological patterns of understanding, and geographic proximity. Grammar among the Wichita people relies on the verb form; many sentences contain nothing more than a verb. Action is emphasized in all statements, even in naming, so that nothing is defined in a static way. Images and concepts for the Wichita relate to one another much as water and soil came together in the river systems near which the Wichita people lived. Wichita logic makes it possible to recognize things and situations even when they are not exactly in the originally known form. Thus the Wichita language is excellent for perception as well as for description. Wichita and Caddoan grammar and logic continue to be based upon common understanding rather than upon a black and white analytical approach and an advocacy of one truth to the exclusion of all else.[3]

Relationships represented those of the family as a whole, not merely of pairs. Family behavior was based on cooperation between members of several families. Marriages were arranged between two families; most often the young man's family initiated interaction through a mediator though occasionally a woman's family recognized a desirable young man and would start proceedings in a similar manner. Gifts of horses or other material objects were given to the elder male of the woman's family. When the union between two elite families was announced they would host a joint feast. This exchange as a part of bonding and celebration of rites of union provided a pattern for intertribal behavior.[4]

In the hunting and gathering stage of existence on the Southern Plains people had times of bounty. Without disaster they could preserve enough to satisfy their community needs until the next period of abundance. Excessive rainfall for extended periods of time or prolonged drought, however, could make their accustomed patterns difficult, if not impossible, to maintain. Starvation could and did occur in one region while there was relative abundance in another ecosystem within a relatively short distance. Until there were agricultural surpluses that could be drawn on for extended periods of time, danger of starvation was a reality for bands and tribes. But the wealth of new foodstuffs from the south provided for a more secure system of management.[5]

Mythology provided the patterns of life for the tribe. The spiritual presence on the Southern Plains was a part of civic life. The Wichita sensed spirituality in nature and simultaneously in the soul of the tribe. What occurred in the tribe was not merely politics or economics or structure; it was environment, context. The Wichita knew that everything was the community and that the community was part of everything. The mythology of the Wichita allowed the people to see that the soul endlessly repeats in different guises its own fundamental pattern. The innate dignity, beauty, and integrity of any act and any thing was shared in a way that would keep the earth on its course. All of creation was alive. Tribes and villages were no more self-sufficient than were individuals and families; only the whole was self-sufficient. Thus the Wichita always knew that they had to look beyond the immediate to each larger system sharing responsibilities.[6]

Reaching beyond the Southern Plains, the Wichita maintained continuing relations with the Pawnee. The two tribes believed that they were originally one people who had split into separate communities on the plains, perhaps in the late eleventh or early twelfth century. Despite the physical separation the Wichita and Pawnee have maintained interaction and intermarriage since then. The Wichita-Pawnee Annual Visitation remained as the visual manifestation of this long-term relationship and provided added strength to the intertribal heritage of the combined whole.[7]

According to Wichita tradition, the people were located in relation to a population concentration named Village-by-the-side-of-the-big-elm-tree in the early years of the twelfth century and were the target of attacks from Apache raiders, who were moving into the area. These became so distressing that the Wichita moved farther south around Perched-upon-a-mountain, where they were threatened by unknown intruders from the north and east. After some time the community leaders decided that their people might fare better if they separated. One community moved north and west into the Republican and Platte river valleys; the other turned southward into the Arkansas River valley and became known as the Wichita. Niastor of the Wichita stated in 1885 that the division occurred on the Arkansas River; he said that an advance party sent out by Todekitsasie, or Boy Chief, selected a site for new villages in the Washita River valley and the Wichita Mountains that they had known from a much earlier time. The people moved overland on foot along the Wichita Trace with their goods packed on themselves and on their dogs.

Boy Chief's people settled for a period immediately north of the North Canadian River, where there were fresh-water springs. The principal Wichita community was named High-hills-extending-into-the-river. When the Wichita left this site, they divided once more and established villages to the south. From there, on a clear day, they could see the Wichita Mountains to the south. According to Niastor, subsequent settlements grew along the Washita River and its tributary Sugar Creek and in all directions from the Wichita Mountains, which were known as Our Mountains.[8]

The Caddo Tribe shared a culture superbly adapted to the conditions of the Southern Plains. Their villages located on the natural terraces above the river courses of the Red, Sabine, and Neches were ordered communities. Trees provided the fuel for heating and manufacture. In this village- and ceremonial-center-based society, peaceful maintenance of commerce was the central focus of life, and tribal values of respect, humility, and strength provided the means to sustain it. Their intertribal relations at the beginning of the modern era looked to the west, primarily to the Wichita and the Pueblo peoples of the Rio Grande valley.

Spirits guided events in the material world and from an early age tribal members sought spiritual help in all things. The nature of a mythic vision was critical to purpose in life and within the community. Ceremonies were conducted by elders whose spiritual leadership patterns formed their life's purpose. Bundles of sacred objects signified tribal mythology that established the patterns for action. Responsibility and argument were expressed in community, family, and individual songs. The people used songs, stories, prayers, and rituals for communication. As the Caddo and Wichita continued their intertribal relations and engaged other tribes outside the Southern Plains, they found assimilation and accommodation the prime means of initiating communication so that it was healthy and open. Assimilation was the process of exploring the context in which something was said. As interchange was made the tribes acted on those exchanges and transformed them into new patterns that would fit into the existing tribal structure of understanding. Accommodation was the process of adjusting the structural belief system so that individuals could adapt each new perspective of the world into a spiritual context.

For the Caddo, interdependency was encouraged on individual and community levels. There was no dichotomy between work and leisure. Moreover, Caddo people tended to work through intermediaries to avoid losing face. The present was stressed in community life although future generations were always taken into account during decisionmaking.[9]

At the beginning of the modern era, tribal technology was changed dramatically by contact with the Western Europeans. Tools and weapons had been crafted from bone and stone by the Wichita and Caddo people, and ceramic pottery had been used along with gourd vessels for centuries. Then iron tools and weapons were introduced into the Southern Plains by the foreigners, and metal pots and vessels became increasingly important. These technological innovations, along with the introduction of horses, brought about strategic changes in Wichita and Caddo life. As the tribes began to trade for the imported items and obtained greater numbers of horses, they became involved in imperial schemes of colonial empire manipulated by the Western Europeans. Further, diseases carried by these people from across the Atlantic Ocean caused increasing numbers of deaths among the Wichita and Caddo, who had no immunity to the bacterial and viral strains of smallpox, measles, influenza, venereal diseases, tuberculosis, yellow fever, cholera, bubonic plague, and myriad other illnesses. The Wichita and Caddo continued in their traditional styles of life characterized by their stable population centers, intensive agriculture, and selective hunting, but the quality of their lives was altered through the expansion of trade in foreign-made objects of metal. They no longer controlled the basis of important industries; the center for this powerful aspect of society had shifted far beyond the limits of the Southern Plains. There were short-term profits to be made, but increasingly this became a difficult time for the people of the region.

The bands of the Comanche Tribe made the first great migratory moves of the modern era into the Southern Plains, a move made more dramatic through their acquisition of horses while they were still in the Southern Rockies. Within a relatively short period of time, a few decades, they rivaled the best riders in the world. Integration and accommodation came into play within a few years on the Southern Plains as the Ietan division of the Kotsoteka band allied themselves with the Wichita people. The Peneteka band formed similar relations on civil, commercial, and spiritual planes with the Waco and Tawakoni bands along the Brazos and Trinity river valleys. These alliances provided for expanding relations between the Comanche and the Wichita, with the Wichita villages serving as important centers of trade in the east and the Comanche maintaining their connections among the Tewa Pueblo villages in the Rio Grande valley in the western plains.

Modern era migrations throughout the Southern Plains increased in frequency and number as more people obtained horses. Horse culture transformed peoples' understanding of travel and communication, but more important, it changed their relations with the earth. After the Comanche push south and east came the joint moves from the north by the allied bands of the Kiowa and the Plains Apache. Their accommodation for each other on the upper

Missouri River lasted through the changes and challenges made in their trek to the Rainy Mountain region of the Wichita Mountains. Their great circle was placed and replaced at the time of the Sun Dance as the center of the earth moved in relation to the image of creation found within the people. In this circle the people camped as the Kata, or Rees; the Kogui; the Kaigwu, or Kiowa Proper; the Kingep, the Kongtalyui, or Sindiyuis; the Kuato; and the Plains Apachc, or Semat.

The Kiowa and the Plains Apache maintained their relations with the Crow Tribe in the Northern Plains. This alliance was cemented through the gifts of the Tai-me or Sun Dance medicine and the sacred arrow lance, given by the Crow to the Kiowa during the early years of their interaction. The rituals associated with the mythic symbols as well as with the ten medicine bundles held among the Kiowa and the Plains Apache tied these people together in a responsible manner.

The meaningful bond between the two tribes made it possible for a configuration of relationships and beliefs in which either tribe's problems and issues made sense. To see the problem in the engagement process as problems in the tribe led to notions of resistance and lack of cooperation; thus the engagement process in the context of these two tribes with larger systems was at first a negative experience. But over time the larger-systems relationships were enhanced through effective engagement and relevant intention in what became an appropriately wider network of relationships. After initial confrontations, the Wichita and Comanche allied themselves through the leadership of people who were willing to understand tribal systems other than their own. The leadership of Wolf-lying-down, a Kiowa, and Afraid-of-water, a Comache, brought about assimilation and accommodation involving concepts and images so important to engagement. Once the Kiowa and Plains Apache were allied with the Comanche, then they were led into alliance with the Wichita. As with the Comanche, the Kiowa and Plains Apache sensitively engaged the ecological system so that they maintained sustainable relations with the earth on spiritual and material levels. These tribes, too, came into the larger commercial system maintaining relations with the Tewa Pueblo and the Spanish colonial systems.[10]

Given the advantages of the horse culture, the Comanche, Kiowa, and Plains Apache made long expeditions into Mexico. They established base camps and lines of supply from the Sierra Madre Oriental from where they ventured as far south as Durango, Sonora, and Sinaloa and as far west as the Gulf of California. Some of these efforts took as long as two years.

The arrival of the French in the eighteenth century increased the material vitality of the Wichita and Caddo villages. The French brought goods technologically superior to those of native peoples and the Spanish and traded metal cookingware, mirrors, guns, rifles, powder, metal knives, and hoes. In turn the French sought Lipan Apache slaves and buffalo hides. The Comanche, Kiowa, and Plains Apache served as trading allies, bringing horses, mules, and slaves from the Spanish of the Rio Grande valley. The Wichita and Caddo continued to process dried and plaited pumpkin, leather pouches, and cured tobacco, and they became wholesale distributors of French manufactured trade items.

By the late eighteenth century, the civil and commercial alliance among the Wichita, Comanche, Kiowa, and Plains Apache had reached a new plateau of engagement, but increasing hostilities caused by forced movement of tribes from east of the Mississippi River began to cause havoc. Osage and Quapaw raiders disrupted lines of communication and endangered village life in the Arkansas River valley. By the early nineteenth century, disease and military conflict caused extended recession in commerce and agriculture. Increased attention continued to swing to the West, as the Latinos and their tribal allies waned in coercive power. It was during this period that the Anglo influence extended into the Southern Plains.[11]

Much academic and popular attention has been focused on military conflict and aspects of warrior life among the tribes of the Southern Plains as well as on the various Latino and Anglo engagements in the region.[12] The military aspect of life on the Southern Plains was more the projection of the military-minded Anglo-American society, however, as it garnered its resources to take control of the region by military conquest. The tribes were forced to allocate more resources, spiritual, human, and material, to the struggle. Yet military concerns never took more than a fraction of the time and efforts of the Southern Plains tribal peoples as they continued to concentrate their energies on mutual aid and support among the tribes and nations. Voluntary alliances among the various tribal peoples softened the harshness of change in the modern era. The period of change was still a progressive one in the early years of Anglo engagement in the Southern Plains; alliances for mutual assistance rather than meaningless competitive rivalries provided for life paths attuned to the larger systems of the region.

Feelings of sociability as well as material benefits of commercial concern moved the Wichita, Comanche, Kiowa, and Plains Apache to act in concert with one another and with peoples outside the immediate region. Each tribe learned by observation of and by vision from the various systems, ecological and social, that solidarity was necessary for meaningful existence and for the true empowerment to maintain it. In the traditions of these tribes, individual self-assertion was counterproductive; they wanted larger images for which to strive. The mutual aid within and among the tribes brought about a humane sense of being on the Southern Plains.

Valued aspects of life were viewed with mutual concern among the peoples of the region, bringing about the possibility of attaining old age with respect for accumulated experience, higher spirituality, growth of social habits, secure maintenance of family and tribe, and extension of progressive community development. The alliances among the tribes provided for development of still wider, more inclusive circles of customs, habits, and institutions. These valued aspects of life were fostered by the principles of common sustained living in the Southern Plains and by spiritual outreach through all of creation.

The alliances were facilitated by tolerance through cross-cultural understanding. During the early centuries of the modern era on the Southern Plains the tribal leaders faced the task of finding the invariant elements among the superficial differences. They sought a means of translation—a method to translate the meaning expressed in one language or by one grammatical foundation into a meaning expressed in a different cultural sphere. The longest and closest alliances were those of the Wichita and Caddo and the Kiowa and Plains Apache. Yet in each alliance tribal languages were maintained. Instead of being seen as a cultural barrier, in each case they were viewed as added perspectives in attaining a sense of the whole of creation. Each tribe looked to their relationships for mutual intelligibility leading to mutual respect and aid.

An important key to intelligibility was found in the images and symbols that could be shared by the various peoples. They were moved by needs and desires to understand the world around them, its nature, and their societies in relation to the ecological systems in which they lived. Myth was not a matter of giving these peoples more material power over the environment; rather, it gave them a sense of understanding of the Southern Plains' ecological system and their respective roles within it.

The growing populations on the Southern Plains brought with them significant images and symbols. Once settled in the region, they maintained special relationships across much of North America, in the far Northern Plains, the Rocky Mountains, and to the coasts of the Gulf of Mexico and the Gulf of California. Through these contacts with the land and the people they shared myths over the continent. In truth, many of these were Pan-American images rather than scattered fragments in different parts of the continent. These images and symbols provided for a greater flow of communication and understanding.

In language as well, ideas and concepts were shared across cultural boundaries. Even though the identity of the Southern Plains tribes was tied up in their respective languages, most people knew more than one language, sometimes as many as five or six. On the Southern Plains, the universal language was Comanche, along with sign language. Thus as many tools as possible were used to move across cultural boundaries.[13]

The vocabularies of the native languages were very different. But in the logical substructure, their inner force, they were strikingly alike in the use of pronominal forms, an abundance of generic particles, a preference for concepts of action and verb forms rather than a static sense of essence or nouns. Subordination of nouns to verbs in a proposition was important, a characteristic called incorporation.

The native languages of the Southern Plains are essentially incorporative languages. That is, they formally include both subject and predicate in the translative element and its oral expression. Languages are said to be cognate when relationships between them show that they have descended from a common ancestral speech, evidence of which is derived almost exclusively from the vocabulary. Grammatical similarities are not supposed to furnish evidence of cognation but are considered as phenomena. Not only for the Southern Plains but also throughout the Americas the scholarly custom is to classify American Indian languages into categories, neglecting grammatical structure and considering lexical elements only. This approach stems directly from the Western European dependence upon analysis, using division, definition, and categorization that relies upon Greek and Latin grammatical forms that were imposed upon various Western European languages, including English. These grammatical forms provide for the application of classical Greek logical methods, which is inherently more limited in logical form than that which arises from the American Indian incorporative form and its resulting grammars.[14]

The words in a language change. Migration introduces a potent agency for modification. A new environment impresses its characteristics upon a language more by a change in the meaning of words than by a change in the grammatical forms. For example, the Kiowa's failure to establish linguistic relationships may be based upon vocabulary relating to Kiowa custom more than on any other factor. The tribe requires the dropping from common expression the use of any word that might suggest the name of a deceased person; another word is substituted for the dropped word. This practice introduces a new inclusive combination in existing roots even though the overarching grammatical form remains essentially the same.[15]

Verb construction is the primary concern in most Southern Plains tribal sentence constructions. There is much more emphasis upon action in these languages than in the Western European languages. In the Southern Plains languages, including Wichita, Caddo, Comanche, and Kiowa, the verb consists of a stem with a series of prefixes and a set of suffixes; both the prefixes and suffixes are attached to the verb stem in a specific order.[16]

In addition to verbal communication, sign language added other dimensions to cross-cultural communication, a practice that allowed concepts to be disclosed that might otherwise have remained obscure. An officer in the U.S. Cavalry, W. P. Clark, commented on this form of communication:

> I have heard Indians declare that they had always located the
> Great Spirit in the heavens, and yet in gestures that would

indicate that this was the location of the white man's God, and for their Great Mystery would point to the north, south, or east for its location.

The sign for the Milky-Way led me to make special inquiry in regard to this starry pathway, and I was rewarded with the story of its being the direct and easy trail to the Happy Hunting-Ground, made by those who had been killed in battle.

The mysteries of their myths are illuminated by this language, and traditions, which otherwise would have long since passed into the shades of forgetfulness and oblivion, are kept alive and green in the memories of the present generation.[17]

Sign language clearly served the peoples of the Southern Plains as a sophisticated means of communication.

Through common understanding of symbols and elements of language, the tribes engaged larger systems, including the environment, in concerted ways. Their shared feelings and cognition provided a strong basis for civil and commercial solidarity. In turn, these elements were bound up in spiritual and religious communion.

Each tribe and often each band remained self-governing and autonomous. As the tribes found cooperative understanding and communication, the necessity for hegemony did not arise as it did in colonial cultures. Family and band elders exercised the most direct influence upon community members, even though community forms varied from nomadic extended local families to highly structured village associations. Leaders functioned as managers and decisionmakers in society, sometimes mediating conflict between individuals, families, and bands as well as among tribes. Leaders were usually heads of large, extended families, which ensured support from their members. They were most often individuals whose achievement reflected their spiritual and material success but most singularly their ability to promote and execute cooperative efforts. Leaders led through their status within the community in terms of personal appeal rather than by coercive force. Each person received respect according to his or her recognized wisdom.

Leaders functioned as intermediaries between tribes, especially in terms of commerce and ceremonialism. Marriages often linked the families of leaders in the Southern Plains societies, but marriages among leaders functioned everywhere to link peoples across local cultural boundaries. Ceremonial and other dances also provided a context for cross-tribal interaction, and tribal peoples in the Southern Plains almost always interacted peacefully. Social and political arrangements were made or reinforced. Conflicts that did arise involving large numbers of people of one society against those of another sometimes led to military conflict, but a state of war was never sustained for a long time. Hostilities would be forgiven—but not forgotten. They became an important part of tribal tradition and were expressed within the community through the Scalp Dance or the Turkey Dance. Families exerted considerable influence over members and set the context for social interaction; band interaction was central to ceremony. Spiritual interaction among people and between people and the environment guided activities involving the earth, water, plants, and animals.

8

EXTERNAL DEMANDS

Throughout the nineteenth and twentieth centuries the Southern Plains tribes have continued to validate their traditional knowledge of themselves and their interaction with larger systems. Yet in that same period a radically different point of view was imposed upon them. Anglos, through the collective power of the U.S. government, advanced militarily and commercially, using colonial methods to subjugate the native populations and the environment. Western European social and commercial ideologies as well as religious theologies were used in attempts to sever the tribes from their sense of self. As this intervention proceeded, the Wichita, Caddo, Comanche, Kiowa, and Plains Apache were redefined by the Anglos as exotic beings or as savages. Anglo academic disciplines have justified the policy decisions by defining cultures as "civilized" or "primitive," and studies of a historical, ethnological, anthropological nature were partial and inaccurate. The Anglo point of view imposed on the Southern Plains peoples was ethnocentric and served as a tool to dominate the native peoples.

The Anglos clearly recognized tribal organization as a defining element of native identity. Destroy it, the argument ran, and the coherence of the native ways of life would be destroyed. Anglos attempted to supplant native traditions through military repression and colonial institutions. Always in the picture were pieties of civilization and Christianity, but the imperatives of politics and economics were foremost in policy decisions. The native people were exhorted to sustain the habits of industry and thrift within the colonial system as if they had never practiced them. Where there appeared to be lack of understanding or resistance, policies of extermination and assimilation without accommodation were effected by U.S. policy makers.

The basic issue for the new intruders remained an obsessive desire to acquire land at any cost. The land and the native peoples had to be brought into a more efficient, exploitable framework according to the orderings of "civilized existence." The Western system of logic was applied and dichotomies were established: right and wrong, us and them, friend and enemy, principled and unprincipled, natural and unnatural, civilized and barbaric, capitalism and communalism. People express their experiences through perceptions and languages; every native community understood that. But in the Anglo point of view, the opposite of a concept or an object was a deliberate construction and meant only the opposite. The American Indian peoples on the Southern Plains did not understand this or the system of logic that dealt only in either/or constructions. For the Anglos, the principle of contradiction applied if two proposed categories were made to be mutually exclusive, a construct totally foreign to the native peoples of the Southern Plains. To them dichotomies imposed a false and sharp polarization and allowed no middle ground, a position they considered not only dangerous but insane.

In the early nineteenth century U.S. military expeditions ranged over the Southern Plains and were followed by highly capitalized Anglo-American and British corporate efforts in the region. Industry in the East and in Europe reached out to extract needed natural resources. Growing numbers of people and the search for added raw materials brought new pressures on the Southern Plains. The monopolistic industrial powers sought access to the region in order to meet the needs created by their increasing levels of investment and production.

The Southern Plains provided further access for the expansion of U.S. capital and for industrial and trade expansion in the Far West and into Mexico. Mexico, with its common border, inexpensive labor, vast mineral wealth, oil on the Gulf Coast, tropical agriculture, and possible railroad and canal routes through Tehuantepec, was of major importance to a developing global power. By the latter half of the nineteenth century, half of all U.S. foreign investments were in Mexico.

By mid-century, U.S. Secretary of State William Seward envisioned an American-controlled empire that embraced both North and Central America, and later, Secretary of State James G. Blaine would push for the same end. Blaine wanted pacification of the Southern Plains so that the budding railway system could play its central role in establishing U.S. economic hegemony throughout the region and Mexico. The self-governing Southern Plains tribes were seen as a barrier to the economic growth of the United States.

The expansion called for the elimination of the buffalo on the plains, which had served the Indian nations for centuries as a mainspring of their economic well-being. The United States initiated treatymaking negotiations, then warfare, then enforced concentration on reservations and allotment of lands in severalty followed by complete U.S. hegemony in the Southern Plains. Each of the Southern Plains tribes underwent ever-increasing abuse as the United States expanded its influence. Subordinations entailed social, political, cultural, and economic displacement of tribal and local leadership as well as of native artisans. Paralleling these military-supported policy decisions, silver was devalued, fiscal crisis spread over the global economy, and rising interest rates created an increasingly erratic cycle of inflation and depression that deeply affected the Southern Plains tribes since they were restricted in their primary economic efforts.[1]

During the nineteenth century the U.S. government developed its military strength. By mid-century the United States and the United Kingdom had peacefully resolved their differences, and English financial investments were becoming more extensive in land, cattle, mining, and railroads to exploit the natural resources of North America. The British assisted the United States by providing military advisers and expensive armaments and by generally agreeing on global strategies. As early as 1835 the U.S. military presence in the Southern Plains was direct and inescapable. The Leavenworth–Dodge Expedition engaged the Wichita and Comanche peoples in the area of the Wichita Mountains, after which the United States sought to impose a redefined system upon the Southern Plains. Agreements were negotiated that brought about new international recognition of changes in power in the region. Anglo traders took on new status, extending their commercial advantages from the government-sponsored factories in the Arkansas and Red river valleys in concerted efforts to eclipse the trade relations with Latino and Pueblo peoples in the Rio Grande valley. After 1848, all competition was eliminated when the United States defeated the

Republic of Mexico in the Mexican-American War of 1846–1848 and the Anglos assumed power over the northern states of Mexico. The Southern Plains tribes came under the influence of the United States because their traditional trade relations were disrupted; thus Anglo trade became the primary recourse for the tribes, which had become dependent upon the new technologies in common trade goods and military armaments.[2]

The latter half of the nineteenth century saw a major surge of Anglo intrusions into Southern Plains tribal affairs. Treatymaking with all the tribes after the American Civil War provided a new foundation for Anglo–Native American interaction. In 1867 a series of U.S. military assaults were launched on the Southern Plains to enforce new, special trading rights and cession of land claims. In 1871 the railroads began to open Indian Territory on the Southern Plains to larger numbers of non-Indians by reducing the time and difficulty of travel and communication in the region. By 1889 a telegraphic communications network was established that connected the growing number of towns along the several railroad lines, making communication instantaneous.[3]

Concessions were given to Anglo-held corporations for additional telegraph lines, railroad rights-of-way, toll roads, ferry and warehousing facilities, banks, mining leases, and oil development and even to oversee archeological sites. The growing road system reflected the fundamental regional social and economic transformation that was under way. Anglo shippers and merchants conducted all the import and export trade on the Southern Plains as a result of the displacement of the Wichita, Caddo, Comanche, Kiowa, and Plains Apache trade system. The Indian nations and tribes resisted this displacement but to no avail. Moreover, the tragic loss of life in recurring epidemics among the tribes weakened their commercial and political institutions and structures as they had little or no resistance to the strains of diseases introduced by the Latino, African, and Anglo populations.[4]

Agricultural surpluses gained through the traditional native intensive-farming methods of former times were diminished in scope; the Wichita, Caddo, and Delaware cultivated corn or maize, pumpklin, beans, and squash but in reduced amounts. The Anglo corporations supported the raising of wheat and cotton to the exclusion of Native American crops. High costs of equipment needed for the cash crops, tribal resentment of pricing and cost abuses, and government interference prevented the agrarian-based tribes of the Southern Plains from entering the cash-crop system. The Comanche, Kiowa, and Plains Apache were saddled with bureaucratic farmers hired to teach them to cultivate wheat and to herd sheep. The Chiricahua and Warm Springs Apache were taught to cultivate hay for the U.S. Army mules and horses on the Fort Sill Military Reservation after they became prisoners of war.[5]

Between the 1860s and 1905 the total trade in constant dollars more than quadrupled in the region, largely because of agricultural and raw material delivery. By 1905 the Anglo private and corporate interests, either directly or in trust through the U.S. government, controlled 100 percent of the commercial agriculture and manufacturing in the Southern Plains. In half a century the Anglo population had completely dominated the market to the exclusion of the native populations. Only seventy years earlier the U.S. military had ventured onto the plains to negotiate their first treaties with the tribes.

In many rural locales native tribal and community leaders felt the challenge to their efforts although in civil and spiritual matters their power was still very much a matter of importance. As U.S. Indian policy forced people onto reserve areas, the tribal leadership still held arable properties amid band-defined tribal memberships. But during the course of the latter half of the century, the Indian Service of the United States increased national hegemony at the expense of these tribal leaders. One of the techniques the government used was to issue leaseholds to Anglo ranchers, with little return to the tribes.

Thus traditional native lands—and the possibility of their continued use and occupancy by their indigenous inhabitants—were reduced to ever smaller splotches on the national maps. These restricted ethnic enclaves made it increasingly difficult for the native tribal alliances to communicate and to trade with one another. The illusion of recognition of native tribal sovereignty was rudely shattered. Land became a commodity, and disputes over proprietorship were growing between numbers of immigrants and displaced occupants. The continued subjugation of the tribal peoples was harsh, with extreme force used against dissenters.[6] The process of the United States' increasing involvement in the global market at the beginning of the twentieth century contributed to the impoverishment and displacement of Anglo and African-American people, urban overcrowding, and unemployment. But the opening of lands in the Southern Plains for settlement by non-Indians created havoc for the Indian nations.[7]

The depressions of the 1870s and 1890s and the recession of 1914 increased pressure to open the Southern Plains further within Indian Territory to Anglo capital and immigration. Economic pressures required new concessions to special interests, especially in oil and gas. Increasing economic complications wrought by American and British financial shortages and higher interest rates were severe. During this period the reservations of the Wichita and Affiliated Tribes, including the Caddo and Delaware, as well as the Comanche, Kiowa, and Plains Apache were opened to non-Indian settlement. The ever-greater spending policy of the U.S. government further compounded the affliction.[8]

Costs incurred in the development of the transportation and communication infrastructure increasingly drained government revenues. Federal obligations included the construction and improvement of military and post roads connecting Fort Sill, Fort Reno, and the towns of Old Oklahoma Territory, or the unassigned lands. Added governmental expenditures covered the purchase of materials for the construction of federal offices, support for the telephone and telegraph concessionaires, and indemnities to merchants and manufacturing interests. Other outlays went for the dredging of rivers and creation of port facilities.

The western lands were opened for settlement for the common good of the citizens of the United States. The tribal peoples, who had retained the lands by treaty negotiations, were not U.S. citizens; they were members of their sovereign nations and tribes and were so recognized by the U.S. government. The U.S. land policy and encouragement of Anglo and African-American immigrants to settle in Indian territory was an immediate threat to political power for the tribal leadership and undermined further the economic position of the American Indian peoples. The opening of their lands also stimulated a commercial revolution in agriculture. The cultivation of wheat and cotton encroached on their agricultural fields that had long been available for corn, pumpkins, beans—the food products that had supported the tribal peoples for centuries. The availability of staple foods diminished while the population grew and prices rose. At the turn of the twentieth century local food shortages and price increases caused real hardship for the Indian peoples. Diet changed for the worse as it was underwritten and controlled by the U.S. government, and dependence upon the rations provided by the Indian Service continued to be a disturbing reality.[9]

Throughout this period the United States was acting unilaterally in Indian affairs without the consent of the tribes. The growing hegemony was upheld in the U.S. Supreme Court in *Lone Wolf v. Hitchcock* (1903). Lone Wolf, a Kiowa leader, attempted to use the U.S. court system to prevent the government from taking tribal lands without agreement from tribal leadership. His efforts failed, just as had the Cherokee Nation's attempts to prevent forced removal and alienation of lands in the 1830s, as U.S. officials stated their interpretation of the Supreme Court decision: "Such Indian lands as it saw fit to take might be appropriated and the owners left to obtain such redress as Congress might be willing to make."[10]

The response of tribal and local native leaders to U.S. economic, political, and cultural penetration was widespread and negative, but it was ignored. Tribal diversity and degrees of local autonomy stimulated regional and local opposition to the encroachment but only with nominal effect. The U.S. government's concessions to special interest groups outraged all but the few who were directly benefiting from the Anglo-American entrepreneurial enclaves. The destabilizing effects of material shortages and higher interest rates seriously undermined the tribal economies. The failure of the Indian Service to protect tribal interests provoked indignation, scorn, charges of corruption, and demands for renewed respect for treaty obligations. As always, a number of grievances converged: the nature of the treaties; native administrative priorities; attempts to assimilate American Indian peoples with no accommodation; the decline of traditional native means of sustenance; the spread of nonnative habits, primarily the abuse of liquor; and the spread of diseases to which the American Indian peoples had little immunity.

During the latter half of the nineteenth century and the first decade of the twentieth, tribal leaders strove to retain their hold on the land and on local resources as well as to control resource management for intensive forms of agriculture; they also tried to maintain a reasonable share in the trade of all agricultural products.

Despite the grim realities of Anglo- and African-American encroachment upon their lands after the close of the Indian wars,
tribal and local native leaders orchestrated community affairs involving tribal members in efforts to prevent utter collapse of their
traditional life ways.

Tribes and their members obtained additional identities by virtue
of their involvement with the United States. Demeaning labels
were used repeatedly by the larger political and economic bodies in
reference to the tribes, such as "savages," "redskins," "gut eaters,"
in attempts to stereotype the people, to reduce the complexities of
tribal societies. The labels not only alienated one culture from
another but also projected an image of the American Indian peoples
in the growing colonial economic system that limited perceptions
and narrowed choices for solutions. Further labeling of the tribal
peoples frequently occurred when the United States carried over
academic and legal terms such as "primitives" and "wards" to the
political and educational systems, where differences between tribal
and colonial systems were submerged. Unquestioned terminology
served as a means to calibrate the relationships within the tribes
and between the tribes and the larger colonial system, which had
replaced the existing tribal systems of commerce and interchange.
Behavior that was different from Anglo-American expression was
seen as negative and unpredictable so that options for cross-cultural
exchange became constrained or unavailable.

The tribal leadership was engaged with the U.S. military system,
the reservation system operated by the Indian Service, and the
colonial economic system. It was not unusual for the leaders to be
the recipients of simultaneous and contradictory ideas from the
various levels of authority, a situation that resulted in confusion,
thus paralyzing the leaders' attempts to act. The tribes were facing
the fact that they were being required to interact with larger systems and with multiple authorities over which they had little or no
influence, a state of affairs that would clearly last into the future.
Thus those leaders who were already under stress because of the
destruction of their economic systems through the alienation of
land, annihilation of the buffalo, tremendous loss of life through
disease, and unsettling effects of continuous military harassment
had the additional stress of dealing with the hegemony of the
United States in all its policies.

U.S. agency personnel rarely, if ever, viewed their work with any understanding of the tribes and their existing complex systems. The military engaged the tribes as enemies to be destroyed or subjugated. The Indian Service, apart from its gross corruption, ostensibly was organized to assist tribes; however, it frequently fragmented them through practices and policies that lacked appreciation of diverse tribal forms and that failed to realize the impact of intervention upon tribal systems. Educational and medical agencies, both operated directly by the U.S. government, generally viewed their efforts as being on behalf of the tribes. Interaction with the tribes was required, yet this often was not seen as the heart of the matter but as a necessary evil. The U.S. agents' purposes were to correct technically whatever problems they defined as those existing among American Indian peoples.

The boundaries between the tribes and the U.S. agencies that existed over long periods of time showed increasingly unusual combinations of diffusion and rigidity. Tribes were required to share much more information with the government than it was required to share with the tribe. Access to the tribal systems was forced to remain open to multiple authorities in order for the tribes to receive needed services, but government bureaucracies were less open to the tribes because of their highly regulated formal and complex processes.

In order to deal with the presence of these bureaucracies over long periods, tribes appointed one person to carry on most of the interaction; he became the conduit between the tribe and the larger system. U.S. officials made the error in many cases of assuming that this person was also the major decisionmaker for the tribe when in fact he may have been simply a message carrier between systems. The role was difficult and stressful. Furthermore, secrecy between tribes and the U.S. government represented metaphorical boundary markers. Officials promoted patterns of secret-keeping through their approaches to particular problems or issues; such secrecy generally reflected wider social values and shifted as values shifted. Information was seen as power by the authorities, not used as a means to facilitate more reasonable living conditions on the Southern Plains.

The framework introduced into the Southern Plains by the United States was one largely of intensity and crisis and was confused further by the lack of shared information between the tribe and the larger system. The tribal leaders could not impart traditional wisdom to the bureaucrats in the military, Indian Service, teacher corps, or medical profession because the Anglos were unprepared to hear what was being said. By definition the "civilized" people could only regress if they listened to the teachings of "savages." At the same time, the government professionals would waste their time by spelling out their plans to "primitive" peoples to assist in their own assimilation into the larger system. There was little advantage in teaching the Native Americans the American Dream; it was an immigrant's dream: change the world and you change the subject.

Given the military subjugation and the economic and social repression, the tribal peoples seemed to be at the point of annihilation. Many Indian peoples were already at the point of extinction because of the diseases that continued to ravish them into the early years of the twentieth century; the Indian Service medical doctors actually predicted the end of some tribes. Assimilation without accommodation was seen by Indian Service bureaucrats as the path on which Indian people would travel so that they would no longer function as tribal members. War, pestilence, and abuse in the name of education seemed to be taking their toll.

Although there was seemingly nowhere to turn, the Southern Plains tribal peoples knew to turn to their mother, the earth. The physical intensity of the people enabled them to extend themselves in the symbols of the earth—in its compassion and its visionary power, forming the beauty of its images. The earth was alive; the people had but to respond to it. The aesthetic response saved the phenomenon, the face of the earth. What remained when all else perished was the face of things as they existed. When there was nowhere to turn, the Indian people turned back to the face before them, to the Southern Plains—the earth. Here was the power that gave a sense of existence that was neither myth nor meaning. Instead, that immediate presence in their lives as image, its metaphor, brought sustenance and beauty that was healing in nature.

9

PEACEMAKING

As the native peoples of the Southern Plains were brought into the sphere of U.S. influence during the middle and late decades of the nineteenth century, other tribes were brought into the plains region through forced removal under the authority of the federal government. Despite disruption forces, the Delaware Tribe was able to retain a strong sense of identity while integrating itself with the other tribes of the plains.

The Delaware made discerning choices as they moved before the onrush of Anglo immigrants all the way from the Atlantic Coast, assessing the meaningful systems of the Caddo and Wichita as they moved into the region. The configuration of relationships and beliefs they found there made sense within their specific frame of reference. The Delaware based their assessment on their strong sense of tradition formulated in the *Walam Olum,* or Red Score. This configuration of tribal heritage provided for a process in the context of tribal–larger-system relationships that enhanced the possibilities for effective engagement and for relevant moves into an appropriately wider network of relationships among the tribes while maintaining cultural boundaries. This same process was restricted, however, when the United States intervened and imposed colonial practices colored by Anglo ethnocentrism.

The Delaware people exhibited a strong sense of their presence in the world, which extended back into the far reaches of space and time. They have an oral tradition that includes a tribal memory of common life before their entry into North America: The *Walam Olum* speaks directly of the move across the ice sheets into America as a part of their migration story. The Delaware occupied the east coast of North America in the early seventeenth century. According to their own tradition, they had lived on the Atlantic

Coast for seventy-six generations when the first contact with the Anglo explorers and colonists occurred. Their arrival on the Southern Plains did not take place until the early nineteenth century, and their record was extraordinary:

I

There at the edge of all the water where the lands ends,
. . . the fog over the earth was plentiful, and this was
    where the Great Spirit stayed.
It began to be invisible everywhere, even at the place
    where the Great Spirit stayed.
He created much land here as well as land on the other
    side of the water.
He created the sun and the stars at night.
. . . all these he created so that they moved.
Accompanying good deeds the wind blew, the sky cleared,
    and water rippled in many places.
It looked bright, for he made islands, and having done so
    he remained.
Then again, the one who is the Great Spirit, a manitou,
    created manitous
. . . and persons who die, and souls for all of them.
Thereafter he was a manitou to young men, full grown
    men, and their grandfathers.
But another powerful manitou created powerful men and
    those water monsters.
. . . he created the flies and he created the mosquitoes.
Everybody behaved, seeing friends everywhere
. . . and was happy, staying with the manitous.
Those young men, the first men went after the mothers,
    the first women
. . . who went to pick berries, the first food, while the
    young men followed them.
Everyone was glad and pleased, everyone felt nicely,
    everyone was happy.
But when the snake god, the guardian spirit, its worship
    did things secretly on the continent,
. . . he did mean things, he did destructive things, and
    black deeds came there,

. . . bad weather came, killing came, death came.
Everybody from over there across the water stayed in the
large villages of the first land.

II

Long ago there was a strong snake when men, the big
men stayed there.
The strong snake, who was hated, those young men
stayed there; the hated one tried to go about to
forbidden places.
Each of the two were destroying things, each of the two
were in bad circumstances: the two of them did not
keep peace with each other.
They were quarrelsome as they lived there; they were
lazy and they were fighting.
The strong snake quickly made up his mind about the
men; he destroyed possessions of the people,
. . . he brought these things: he brought great
quantities of water, he brought rapids
. . . so that the water ran and ran, spreading in hollows
and making hollows, penetrating here and penetrating
there, destroying something here and destroying
something there.
Nenabush [Big Rabbit] stayed on Turtle Island: he was a
powerful rabbit, the grandfather of people,
the grandfather of men.
The wind was blowing but he crept along and untied the
young turtle.
The people and the men all kept going on: they crept
along the river of rapids there downstream on Turtle
Island.
The water monster ate some of them but there were
many people.
The daughter of the manitou helped them with a canoe;
and as they came from the opposite direction, another
one helped them all,
. . . he who was Nenabush, Nenabush the grandfather
of all, grandfather of people, grandfather of men,
grandfather of the turtle.

The Delaware were there where the turtle was, where the
turtle had a tie-line about his waist.
. . . where the turtle was they experienced fear, where the
turtle was they prayed: that the other one cease doing
what he was doing, that he repair what he had done.
As the water rippled, one long extended area became
dry even where there were hollows and in caves: the
powerful snake went some place else.[1]

The Delaware lived after that time on Turtle Island, or North
America, never returning to their former land. The remainder of the
Walam Olum records the movement of the Delaware, their leaders'
achievements for the tribal community, and the structural changes
within the tribe with the creation of the clan system. An extension
of that record reflects the real and apparent dangers of the modern era:

We shall be near our foes the *Wakon* (Ozages [sic]) but they are
better than the *Yankwiakon* (English Snakers) who want to
possess the Big Island. Shall we be free and happy there? At the
New *Wapahani*, We want rest and peace and wisdom.[2]

The Delaware people suffered tremendous population losses in
eastern North America in the eighteenth century from smallpox,
influenza, and measles, diseases that accompanied the European
immigrants.[3] With continuing hope, the Delaware moved westward
through the Ohio Valley into the lands claimed by the French and
the Spanish, the clans system providing structure for the people as
they moved. According to tradition, the Delaware survived in three
clans—the Turtle, the Turkey, and the Wolf, but references to other
clans include the Eagle and the Beaver.

Two significant bodies of the Delaware survived in the West. One
part of the tribe became known as the Eastern Delaware; they were
forced by the United States to become citizens of the Cherokee
Nation in 1867 as a part of the Reconstruction Plan for the tribes
negotiated in the treaties entered into after the Civil War.[4] The
people who became known as the Absentee or Western Delaware on
the Southern Plains associated themselves with the Wichita and

Caddo tribes. Formal recognition of this alliance was made by U.S. agents on the Wichita and Affiliated Tribes reserve in 1874.

The Delaware adapted to the larger systems. First there was a new environment: industries were carried on in different circumstances and with new materials. For example, basketmaking used willow, hackberry, slippery elm, dogwood, cat-tail, swamp grall, soapweed, and beargrass. There were three standard grades of baskets, each one having a special purpose. Hackberry was used primarily in baskets for shifting corn and washing it with lye to produce hominy because it did not leave a bad taste on the corn. Baskets made from the other materials were used as containers. Dyes for these baskets were made from the bark of the slippery elm, blackjack, walnut (also its leaves), pokeberry, and elderberry. The dye was made by boiling the leaves or bark in water, straining it, and soaking the material in the heated liquid. Pottery was made from the red, yellow, black, blue, and white clays found in the river valleys throughout the region. The clay was pulverized, sifted through a fine basket, and then crushed together with shell aggregate. The mixture was moistened and worked into shape. These vessels were sun-dried, polished with stone, and baked in ashes heated with buffalo manure. Most pots were lined with dipper gourds and fired, but some were filled with tallow before firing. The pottery was used for cookware and containers. Hides were prepared for a number of uses. First they were stretched and the flesh removed; then they were soaked in an ash solution and dried. The hair was removed by passing the hide over a clean log. Brains were boiled and the liquid was used to clean the skin; then the hide was hung on poles to dry in the sun and wind. The final process was smoking, which darkened the skin of the deer or buffalo. In the Southern Plains, the Delaware learned to work silver, obtained through trade from the mines in Chihuahua in northern Mexico. Each adaptation made for a more responsible existence.[5]

Just as the Delaware adapted to the new ecology, they also adjusted through their alliances with other peoples and nations. The role they intended to play was that of peacemakers. In the nineteenth century, the Southern Plains were terribly unsettled. The Mexican Revolution in 1821, the U.S. military expeditions onto the plains in 1834 and 1835, the Texas Revolution in 1836, the

Cherokee-Texas War in 1839, the Massacre of the Comanche Chiefs in 1840, the Mexican-American War from 1846 to 1848, Bleeding Kansas in 1854, forced Indian removal from Texas in 1859, and the Civil War from 1861 to 1865 created unrelenting turmoil on the Southern Plains. Throughout this period the Delaware leaders emerged as significant figures among the peacemakers: McCulloch, James St. Louis, Roasting Ear, Red Horse, Captain Stump, Black Snake, Jack Ivy, Jim Ned, Menchara appeared in peace negotiations records regularly.

The Delaware suffered terrible losses in the Cherokee-Texas War in 1839 but returned to Texas in the mid-1840s. With the aid of the Delaware and the Wichita, the Texas government was able to conduct the Tehuacani Creek Council in March 1843, at which the majority of American Indian interpreters were Delaware. Commissioners from the Republic of Texas and the United States joined representatives from the Delaware, Shawnee, Caddo, and Wichita tribes. The Delaware were prominent in the negotiations that led to the Treaty of Bird's Fort as well as to the intertribal councils of 1844 and 1845. A measure of peace was achieved when Texas was granted statehood. The Brazos Reservation was created, but by 1859 the Texas tribes were forcibly removed to Indian Territory.[6]

In the latter half of the nineteenth century and throughout the first half of the twentieth, the Western Delaware maintained their identity and language but were part of the Wichita and Affiliated Tribes. The Delaware survived as a part of a critical intertribal alliance, integrated into the ecological system of the Southern Plains. The people were interdependent by their nature through the images that sustained them across two continents. At the core of their social organization lay social adhesion, and their solidarity had its strongest roots in Delaware spirituality.[7]

The Western Delaware knew that they were no longer self-sufficient by any definition of the term and increasingly demanded to transcend sovereign jurisdictions to meet their responsibilities. As the United States continued to influence interaction on the Southern Plains no tribe could provide exclusively for its own general well-being, including upholding the rights, powers, and privileges of its people. At the same time, the actions of the smallest and apparently weakest tribes could and did act to the benefit of all at critical junctures. To cope with the acute problems precipitated by the ever-growing colonial system, Delaware leaders followed a vision of effective intertribal and international cooperation. They devised a network of contacts in concert with the peoples of the Southern Plains, even under the growing influence of the United States. Through intertribal organization, which supplemented the bilateral relations demanded by the United States from the tribes, the peoples tried to maintain sophisticated linkages to meet specific problems.

Intertribal councils lacked the powers of the sovereign tribes, especially after the Native American peoples could no longer determine the processes of the institutions that governed much of the material direction of their lives. Because of lack of effective communications and given the actively disruptive tactics of U.S. officials, intertribal councils sometimes lacked active participation and support from all tribes. Yet it was generally believed that intertribal organizations provided necessary insurance against economic and social disarray.

The behavior of the tribal leaders provided a functional system through which relations could be examined. Indeed, centering forms of synthesis offered needed perspective in identifying the span of Delaware diplomacy and provided a means of tracing the web of interactions among people. Decisionmaking formed a cycle by which needs were met in context; successes and failures resulted in adjustments in the leaders' actions: identified need, intertribal action, larger-systems response, and adjusted action. This basic framework provided a simple method by which to interpret intertribal efforts. Not only did the focus on Delaware leadership serve the Southern Plains tribes during a very difficult period, but it also seemed to give Anglo policymakers and their bureaucratic extensions in the field a sense that the United States was successful in its efforts.[8]

Power and welfare were not inseparable interests. The political and functional aspects of tribal behavior increasingly were intertwined and remained so. Under the institutional pressures and demands of the larger system, important political and developmental needs became driving forces behind intertribal actions over time.

Intertribal relations were carried on by the tribal governments recognized by the United States. The federal government's interests dictated that tribal jurisdictions be forced into specific enumerated lands. U.S. policies were formed in response to those who had special interests or who hoped to extend their interests into the Southern Plains: railroad corporation boards, wheat buyers, and large numbers of people who wanted a second and third chance to own land and take part in the American Dream.

The fluidity and variation in the actions of the Delaware and other plains tribes in responding to these complex pressures generated by human need belied the impression of intertribal unity. In the world of intertribal relations, the sources of action were to be sought in the motivations and perceptions of the people who were responsible for public authority, leaders such as Roasting Ear, McCulloch, and James St. Louis. The United States was not successful in its stated policy changes because it chose not to take time to understand these community motivations and perceptions.

There was no shirking of personal responsibility for policy decisions in the Delaware worldview; the leaders were clearly identified with their decisions in the tribal community. Policy formation was very much the focus of social control. Yet people's needs continued to be diverse, and the priorities people attached to demands upon themselves varied. To satisfy the needs of one person denied in part the satisfaction of others. As the material wealth of the tribe was reduced because of the imposition of U.S. policy decisions, an inescapable factionalism in social and economic efforts resulted within the tribe and certainly within the larger intertribal systems. In the rapid pace of affairs consensus was rare.[9]

The choices of international and intertribal arrangements to satisfy human needs were causing conflict because logical systems were being imposed upon the tribes that were foreign to them. Forcing all conventions to be carried on in English as the language of diplomacy proved a barrier to workable outcomes. In the system imposed by the United States, the Anglos were the masters of the dependent "wards." The Anglo operatives determined in godlike fashion what was right and what was wrong, despite the imperatives of the larger ecological system. Moreover, as events progressed in this fashion the tribes were blamed for their anger; the Anglo citizens of the United States were to be shielded at all costs. The tribes' life-affirming feelings were seen as posing a threat, and the tribal communities' will had to be broken.

The relativity of values emerged as the tribes engaged the larger general system enforced by the United States. The degree of power—not in the sense of medicine but in geopolitics—determined whether actions were to be judged as good or bad. As the victor in war, the stronger nation dictated the outcomes, regardless of the hurts that were committed on the path to victory.

The Delaware had learned that in experiencing collective changes, survival depended in the long run on the practiced values that tended to contradict the idea of "might makes right." Among those values were respect for the weaker among the whole and respect for life in all forms, without which all creativity would be stifled. The interplay of tribal tradition, ethnocentrism, prejudice, stereotypes, and images and concepts with their supporting or contradictory intentions played a critical part in the decisionmaking during this era of political and economic transition. Attitudes of suspicion or trust, fear or assurance, and loyalties affected the process. Yet a steadfast commitment to cooperation remained the means most likely to secure satisfaction of basic needs. Cumulative evidence pointed to the development of integrative processes among the tribes, a development facilitated by the Western Delaware. It would provide an important foundation for supportive society in the harsh reality of their new environment.

10

RESERVATION SYSTEM

Reservation policy emerged as the principal means of political hegemony on the Southern Plains during the nineteenth century. More tribes, over fifty, were forced from their homelands in the southeastern United States and from the Old Northwest into a concentration of peoples in Indian Territory. The U.S. military established themselves to ensure the imposed order. Although the agrarian peoples such as the Delaware, the Wichita, and the Caddo could manage despite the added restrictions on their movements by using their traditional methods of sustenance, they still suffered from the loss of buffalo and other game that were being destroyed on an unprecedented scale. The other tribes that had crafted their life ways within the outlines of the horse culture and the buffalo hunt found that this strict enforcement of reservation policy made it difficult if not impossible to survive.[1] During these difficult times two tribes from the north were forced by the United States into the Southern Plains—the Cheyenne and the Arapaho. Their stories illustrate the killing force that fell upon the peoples of the Southern Plains during the latter half of the nineteenth century.

The Cheyenne, whose name for themselves is Tsitsistas, and the Arapaho, or Hinanaeina, migrated from the Great Lakes region onto the Great Plains in the seventeenth century, with the Arapaho preceding the Cheyenne in living on the plains west of the upper Mississippi River valley. Both tribes had an agrarian economic base until they adopted the horse culture and followed the buffalo herds to provide for their needs. They had raised corn, collected wild rice, hunted water fowl, and fished for the mainstays of their diet in the lakes area. When the Cheyenne first moved onto the plains, one band turned back, saying that they were hungry for ducks and that the ghosts of the buffalo came to them in their dreams and stared at

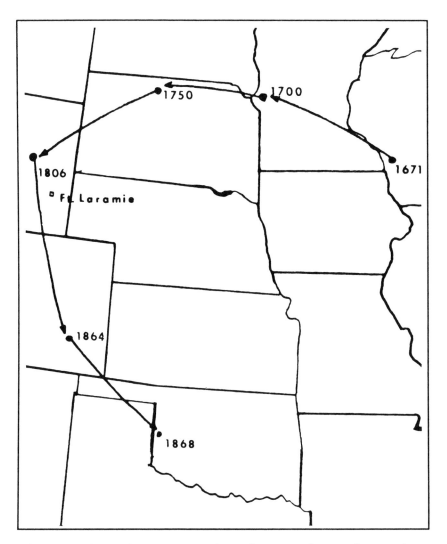

Cheyenne and Arapaho migration in the modern era, indicating the general movement of the Southern Cheyenne people, with approximate dates noted along the line of tribal migration. Modern political boundaries are used for reference purposes only.

them with their great brown eyes. These people never wanted to kill them from that time forward. But the majority of both tribes moved west and south farther into the plains. Each tribe maintained its own tribal and band organization, language, camp circles, and Sun Dance ceremonials; however, they cooperated in hunts, raids, and protection throughout much of the modern era.[2]

Family and band structures provided for social and economic stability through most of the year. Tribal and intertribal organizations and societies maintained order during times when the tribes met in common. Formal governmental structure among the Cheyenne was the gift of Sweet Medicine. Separate tribal Sun Dance societies provided for peace during the height of the summer activities.[3]

The spirituality of the Cheyenne focused upon the ceremonies of the Sun Dance and the Sacred Arrows. The Sun Dance or medicine lodge religious form was that shared by the Arapaho, the Kiowa, the Plains Apache, and others, Crow, Blackfeet, Shoshone, and Shoshone-Bannock, throughout the Great Plains and the Rocky Mountains. Possibly, the Cheyenne received the Sun Dance through the Arapaho; however, there is a lasting tradition that the Sun Dance was given to the Cheyenne by the Sutaio, a tribe later incorporated into the Cheyenne tribal structure.

The Sun Dance among the Cheyenne and the Arapaho was a ritual of renewal and prayerful sacrifice, including as a central focus an appeal for the return of the buffalo. The construction of the medicine lodge enclosure required respect and ceremony. The lodge was constructed of cottonwood and willow; the supports and beams were dragged to the construction site by a horse, many times ridden by a man and woman. Each couple would marry a short time after the dance. Song accompanied each timber to the site. The enclosure had an opening directly facing the rising sun, with a second blind opening facing the setting sun. The appointed ones stood the tree trunks in vertical position with the branches and leaves left in place; beams were tied across these standing supports. The enclosure was circular, about twenty-eight feet in diameter, and in the center an upright cottonwood trunk was stationed. Pieces of cloth—yards of calico, red bandanna handkerchiefs, silk scarfs, or bunting—were tied to the branches of this central tree, which served as the axis, the center of the world. Anyone in the tribe could place a streamer of cloth in the branches, which served symbolically as the presence of prayers and assistance for individuals, families, and tribe. A buffalo head or a buffalo robe and bunches of sage were tied at the central fork of the tree. An altar was built on the west side of the enclosure, and gifts were placed inside it for the dancers: food, blankets, clothing, everything crafted with care. Sage was placed on the ground in a half-circle open to the east. Just inside the circle of the enclosure, beds of fresh-cut grass were placed for the dancers to rest on.

The ceremonial brought together the principal elder and the young men, who made a vow of sacrifice for the families and the community. Each dancer wore ceremonial colors over his body and a wreath of sage with pieces of it extending on each side of the head. In the center of the forehead and leaning back against the head were bunches of white feathers from under the wings of a turkey or an eagle. The downy feathers were attached to the end of a whistle that each dancer held in his mouth and blew as he danced. In his left hand he held a small sprig of cottonwood leaves. Some of the dancers carried eagles' wings in their right hands and some held sticks decorated with horsetail hair. They danced barefoot, standing in place on the sage with a springing motion and looking at the buffalo head.

Singers and drummers maintained the songs important to the ceremonial concerns of the ritual. Women sat around the edge of the ceremonial ground, holding cottonwood leaves and waving them in time to the rhythm of the dance; they helped sing the chants. The drums never ceased their rhythmical beat. As the dance neared its end, the gifts were placed at the center pole. Just before the sun set the opening to the west was cleared away, and two lines of men and women formed on either side of the opening, extending for hundreds of yards. After ritual cleansing, there was a feast.[4]

In Cheyenne culture there is the sacred tradition of the origin of the Buffalo Cap medicine from Erect Horns, the cultural hero of the Sutaio; this too was symbolic of renewal and sacrifice. Both the medicine and the tradition still exist and are in the keeping of the priest of the ritual.[5]

The Four Sacred Arrows with its tradition and ritual, were carried to the Cheyenne by Sweet Medicine. This teaching is sacred and cannot be spoken of casually; the whole of existence for the tribe is identified with the Four Sacred Arrows. The teachings of Sweet

Medicine's wisdom offered a means of providing solutions to political, social, and spiritual problems. One important solution was not to rely on one leader but to accept governance by forty-four men, representing the four principal divisions of the tribe. These men represented the consensus of the whole tribe in alliancemaking, allowing strangers to enter land for which the Cheyenne were responsible, mediating disputes between tribal members, imposing penalties, and passing judgments. Trade was conducted primarily through the forty-four chiefs. They were not to seek excesses in profits for themselves and were to live as examples for all to see. A man could not be a warrior and a chief at the same time.[6]

Among the Arapaho the most significant ritual object was the sacred Flat Pipe. It was constructed with accompaniments as it was seen in a dream by the maker, who made it in connection with the Ghost Dance in the same period that the Sun Dance was being repressed by U.S. government officials. On one side of the pipe is a turtle and on the other a duck, the two animals who dived for the earth; they refer to the symbolic origins of life in the north. Feathers from crows, ducks, and geese are attached near the mouthpiece. Other figures important to the Arapaho are carved on four accompanying sticks, two green ones and two red ones. This is a model of the pipe that is with the Creator.[7]

Through a series of negotiated settlements, the Cheyenne and Arapaho moved further south. The Treaty of Fort Laramie in 1851 provided for a reserve between the North Platte River and the Arkansas River. The Treaty of Fort Wise in 1861, made through the initiation of the Cheyenne and Arapaho chiefs, ensured a reduced reserve in the upper Arkansas River valley. The Treaty of the Little Arkansas in 1865 created a reservation between the Arkansas River and the Cimarron River that was reaffirmed in the Treaty of Medicine Lodge in 1867. Finally, a reservation was guaranteed by executive order for the Southern Cheyenne and Arapaho in 1869. During this period of agreement and movement the Cheyenne and Arapaho were attacked, even under a flag of truce at Sand Creek and again on the Washita River.[8]

The Cheyenne, Arapaho, Kiowa, Plains Apache, and Comanche broke out of their reservations in 1874 in a military effort to end the extermination of the buffalo. The killing of buffalo by Anglo-American hunters had been given fresh impetus by the development of the railroads on the Southern Plains. The effort to bring about the slaughter of the buffalo, which were so important to the Indian peoples, was a commercial enterprise to the Anglos. The buffalo were in the way of the railroads, and the hides could be used in the manufacture of harness. It is estimated that over 4 million buffalo were killed on the Great Plains between 1872 and 1874 by the Anglo buffalo hunters. The tribal peoples attempted to protect the remnant of the southern herd on the High Plains, fighting engagements at Adobe Walls, Anadarko, and Palo Duro Canyon. After they surrendered, members of each of the tribes were taken as prisoners to Fort Marion in Florida, where they were held for years.[9]

Meanwhile, the continuing problems of illegal liquor, a lack of rifles with which to hunt, a lack of annuities that were pledged by the United States, and disputes with tribes including the Ponca and Kaw added even more difficulties. White Antelope, Roman Nose, and Black Kettle, among the Cheyenne, and Left Hand, of the Arapaho, were among the great men who had been killed during this period. The buffalo were nearly gone by the mid-1870s. Anglos wanted the land, both the right to move through it and to exploit the wealth it contained. The native populations could not be exploited efficiently for the economic purposes of the time except through the expropriation of their lands.[10]

Cheyenne and Arapaho leaders were confronted with numbers of problems. Ultimately they were hit with the U.S. policy of allotment in severalty to take so-called "surplus reservation lands" for Anglo and African-American settlement. The timing of this policy change was coordinated with U.S. military efforts to stop the Sun Dance, which promised world renewal, thus stripping Cheyenne, Arapaho, and Kiowa people of their spiritual ritual expressions. In 1889 the Indian Service sought to provide the Cheyenne and Arapaho with beef, but because the agency sold the hides the tribal peoples received no monetary benefit. The Cheyenne and Arapaho peoples demanded the hides as well as the meat; so much had been taken from them they could not afford to lose the hides. The distribution of only the meat without the hides would deprive them of more than $5,000 that they could obtain from the traders. The Cheyenne and Arapaho were also disturbed by the arrival of so many Anglos on the eastern portion of the reservation as a result of the Oklahoma land rush in spring 1889. The prohibition of the Sun

Dance in 1889 made the advent of the Ghost Dance in 1890 that much more important to the reservation. Two Arapahos, Black Coyote and Washee, had been sent to learn of the vision given to Wovoka; when they returned, all the people turned their attention to the message. Carefully the Arapaho made their Ghost Dance shirts and gathered in the hills and bluffs north of the North Canadian River, where they camped, danced, and sang. Other tribes, including the Caddo and Kiowa, joined in the sacred vision dances and carried them back to their own tribal camps.

The opening song of the Arapaho version of the Ghost Dance ceremony provided this proposition:

> O, my children! O, my children!
> Here is another of your pipes—He-eye!
> Here is another of your pipes—He-eye!
> Look! thus I shouted—He-eye!
> Look! thus I shouted—He-eye!
> When I moved the earth—He-eye!
> When I moved the earth—He-eye!

The pipe served traditionally as the means of communicating truth. A second Arapaho song further delineates the theology of the Ghost Dance:

> The sacred pipe tells me—E-yahe-eye!
> The sacred pipe tells me—E-yahe-eye!
> Our father—Yahe-eye!
> Our father—Yahe-eye!
> We shall surely be put again (with our friends)
> E-yahe-eye!
> We shall surely be put again (with our friends)
> E-yahe-eye!
> Our father—E-yahe-eye!
> Our father—E-yahe-eye![11]

In all aspects, the dance was one of renewal. It recognized the spirits of all those around them and the movement to a world of ecological understanding and harmony. But Indian Service Agency officials and Christian missionaries were threatened by the theology and by the large gatherings in Cheyenne and Arapaho country.[12]

Controversy continued over the carrying of Cheyenne and Arapaho children away to boarding schools, where they were educated along Western European lines of thinking and also abused. The children were subjected to corporal punishment for the first time in their lives, chained at times to their beds, forced into western military regimen, and given inadequate rations. Each new issue or concern directly affected the peoples on the reservation, taking added strength to face and to try to resolve. Constantly there was the threat of U.S. military intervention to enforce Washington-based policy on one issue or another.[13]

Through the Springer amendment to the Indian Appropriations Act of 1889, the president of the United States was authorized not only to open the unassigned lands in Oklahoma to settlement but also to appoint a three-man commission to negotiate with the tribes in western Indian Territory to end the exclusive use of the reserves of tribal members. Moreover, the Southern Plains tribal peoples were to be forced from their tribal associations and made to settle on restricted land allotments, a plan carried out by the Jerome Commission chaired by David Jerome, former governor of Michigan. The commission arranged for the dispersal of the "surplus" lands of the Sac, Fox, Potawatomi, Shawnee, and Iowa tribes before approaching the tribes of the Southern Plains—the Cheyenne and the Arapaho, the Comanche, the Kiowa, the Plains Apache, the Wichita, the Caddo, and the Delaware. The meetings began at Darlington, an agency station in the Cheyenne and Arapaho Reserve on July 7, 1890. It was U.S. policy to preempt the ethnic enclaves that were due to families and individuals so that there would be less defense of the land.

All the conditions were right: the Cheyenne and Arapaho tribes were divided into contending factions, key chiefs had been deceived by supposed friends, U.S. policy was nonnegotiable, railroad corporations demanded such a policy, and land-hungry Anglos and African-Americans stood ready for the reservation to be opened for settlement; easy money waited for Anglo-American spoilsmen. From the outset, the commissioners used both threats and promises to influence the two tribes, to which Old Crow, a Cheyenne elder, responded:

The Great Spirit gave the Indians all this country and never tell them that they should sell it. . . . See, I am poor. I have no money; I don't want money; money doesn't do an Indian any good. Here is my wealth [pointing to the ground]. Here is all the wealth I want—the only money I know how to keep.[14]

U.S. spokesmen explained the policy, after which a bitter debate took place between Old Crow and Commissioner Jerome. Old Crow said that the Cheyenne did not want the reservation cut up into small acreages and that if individual leaders violated the wishes of the majority of the chiefs, "we will punish them." Jerome reminded Old Crow that the Dawes Act could be imposed on them without their consent and that the U.S. Army was available to enforce the law. Old Crow replied, "Now I am going to speak my mind to you if I am killed for it. . . . We have been robbed of our land and the worth of our land ever since the white man came into the country and they ought to be full of it."[15]

Arapaho chiefs Left Hand and Cloud Chief knew they had received an offer they could not refuse, so they brought forward counterproposals, demanding more money and large blocs of land instead of the individual allotments in the proposal. The Arapaho were being advised by the young men of the tribe who had received education at the boarding schools. Even the counterproposal was refused because the United States had created a system by which they could force the issue regardless of the terms. The Cheyenne and Arapaho cession agreement was approved by Congress in 1891 over the protests of the Cheyenne chiefs led by Old Crow, Little Whirlwind, Little Big Jake, White Shield, Red Moon, and Wolf Face and of the Arapaho chiefs led by Left Hand and Cloud Chief; the Cheyenne Dog Soldier Society leaders Mad Wolf and Howling Wolf also protested.[16]

By 1907, the year of Oklahoma statehood, it was incontestable that the Southern Cheyenne and the Arapaho had not benefited from the allotment process; rather, the reverse was true. Irreparable damage had been done to both tribes' peoples as well as to the Anglo settlers who were set up for failure in trying to farm 160-acre plots in semiarid conditions. Clearly the Cheyenne and Arapaho could not effectively cultivate and farm their allotments any more realistically than the Anglos, given the technology and methods imposed upon them. The U.S. government inadequately funded and overmanaged Indian agricultural efforts and then leased the land to Anglo ranchers. Indian land policy was a dismal failure because ideology won out over sensitivity to ecological systems, tribal systems, and the general systems of the Southern Plains.

Despite the educational policy and the other crushing burdens of the assimilation policy, the Cheyenne and Arapaho retained their tribal identities. All else had failed, but the chiefs were still respected, the earth was loved for the joy it afforded, children and elders were cherished, friends were welcomed, food and hospitality shared: eternal patterns were not forgotten.[17]

The Jerome Commission did not stop with its Cheyenne and Arapaho dictates. In the early 1890s the commission visited itself upon the Comanche, Kiowa, and Plains Apache reserve and later to the Wichita, Caddo, and Delaware reservation to the north and south of the Washita River. Commissioners had grown anxious to complete their work and were far less tolerant of opposition than they had been in 1890. When the tribal leaders grasped the import of the proposed agreements that were thrust upon them, they protested and the commissioners departed. But once away from the negotiating grounds, the Anglos simply smudged thumb prints and testified that tribal leaders had agreed. The terms of the agreements were altered to suit the U.S. government, and congressmen willingly enacted each agreement. Tribal protests through the courts did delay enactment until the twentieth century, however.

Cheyenne and Arapaho incomes as measured within the larger system were too low to support families, so the Indian people borrowed from bankers and money lenders and obtained credit from merchants. The system was unmerciful to the Indians, who lost what little they had in many cases. Economic conditions among the Cheyenne and Arapaho peoples were depressed. Sale of liquor, although illegal on the reservation, was never controlled so that chemical dependency took an ever-increasing toll on many tribal families. Every band or family within both tribes was affected by addiction in some way. The leasing of Indian land held in trust by the U.S. government was abused on a broad scale. Farming, which was the keystone of U.S. policy measures, brought in less than 2 percent of the total income of the two tribes in the first decade of the twentieth century. The federal Indian land policy and educational policy were dismal failures.[18]

Promised safeguards to protect the tribes of the Southern Plains had failed. Government-controlled leasing gave the tribal members a pittance in rental. All too often, farmers and ranchers overgrazed and one-cropped the leased trust lands to the point of destroying the soil; lumbermen lessees stripped timber from the land, leaving eroded barrens. At the end of the allotment period, over half the Indian lands that had been held in trust were critically or severely eroded, and the Dust Bowl was a terrible reality. The fiduciary responsibilities of the United States were largely ignored or strained beyond recognition. But through it all, reservation boundaries remained intact.

The reservation system that led to the enumeration of the lands of the Southern Plains provided the means to dismantle the tribal land bases through allotment in severalty. A national paternalism replaced the legal procedures expressed in treatymaking that had prevailed through much of the modern era. By the last half of the nineteenth century the United States had defeated the Indian nations militarily. Given the importance of the metaphor of war in Anglo-American cultural affairs, U.S. officials ignored the tribal members' needs, failed to respect them as people, and overlooked their position in a nation of laws, focusing instead on ethnicity and personalities. The people, on their significantly reduced land base, were wards in an ever-increasingly paternalistic system.[19]

The U.S. military, the Indian Service, and the Congress demanded obedience. First, the Southern Plains tribal peoples had to willingly do as they were told; the measure of their compliance was no longer the Native American sense of spirituality but socially and commercially correct behavior. Regulation of their lives was to be determined by a Western European sense of civilized behavior. For example, to be religious one had to have short hair and dress in a stylish manner accepted in Western society. Second, the Indian people had to willingly refrain from doing anything that was forbidden by Indian Service interpretations of U.S. policy. For example, the Southern Plains peoples had to stop the Sun Dance ritual practices that were central to their lives and their sense of renewal. The Indian Service agent threatened the Kiowa people with military force when they attempted to hold a Sun Dance in 1889 at Medicine Bend of the Washita River, and the Kiowa and Plains Apache have never danced the Sun Dance since that time. The United States intervened to destroy the centeredness so important to Kiowa, Cheyenne, and Arapaho civilizations. As a result, only the Cheyenne still dance the Sun Dance on the Southern Plains in the twentieth century, and the Arapaho dance with the Northern Arapaho on the Wind River Reservation in Wyoming. Third, the Indian peoples were forced to accept the rules made for their sake by Anglo-American officials and were no longer allowed to influence the institutions that directly affected their lives. Thus did the paternalism of the Anglos expand into most aspects of the tribal peoples' material and spiritual life.

The Indian Service consciously used humiliation to destroy the Indian peoples' self-confidence, both against the children who were separated from their parents in boarding schools and against the adults through the detailed management of their lives, which set them up to fail in small farming operations. The suppression of native spiritual expression inhibited the people, leaving them insecure even though the action was touted as beneficial. Feigned friendliness helped to conceal this type of cruel treatment, deception apparently being a universal method of control. In the political sphere the government's ultimate victory was presented as the successful solution to the cross-cultural conflicts.

The general system was established so that the Anglo-Americans were the masters of the Indian wards of the state. The Anglos determined right and wrong according to "enlightened" thought. If the Indian peoples showed anger they were held responsible in the most exacting manner; the Anglo-Americans were to be shielded from any sort of retribution. Any tribal member's life-affirming feelings and expressions posed a threat to the U.S. system. Assimilation policy required that the will of each tribe had to be broken so that there could be no resistance.

Isomorphism emerged in two ways during the allotment policy period. First, when the process began, the tribes were overprotective toward those members who could not make changes in their lives to accommodate the dictates of the larger colonial system that sought to assimilate them, but the younger people instead became exasperated with them. In turn the larger system, dominated by the

United States, was overprotective through its restrictions and grew exasperated with tribal members among the Cheyenne and Arapaho. Each plan imposed by the United States was met with quiet resistance in the middle decades of the twentieth century. Yet this position led to periods of intense frustration and anger followed by periods of confusion and disorientation. Second, within the tribe there was covert competition among different fractions over the eventual leadership in Cheyenne and Arapaho affairs. The power of tribal chiefs, although never eliminated, was substantially lessened. Among the older Cheyenne Peace Chiefs and Dog Soldier Society members, many had died, and their successors never attained the prestige of the older leaders. The Indian Service agents ensured this situation through appointments and by select distribution of material goods. The covert tribal competition was mirrored in a subtle symmetrical struggle among the outside systems, including the Indian Service, the Christian missions, and the local institutions of governance and finance, in their attempts to provide the appropriate answers for the Cheyenne and Arapaho. Simultaneous and often contradictory ideas from various Anglo institutional agents resulted in confusion, paralyzing any efforts for action. Just as the dominant larger system highlighted only the perceived deficits in the tribes, tribal members primarily saw only the negative aspects of this system that was being imposed upon them by the United States.

Six Kiowa-Apache children, c. 1984–1985. Mrs. Don Paddlety, as a child, holds a doll in a cradleboard. Photo by Irwin and Mankin, Chickasha, IT. (Archives and Manuscripts Division of the Oklahoma Historical Society)

Cheyenne Indian children at school with a miniature plains Indian village, c. 1895. Hickox Collection. (Archives and Manuscripts Division of the Oklahoma Historical Society)

Arapaho school at Anadarko, OT, 1891. (Archives and Manuscripts Division of the Oklahoma Historical Society)

"Commanche [sic] & Kiowa Indians painting history on buffalo robe, Indian Territory 1875." Photo probably by Jack Hillers, near Okmulgee, IT, May 1875. C. W. Kirk Collection. (Archives and Manuscripts Division of the Oklahoma Historical Society)

"*Caddo & Delaware Club,*" *women and children. Kiowa agent's report, 1938.*
Parker McKenzie Collection. (Archives and Manuscripts Division of the
Oklahoma Historical Society)

Mission Board representative from New York by a Wichita grass house and
arbor. (Western History Collections, University of Oklahoma Library)

Wichita danceground on Camp Creek, near Gracemont, Okla. (Western History Collections, University of Oklahoma Library)

Fort Sill Apaches waiting for train from Fort Sill, after their release in 1913 as prisoners of war. (Archives and Manuscripts Division of the Oklahoma Historical Society)

Jack Harry, a Delaware, and Bar-cin-de-bar, a Caddo. (Archives and Manuscripts Division of the Oklahoma Historical Society)

Zachory Taylor, or "Old Sack." One of the last of the Caddo road chiefs, or Peyote leaders. (Western History Collections, University of Oklahoma Library)

Geronimo and Natchez, at Fort Bowie, Ariz., after surrender to General Nelson, 1886. (Western History Collections, University of Oklahoma Library)

Chief Al-ika and Laughing _____,
Kiowa Apaches. (Archives and
Manuscripts Division of the
Oklahoma Historical Society)

Quanah Parker on horseback.
(Archives and Manuscripts Division of
the Oklahoma Historical Society)

Indians in Sun Dance costume. Observers in large tent around them. Cheyenne.
Clinton, Okla. (Western History Collections, Univeristy of Oklahoma Library)

Chief Hail, an Arapaho, in Ghost Dance costume. Hickox Collection.
(Archives and Manuscripts Division of the Oklahoma Historical Society)

"Flashlight photo of Sacred Dance of the Geronimo Apache Indians, only photo made of this dance. Copyrighted 1910." Photo by Eugene Bates. (Archives and Manuscripts Division of the Oklahoma Historical Society)

Participants in the Kiowa mud race, a religious ritual. July 4, 1900, Anadarko, Okla. (Western History Collections, University of Oklahoma Library)

"Apache Indian women with their gifts for their guests, the Comanches."
Postcard printed c. 1918–1922. Photo by Eugene Bates, Lawton, Okla. (Archives
and Manuscripts Division of the Oklahoma Historical Society)

"Comanche Indians dancing in response to the dance of welcome by the
Apaches at Apache Camp near Apache, Oklahoma." Photo by Eugene Bates,
Lawton, Okla. (Archives and Manuscripts Division of the Oklahoma Historical
Society)

A council of the Comanche, Kiowa, and Apache chiefs: (1) Quanah Parker, Comanche; (2) Ahpeatone, Kiowa; (3) Lone Wolf, Kiowa; (4) Koon-kah-zah-chy, Apache; (5) Ca-va-yo, Comanche; (6) Pah-ka-toquodle, Kiowa; (7) George Hunt, Kiowa (interpreter); (8) Mo-ziz-zoom-dy, Apache; (9) Soontey, Apache; (10) Arrushe, Comanche; (11) Es-i-ti, Comanche; (12) San-ka-do-ta, Kiowa; (13) Otto Wells, Comanche (interpreter); (14) Delos K. Lonewolf, Kiowa; (15) Tennyson Berry, Apache (interpreter); (16) Pe-ah-coose, Comanche; (17) Eustace Merrick, Comanche; (18) Kline-ko-le, Apache; (19) Max Frizzlehead, Kiowa; (20) Ko-mah-ty, Kiowa; (21) Henry Tse-lee, Apache; (22) Lt. Stecker, Indian agent; (23) John A. Hendricks, U.S. Indian Bureau attorney. (Western History Collections, University of Oklahoma Library)

Council of Kiowas and Comanches. Left rear, braids wrapped, *Piakusah, Quanah Parker;* left front, *Apehatone;* right front, *Kiowa*. Anadarko, Okla., June 17, 1899. (Western History Collections, University of Oklahoma Library)

Old Man Tippeconnic and son, John Tippeconnic, the first Comanche to graduate from a four-year college. 1930. (Western History Collections, University of Oklahoma Library)

Comanche Indian memorial service for President Harding, c. 1923: (1) Os-ea;
(2) Ouas Ana; (3) unknown; (4) Mrs. Chief Yellow Wing; front row, far left,
Mam-sook-a-wat. Photo by G. W. Long, Hobart. (Archives and Manuscripts
Division of the Oklahoma Historical Society)

Kiowa Indians. Left to right, rear: *Linn Pauahty, unidentified minister, Delos*
Lone Wolf, Conrad Mausape, Mathew Botone; front: *Ted Ware, Albert Horse,*
Guy Quoetone, Kicking Bird II, unidentified minister. (Archives and
Manuscripts Division of the Oklahoma Historical Society)

11

PRISONERS OF WAR

The last tribe to enter the Southern Plains to live among the other tribal peoples did so in railway boxcars under the control of the U.S. Army as prisoners of war. The entire Chiricahua and Warm Springs Apache people—men, women, and children—were held as prisoners of war for twenty-six years by the United States. These were the people who had followed Naiche and Geronimo in their struggle for freedom against U.S. hegemony in the desert Southwest. The Apache's primary concern was to live responsibly within their traditional desert homeland in the vicinity of Hot Springs (the area of present-day Arizona and what were then northern states of the Republic of Mexico). There was no doubt of their historical and traditional need for liberty or of their willingness to fight for its achievement.[1]

The Chiricahua Apache persisted in defending their homeland until their surrender to U.S. military forces. Four bands, the Warm Springs, Mimbrenos, Bedonkohe, and Chokonens, or Chiricahua proper, provided the structural strength of the tribe. The military struggle with the United States and with the army of the Republic of Mexico occurred intermittently until the final surrender on September 4, 1886. The Chiricahua people were confined to military prisons first in Florida and then in Alabama, where all the newborn children died within their first year of life. Finally they were interned at Fort Sill in the Indian Territory on the Southern Plains. They remained there until Congress brought about the removal of the Chiricahua prisoners, some to the Mescalero Apache Reservation, some to allotments in the Kiowa, Comanche, and Plains Apache Reservation in Oklahoma.[2]

In the centuries before their capture, Chiricahua people had moved south in their efforts to be responsible to the Creator and to their land. The patterns of their lives related to eternal images that provided for life. Like other peoples on the Southern Plains, they believed that the earth was in darkness in the beginning. There were two tribes, birds and beasts, including many nameless monsters, who fought a long war in which the birds finally won, under the leadership of the eagle. The final engagement was between the eagle and a nameless monster, and the eagle killed the monster with a round, white stone. (The symbol of the stone is used in the Chiricahua game of Kah.) A human correspondingly had to face a monster, which he killed with bow and arrows; this boy's name was Apache, the son of White Painted Woman or Changing Woman. Usen, the Creator, taught him how to prepare herbs for medicine, how to hunt, and how to fight. Apache was the first chief of his people and wore eagle feathers as the sign of justice, wisdom, and power. Usen gave homes in the arid Southwest to Apache and his people.[3]

The Chiricahua and Warm Springs peoples were removed from their land in 1886 by the orders of the U.S. military. In 1885 the Interior Department gave absolute and total control over reservation affairs to the War Department, completely abrogating its responsibility toward the Chiricahua and Warm Springs Apache. Removal to Florida opened the reserve to corporate intrusion for the exploitation of mineral resources.[4]

The restrictions upon the Chiricahua and Warm Springs Apache confused them but did not strip them of their abilities, gained over long years of experience. They had carried on sophisticated commercial relations in the Southwest. Their understanding of the movement of commodities such as gold, silver, livestock, and other precious items provided for a sustainable life in a relatively harsh environment.[5]

Apache association between direct achievement and economic growth should be understood in the context of sequential phases and in the distinction between values and norms. The term values in this context refers to preferred mode of orientation toward specific categories of experience; thus need and value preference were similar concepts. During the course of internment values did not exert the same degree of compulsion on the individual as needs did. Needs certainly motivated the people on basic physiological levels, but values affected choices at the spiritual core of each person.

Santa Fe and Chihuahua Trails in the nineteenth century, showing the
general path of two important trade routes popular in the nineteenth
century. Significant trade centers are noted as well as Fort Laramie.
Modern political boundaries are used for reference purposes only.

Values, in the case of the Chiricahua and Warm Springs peoples,
were forged from the experience of the entire society. The pressure
to conform to Anglo life ways within a military framework for
more than a quarter of a century therefore took a terrific toll.
  Needs were gradually projected into the basic images of the value

system of the Chiricahua and Warm Spring's Apache society, a development that occurred as conformity and technology impacted the various aspects of their lives even more than military policy did. Survival brought about a strong sense of the value of achievement in their renewed concern for traditional patterns of life.[6]

Among the Fort Sill Apache definite concerns provided a measure of motivation of sustainable development. Within the Chiricahua and Warm Springs Apache culture, some socioeconomic groups were more highly motivated by achievement than others, and particular periods in the modern era were characterized by higher degrees of it. Moreover, achievement motivation was associated with some bands and with groups with certain religious affiliation more than with other bands or groups, and achievement images were linked with some religious systems more than with others.

Traditionally, once Apache society had achieved a certain level of well-being, it turned its interest and activity to other nonmaterial needs. Economic well-being was understood in different terms according to images and patterns inherent in Apache society. At various points in the seventeenth, eighteenth, and nineteenth centuries, the Apache people vigorously pursued status and wealth. For example, Geronimo related a number of instances of raiding into the state of Sonora in northern Mexico. The raids were risky and undertaken in pursuit of material gain, i.e., blankets, clothing, cheese, sugar, horses, cattle, and mules; the livestock was then used as exchange items in commerce.[7]

Among the most important of the spiritual rites was the puberty ceremony, a joyful ritual given to the people by White Changing Woman that serves as a blessing for the entire tribe. Regardless of their circumstances, the Chiricahua continued the puberty rite through the years, whether they were at war with the Spanish, the Mexicans, or the United States or living in captivity, on reservations, or among others. The actions and rituals of many individuals who possess certain ceremonial abilities or special knowledge are required to produce an effective puberty rite. Among the most spectacular figures are the Mountain Spirit Dancers, with their extraordinary headdresses and symbolic swords. Their high-stepping dance, accented by its many moments of rigid pauses, brings the girl long life and good health. They bless her, the ceremonial grounds, and the people.[8]

The years of captivity disturbed the concerns of goal attainment among the Apache. Values and symbolic images that motivated activity changed as their environment changed, and values that had been shaped primarily by tribal spiritual practice was stifled. Their conversion to Christianity added certain theological insights. Naiche and Geronimo led most of the Apache prisoners of war into the Dutch Reformed church as a matter of protection as much as from a concern for added spiritual guidance. New technology, new land, and new forms of knowledge impacted the worldview of the Chiricahua and Warm Springs Apache even as religious symbolic systems took on more abstract ideals. They saw the potential for freedom becoming increasingly possible in the twentieth century, and an elemental degree of it was provided through congressional action in 1913, which ended their period of imprisonment.[9]

It was decided that the Fort Sill Apache people who desired to stay in the Southern Plains could do so if they accepted an allotment of land within the Kiowa-Comanche-Apache Reservation. Several of the Apache had become successful stockraisers and had become attached to the land, but War Department officials ruled that the Apache people could not have any part of the military reservation at Fort Sill. The military wanted to send the Apache back to their homeland in the arid Southwest, but the Interior Department did not provide reservation land as had been promised by the United States at an earlier juncture. The Chiricahua and Warm Springs people's release was accepted by Interior Department officials as a part of the Indian Appropriations bill of 1913 by which funds were made available for relief and resettlement though not without objection. The Chiricahua and Warm Springs Apache people then began to live as restricted Indians in the Southern Plains, where they combined intensive and extensive farming methods and practiced cattle ranching. They were the first to raise kaffir corn for forage in Oklahoma. They raised melons and vegetables for their own needs and for local markets, and some continued to engage in seasonal work, cutting and bailing hay under contract for the army at Fort Sill.[10]

Mildred Cleghorn, a Fort Sill Apache born as a prisoner of war, recalled that although the Apache spoke of the tribe's lack of preparation for the continuing crush of events related to the cash economy, no one would listen to them. The tension was reflected in the values of the Fort Sill Apache, which revealed preferences. Apache cultural values constituted the core of their system of symbols; Anglo value systems continuously impinged upon theirs in terms of the economy, the polity, the arts and sciences, and many cultural subsystems. The decay of institutions and normative inter-relations were at the center of the imprisonment experience. Apache values continued to play a significant role in the lives of the people, providing cultural solutions to the problems of absolute and relative dependencies. Norms were shaped primarily by the pressures of organized society. In the case of the Apaches held as prisoners of war, this system was totally distorted. Materialism and militarism impinged not only on the norms but on the values as well. The functional imperatives brought about conditions that forced the people into difficult if not impossible situations.

The higher degrees of freedom allowing discernment in value orientation were no longer present because there were no implications of any utilitarian reward. The Chiricahua and Warm Springs Apache were grounded in their sense of being, which emphasized that good things in life came of their own accord through existing in harmony with the earth. During their quarter of a century as prisoners of war, this worldview was impossible. The government's Indian policy stressed the need for constant activity, energetic solutions to problems, and improvements through technical means for controlling nature and society. The norms of each society, one completely dominant over the other, made interaction difficult.

The United States saw economic growth as a process of continuous evolutionary change and development, a view predicated on a particular perception of the significance of life on this earth. Necessary to this view was the acceptance of the idea of progress, of a present better than the past and a future potentially better than the present. Human ability could legitimately control and improve the natural environment. Western history and logic led policymakers to view Apache ways as being capable of abstract truth, which was so important to the Anglos. They emphasized the study of history, deeming it to be the means of examining human behavior and interaction. Because of cause and effect relationships, hindsight provided the basis of the historical method. Linear thought was justified through classical Greek logic. Western knowledge and critical thinking skills were considered enough to ensure a measure of the truth. Truth in this system was reached by means of argument, through the logic of reason, so that contradictory positions could be eliminated.

Apache tradition held to a sense of truth that grew from experience in which learning took time and repetition. The means of change, which may be radical in nature, came through changed perceptions and values; the steps were small but cumulative. The Apache did not use argument because of their fear of polarizing the community. They emphasized exploration of a subject and creative activity rather than critical thinking. Design skills were paramount, not skills of analysis. The Apache did not share an obsession with history but had a concern for existing patterns and relations. The skills of doing were as important as the skills of knowing. Thus the Apache avoided the direct dangers of crude perceptions, polarizations, misleading language, unnecessary confrontations, aggressive beliefs. They felt that these practices were directly responsible for much of the misery that humans have inflicted on others. They believed the greatest dangers to be arrogance, complacency, and the ability to defend that arrogance and complacency. Apache logic was expressed best in songs and humor; it was a logic of perception.

Apache experience has shown that reason and classical Greek logic can never change a person's perceptions, emotions, prejudices, and beliefs. Hindsight was of little value in identifying a process, and obsession with history at times seemed to reflect a culture of corpses. The Western logical system, its grammar, and the particularly false dichotomies necessary to operate the principle of contradiction had created and crystallized the polarities of "either/or" and "us/them."

The Chiricahua and Warm Springs Apache people understood that a frame of reference was important to understanding and that it was never complete. The only truth in perception was the truth of the eternal patterns and relationships. Understanding the symmetry of patterns allowed the Apache to perceive the phenomena of humor, of insight, and of creativity. The relatively small Apache tribes spent long periods of time together. Because of such close proximity, human relationships became very important and subtle. The Apache had developed a rich language to describe nuances of human relations. A good disposition, believed to be one of the gifts White

Painted Woman confers, promises that the Apache girl in her puberty ceremony will always have the support and assistance of her relatives, a crucial concept in traditional culture. Much of Apache life depends on goodwill among relatives and the community.

Geronimo in his autobiography hoped for goodwill:

> I am thankful that the President of the United States had given me permission to tell my story. I hope that he and those in authority under him will read my story and judge whether my people have been rightly treated.
>
> There is a great question between the Apache and the Government. For twenty years we have been held prisoners of war under a treaty which was made with General Miles, on the part of the United States Government, and myself as the representative of the Apaches. That treaty has not at all times been properly observed by the Government, although at the present time it is being more nearly fulfilled on their part than heretofore. In the treaty with General Miles we agreed to go to a place outside of Arizona and learn to live as the white people do. I think that my people are now capable of living in accordance with the laws of the United States, and we would, of course, like to have the liberty to return to that land which is ours by divine right. We are reduced in numbers, and having learned how to cultivate the soil would not require so much ground as was formerly necessary. We do not ask all of the land which the Almighty gave us in the beginning, but that we may have sufficient lands there to cultivate. What we do not need we are glad for the white men to cultivate.[11]

Geronimo died in captivity in 1909. Even so he gave voice to a multicultural expression that reflected the sophisticated nature of Chiricahua and Warm Springs concerns. His was not the voice of a childlike ward of the government. Geronimo hoped that U.S. policy would permit the Apache the freedom to live not "against" but "with" their past; the Apache people's traditional wisdom could then be in harmony with the "enlightened" knowledge offered them through the auspices of the Indian policy. The false demands of paternalism could be silenced and a true understanding of life could take their place. But this hope was lost on the authorities in Washington.

In the case of the Chiricahua and Warm Springs people of the Fort Sill Apache Tribe, the messages to be understood are the patterns of the land, the experience of the people, and the expression in thought and word of these relationships. The tribe functioned according to a doctrine with a tradition for planning and community action, a precept governing work and leisure, and a reverence for creative forces. The tribal leadership understood the revolution of credit, which involved social ethics, mortgages, development banks, and fugitive money. They also understood the role of tribal justice, responsive civil service, and advanced institutional tribal studies needed to bring about development.

The Chiricahua and Warm Springs peoples want to be involved in their own destinies. They remind one another that as a small tribe in an interdependent world they are restricted in what they can do to guide even internal change. Wars, business cycles, technological discoveries, energy, and changes in food supplies affect the tribe in dramatic ways. The Chiricahua and Warm Springs peoples have had a difficult time making themselves understood by the Anglo-American leadership in the late nineteenth century and throughout the twentieth. This inability to communicate their needs has resulted in extreme loneliness at times. In turn, their relative isolation has made for difficulties and thrown them back upon themselves. Nevertheless, their basic consensus on important values and norms has made intratribal communication both possible and fruitful in the long run. Thus their internal strength has provided a stable foundation for social, economic, and political survival.

12

CONTEMPORARY ALLIANCES

Contemporary alliances between the United States and each tribe on the Southern Plains have been fashioned on a contractual basis with heavy emphasis upon land transfers and material concerns. The United States has served as the dominant party in these alignments for the past 125 years. Indian-white relations have tended to follow models of modern international law, stemming from the Spanish school and the United Kingdom and emulated in tribal affairs. Treaties recognized individual tribal entities throughout the nation's early period and in policy considerations until 1871. After that, U.S. Indian policy was dominated by Washington's unilateral approach—tribe by tribe.

Throughout the period of formal relations between the United States and the tribes of the Southern Plains, the former has enjoyed the proceeds of tremendous economic growth while the tribal reservations have remained underdeveloped. Theories espoused in the United States that progress in the general welfare is based upon rugged individualism, state welfare, or supply-side economics have failed to directly benefit the American Indian people in measurable fashion. U.S. hegemony in the region has been directly accountable for the repression of spiritual expression and commercial overregulation from the late nineteenth century throughout the twentieth.

Sustainable development has become a renewed goal for the Southern Plains tribes only during the past quarter of a century. To stimulate it, a complex but often poorly coordinated network of projects has been devised by the tribes and certain agencies of the United States, largely excluding the Bureau of Indian Affairs, to transfer two kinds of assets from the global economic and social network to the tribal frameworks: information and capital.

Underdevelopment among the Southern Plains tribes is difficult

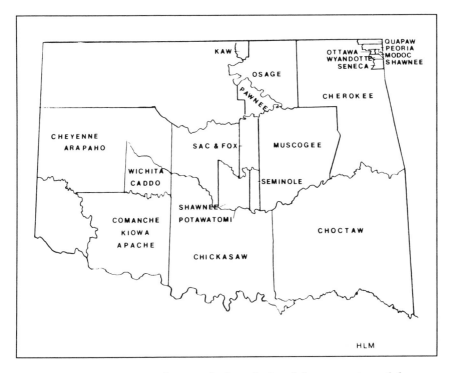

Indian Territory in 1867, indicating the boundaries of the reservations of the various tribes in Indian Territory negotiated in the Reconstruction treaties after the Civil War.

to define on a technical level. Yet its best measure is low human productivity linked to a sustained low level of human consumption. In other words, the tribal peoples have relatively little material gain to show for labor in the underdeveloped Southern Plains regions contained in the reservations or tribal jurisdictional areas. Loss of much of the landbase during the allotment-policy period and continuing paternalism in the middle of the twentieth century curtailed tribal efforts to provide for their populations as well as for Anglo and Latino enclaves living in their midst. The strategy for economic and social development is carried out to the exclusion of any spirituality and is focused upon providing for greater productivity among the various peoples. U.S. authorities define these secular approaches as necessary for a higher standard of living for the tribal populations. Much of this development effort, however, remains alien to the tribal patterns of existence for the Wichita, the Caddo, the Comanche, the Kiowa, the Plains Apache, or the Apache of Oklahoma, the Delaware of Western Oklahoma, and the Fort Sill Apache (the Chiricahua and Warm Springs Apache).

The government took on increasingly significant aspects of Southern Plains tribal affairs, which were confused because of the variation in policy direction or lack of direction in the twentieth century. As the United States vacillated in the third and fourth decades of the twentieth century, creative and intellectual renewal began to have a major impact among the Southern Plains tribes. The continued official U.S. government policy espoused repression of native languages, alienation of Indian trust lands, and restriction of religious freedom. Only the resistance by traditional tribal culture-bearers preserved vital centers of civilization and culture in small, remote pockets throughout the plains.

The resurgence of traditional artistic expression had a tremendous impact upon the tribal peoples, especially the young who had been denied these images. The visual art in traditional styles and the publication of translations of tribal literature, as well as increased interest in native crafts—basketry, pottery, metalwork—grew in importance for the tribal members and also among Anglos. The artistic symbolism had an increasing impact upon American thought. Growing numbers of art buyers traveled to Anadarko and Tulsa, Oklahoma, and others bought traditional Southern Plains art in Taos and Santa Fe, New Mexico, in the period between the two world wars.[1] Young modernists such as Marsden Hartley and others sought to broaden American perspectives in articles on aesthetics and art.[2] Anglo-American history books ignored the inheritance of the Southern Plains Indian peoples; however, the tribal artists presented images of strength and renewal from the tribal heritages for everyone to remember or to appreciate. Their nostalgic call was a major rallying force in contemporary tribalism.[3]

The early founders of contemporary American Indian painting developed a style characterized by high degrees of discipline. Detail in ceremonial dress and in personal articles for ceremony and pleasure was emphasized. Other aspects of painted images such as context and background were reduced in importance or eliminated entirely. Few technical efforts such as shading were used to create a sense of depth in the paintings through foreshortening as was common in popular Western art. Most important, the art was dedicated to portraying the ceremonial systems of beliefs of Indian people.

Significant among the earliest artists to have an international impact were the Kiowa painters Stephen Mopope, Monroe Tsa-to-ke, Jack Hokeah, Lois Smokey, and Spencer Asah. They participated in a special program at the University of Oklahoma organized by Prof. Oscar Jacobson. James Auchian joined the other Kiowas in classes. Their art was nostalgic and colorful. Moreover, these artists were dancers; the sense of performance and motion in their works stemmed directly from their dancing.[4]

The Southern Plains people also felt the power of their heritage in their literatures as well as in their visual art. The literature took the form primarily of song and poetry but also of stories and myths. Traditionally, the people learned by listening to an older person talk through the long winter nights and by hearing a public speaker relate traditional patterns of thought and image at dancegrounds scattered over the prairie. It was this body of literature that related the vision of existence separate and apart from the Western European cosmology they were being taught in the public and boarding schools of Oklahoma. Most important, these mythic images of the tribal songs and stories related directly to the earth in the Southern Plains, not to someplace an ocean away. Traditional literature bound together individuals, families, bands, and tribes as an integral part of creation.[5]

The United States had never been able to overcome the civilized cores of the Southern Plains tribes. For over 100 years the status of the tribes had been considered in matters of law as "domestic dependent nations . . . in a state of pupilage."[6] But in the twentieth century renewed strength emerged from the interaction of the tribes and from the ecological and cultural systems with which they were engaged. This return of strength was recognized to a limited degree in the Indian Reorganization Act of 1934 and its corollary, the Oklahoma Indian Welfare Act of 1936.[7]

The economic depression of the late 1920s and early 1930s shook the Anglo-American belief systems that were so focused on individualism. Large numbers of unemployed people, estimated at times at 23 percent, undermined the idea that the reservation- or tribal-jurisdiction-based Indian populations could be assimilated into a competitive economic system. Thus the depression and the increasing lack of faith in the administration of Indian Affairs made possible a drastic reorientation of U.S. Indian policy. The 1928 Meriam Report depicted appalling conditions among the tribes in the Southern Plains and throughout the western United States. American Indian concerns were highlighted enough so that public opinion favored policy change.[8]

Harold Ickes was appointed as secretary of the interior by Franklin Roosevelt at the beginning of his first term in office. Ickes and his wife, Anna, were well acquainted with the issues concerning needed reform in Indian policy. Anna Ickes spoke Navajo and authored *Mesa Land*, which dealt respectfully with Native American perspectives. The couple had been among the first to join the Indian Defense Association in 1923. Out of Ickes's understanding of Indian policy concerns, he chose John Collier as the new commissioner for Indian Affairs. Collier had been active in Indian policy reform efforts throughout the 1920s, working through the Indian Defense Association and directly with the traditional Pueblo leadership to effect change.[9]

In his first annual report, the new commissioner outlined the policies he proposed to pursue. Not only should allotment be abandoned but allotted lands should be consolidated for tribal use within the reservation areas. Financial aid should be made available to cooperative Indian associations. The American Indian should be instructed in the latest methods of land use. The trend toward removing Indian children from boarding schools and into public ones should be accelerated. Day schools should be employed as a means of improving community welfare through work with the adults as well as with the children. More Indian people should be brought into the Bureau of Indian Affairs, and more self-governance should be encouraged among tribal societies. As a corollary to these measures, the Bureau of Indian Affairs should be decentralized and local officials given more latitude in dealing with the problems of their charges.[10]

Early in 1934 the policymakers in Washington agreed with Franklin Roosevelt's declaration that the time had come to "extend to the Indian the fundamental rights of political liberty and local self-government and the opportunities of education and economic assistance that they require in order to attain a wholesome American life." In 1924 the United States had made all Indian people citizens of the nation; in June 1934 the president signed the Wheeler-Howard bill into law as the Indian Reorganization Act to change policy direction. But the Southern Plains tribes, like the other tribes in Oklahoma, were excluded from the legislation through the direct intervention of Sen. Elmer Thomas.[11]

The Oklahoma Indian Welfare Act passed in 1936 included the provision for a measure of self-governance by the Southern Plains tribes who indicated their willingness to organize under the corporatist policy restrictions of the U.S. government. Also included in this legislation were provisions for tribal self-government and communal ownership of land similar to those in the original Wheeler-Howard bill. Tribal organizations could establish cooperative-marketing and land-management associations. It also reaffirmed trust responsibility for tribal land and allotted lands within the reservation boundaries established by treaty. The act also stated that Congress intended to provide adequate health care and education for Indian people. Unlike previous policy that ignored tribal power, this act set forth the substantive power of the tribes in charters that allowed Indian tribal members to file law suits, borrow money from tribal and federal credit funds, own and manage property of every description, negotiate with federal, state, or local governments, and advise the secretary of the interior concerning appropriation estimates. The system established for the Indian tribes continued to be paternalistic, following controversial corporatist forms, but it allowed for a measure of legislative home-rule. No provision was made for tribal courts, however, although they had existed prior to Oklahoma statehood. The court system of the Code of Federal Regulations was thus extended as a temporary solution.[12]

The Johnson-O'Malley measure to provide for American Indian education was passed in 1934 and was welcomed by the Oklahoma politicians because of the funds it brought into the state for public education. This act allowed the secretary of the interior to provide monies through contracts with the states for local assistance in education. Collier had great hope for the Johnson-O'Malley measure, but its impact was minimal for a number of reasons: the Bureau of Indian Affairs failed to retain any control over expenditure of funds; animosity developed between federal and state administrators; and the public schools refused to establish special Native American programs to facilitate American Indian education.

Various tribal responses arose in reaction to the new policy efforts. The United States demanded to work unilaterally with the tribal communities. The Wichita and Affiliated Tribes did not organize under the Oklahoma Indian Welfare Act of 1936, however, choosing to govern themselves through traditional means on an unwritten constitutional basis. Nor did the Comanche organize under the act. From 1936 through 1963 the Comanche Tribe was governed by a joint resolution and by-laws shared with the Kiowa and Plains Apache tribes. And the Delaware did not organize under the act; they adopted a constitution that was approved in 1937 by the secretary of the interior. Neither did the Fort Sill Apache organize under the 1936 legislation.[13]

A short time after the initiation of tribal homerule, increased global violence began to draw most attention away from domestic reform. But as World War II drew to a close in 1944, the congressional Committee on Indian Affairs undertook a broad-based investigation of policy. It reported that the New Deal Indian reform had in some instances aided the tribal peoples. However, inadequate use of an existing landbase, lack of effective education, poor guidance in health care, and the U.S. government's failure to settle claims and to consolidate landholdings were obvious shortcomings in the efforts to bring about needed change.[14] The reform legislation had been the operating basis for American Indian policy for only a matter of a few years when the United States entered World War II. Many superintendents, reservation officials, and the young Indian leadership then left the Southern Plains for military service, and there were reductions in Bureau of Indian Affairs appropriations. Physical plants, schools, roads, hospitals, telephone systems, and other communitywide systems fell into disrepair during the wartime period of the 1940s.

Land claims became increasingly important for all parties in the mid-1940s to rebuild momentum. Fair settlement would clear title to the land from a legal point of view, redress grievances over the colonial appropriation of land, and offer the possibility of capital being in the hands of tribes and tribal members. In fall 1944 the leadership of various tribes in the western United States met in Denver, Colorado, and formed the National Congress of American

Indians (NCAI) to unite the tribal forces to speak for land-claims legislation. The first president of the organization was N. B. Johnson, a Cherokee from Oklahoma. The NCAI was established as a federated organization basing its representation on tribal entities.[15]

In 1946 the U.S. Congress passed the Indian Claims Commission Act. President Harry Truman, in a message to the NCAI, struck a conciliatory note:

> This bill makes perfectly clear what men and women, here and abroad, have failed to recognize, that in our transactions with the Indian tribes we have at least since the Northwest Ordinance of 1787 set for ourselves the standard of fair and honorable dealings. . . . Instead of confiscating Indian lands, we have purchased from the tribes that once owned this continent more than 90 percent of our public domain, paying them approximately 800 million dollars in the process. It would be a miracle if in the course of these dealings—the largest real estate transaction in history—we had not made some mistakes and occasionally failed to live up to the precise terms of our treaties and agreements with some 200 tribes. But we stand ready . . . to correct any mistakes we have made.[16]

The establishment of the Indian Land Claims Commission in 1946 provided for a regular means of adjusting any claims arising from areas covered by the U.S. Constitution, federal laws, and treaties between the various tribes and the United States. Thus a formal process now existed through which the tribes of the Southern Plains and others throughout the West could research their heritage and tradition. This focus provided frames of reference by which to measure current tribal and U.S. activities in relationship to patterns and images that had remained true throughout their existence.[17]

With the exception of the land-claims corrective process, the period from 1945 through 1964 was a disconcerting time as the tribes and the U.S. government seemed to be working at odds against each other. The tribes were reorganizing themselves on the Southern Plains in accord with the demands of U.S. policy strictures. In addition, each of the tribes worked through the claims process to strengthen the framework by which they could act in a coherent manner, providing something of value for all concerned.

The "friends of the Indians" were at work during this same period. In 1944 the women's societies of the Christian denominations that belonged to the National Council of Churches focused on the domestic Indian mission field. The women were taught about the Indian people in terms of releasing them from wardship, and "experts" indicated that the trust relationship was degrading to Indian people. Commissioner John Collier had resigned in 1945, and although his successors attempted to carry on the policies of tribal reorganization, they had little support from Congress. Meanwhile, women's Christian denominational organizations favored an end to the federal role in Indian affairs.

In May 1950, with the Korean conflict in full swing, Harry Truman appointed Dillon Myer as Indian commissioner. Myer had served as the director of the internment camps for the Japanese-Americans during World War II and had relocated them after the war, not allowing them to return to their homes. He had thus had first-hand experience in carrying out the U.S. policy of resettling people throughout the western states. As he began to act his intention was to carry out a similar policy with the Indian people; in 1951 Myer stated, "I realize that it will not be possible always to obtain Indian cooperation. . . . We must proceed, even though [this cooperation] may be lacking." Both the Democratic party and the Republican party platforms for the 1952 election used the same wording in a misguided effort to break up the tribal communities in order to provide them with "full citizenship."[18]

The disastrous policy of termination surfaced with the congressional Concurrent Resolution 108 adopted in 1953. A few days after this policy statement, Congress passed Public Law 280, giving certain states power to extend their civil and criminal law over Indian reservations. It was not until 1968, after a fifteen-year effort, that a law was passed requiring states to obtain American Indian tribal consent before extending their jurisdiction. Oklahoma never acted under this law to force the issue with the Southern Plains tribes although termination did affect several tribes in the extreme northeastern portion of state, including the Ottawa and Miami tribes. By the mid-1950s, growing numbers of American Indian tribes and intertribal organizations, including the National Congress of American Indians, protested the termination policy. The National Council of Churches began to reverse its propolicy position but not officially until 1976. Ralph Nader presented an influential review of past U.S. Indian policies, current trends, and prospects for the future in the *Harvard Law Review* that marshaled additional resistance to termination as a policy. The National Congress of American Indians in Washington, D.C., the Indian Rights Association in Philadelphia, and the Association of American Indian Affairs in New York opposed the policy and attempted to obtain hearings on it. Ultimately, however, six termination bills were passed into law.

In 1955 the health program of the Bureau of Indian Affairs (BIA) was transferred to the Department of Health, Education, and Welfare. Relocation became a prime program for the BIA in an attempt to separate American Indian peoples from their tribal associations. The first relocation centers were established in Chicago, Denver, and Los Angeles. Oklahoma City was never an official relocation center; however, it ranked first in Indian urban population by 1960. U.S. officials recruited Indian people, paid the cost of the transportation, placed them in jobs, and helped them to obtain housing in the urban relocation center. The relocation effort spelled disaster for some, who drifted to urban ghettos or returned home, but it provided opportunity to others who remained and prospered. Still, the overall costs in human life and community were borne by the Indian people.[19] These separations had a debilitating effect on the tribal communities of the Southern Plains. Many Indian people downplayed their ethnicity in an attempt to better cope with the Anglo-dominated social and economic institutions. But this accommodation left voids in people's lives that were not filled by the elements of a materialistic society.

One of the obvious examples of renewal in response to earlier losses was the growth of participation in the plains pan-Indian dances. In summer bonds among tribes and communities were strengthened: goodwill exchange visits were made; powwow celebrations began to reemerge to honor veterans of World War II and the Korean conflict, featuring new songs as well as traditional ones. Powwow celebrations also were held on an intertribal basis in the urban centers. In the 1950s the position of dance- and songleaders was instituted. Head dancers were selected to draw in entire families and to present extraordinary dancing. The camp crier was replaced with the master of ceremonies; arena directors replaced the traditional whip men; a head singer was able to lead over 300 different songs. The drum was always recognized during a powwow with water, tobacco, and material and monetary donations. The dances grew in number and variety. The Southern Men's Straight Dance had its roots in the societies known as the Heluska among the Omaha, Ponca, Pawnee, Otoe, Kaw, and Iowa tribes. The Southern Women's Traditional Dance was an expression of thanksgiving, and the Men's Traditional Dance grew from old-style Sioux dancing. Oklahoma is the home of Men's Fancy Dance, which evolved from the Omaha Grass Dance.[20]

Another example of renewal was the revitalization of the Kiowa Gourd Dance, which had been preserved by the Tai'peh, or Gourd Dance Society, since its origins. The dance had nearly vanished by the late 1930s. There were unofficial summer dances among the Kiowa even after the intervention of the U.S. military to stop the Sun Dance, but there seemed to be constant loss in the nature of the dances. In 1955 Fred Tsoodle called Kiowas together to renew the Gourd Dance, and since the mid-1950s it has replaced the Sun Dance. It has enjoyed phenomenal growth with broad appeal. Not only was it danced annually on July 4, but it also became linked with the popular pan-Indian powwow, providing a distinct Kiowa contribution to these celebrations. Whole families participate in Gourd Dance activities.[21]

Specific tribal traditional dances continued but with renewed vigor; for instance, the Caddo people continued to dance the Bell Dance and the Turkey Dance. The Bell Dance is considered to be the oldest of the Hasinai element of the Caddo and is normally one of the last dances of the night-long sequence. The leader holds a leather strap with large bells attached, like those found at the Spiro Mound complex and the Davis site. The singing is begun with the statement "Yo Ha-see-ney!" and long lines of dancers reaffirm their presence. The Turkey Dance, which relates the heritage and philosophical outlook of the Caddo people, is done by the women. Songs relate specific events that are increased in number over time. The Fort Sill Apache continued the Fire Dance to drive away evil, heal the sick, and bestow blessings on the people. These and other traditional dances were arguments for the renewal of the Native American pathways that have remained a part of the people and of the earth of the Southern Plains.[22]

The continuing revival in traditional Native American arts and crafts provided significant images to support renewal as new and innovative forms added to the force of native expression. The Philbrook Art Center inaugurated its American Indian Art Competition in 1946, and by the 1950s and 1960s it had an international following. Many artists from Bacone College and the Santa Fe Studio as well as many self-trained artists competed, including Alfred Momaday, Kiowa; Roland Whitehorse, Kiowa; Allan Houser, Fort Sill Apache; Blackbear Bosin, Comanche; Archie Blackowl, Cheyenne; and Elgin Lamar, Wichita. Dick West, a Cheyenne, placed regularly in the competition while he served as head of the Art School at Bacone College in Muskogee. There he helped train another generation of Southern Plains artists that included Dennis Belindo, Kiowa; Sharon Ahtone Harjo, Kiowa; and David Williams, Kiowa and Apache, among others. Traditionally trained crafts people such as Homer Lumpmouth, Arapaho; Edward Parker, Comanche; George Silverhorn, Kiowa; Kish Whitebird, Cheyenne; and the extraordinary Julius Caesar, a Pawnee who moved to Gracemont among the Wichita, added to the collective surge.[23]

Following the period of the New Deal reforms, which ran from 1936 through 1941, new efforts brought about a renegotiated bilateral recognition of the Caddo Tribe and a difficult multilateral agreement with the Cheyenne and Arapaho as one tribal entity. The Caddo Tribe organized under the reform legislation. A tribal constitution and by-laws were adopted and approved by the secretary of the interior in 1938, along with a tribal business charter. The Cheyenne and Arapaho tribes organized as one federally recognized tribe in 1937. During the reversal of policy of the late 1940s and throughout the 1950s, the Delaware Tribe of Western Oklahoma approved the establishment of homerule government by resolution, which was adopted by the tribe in 1958; however, the tribe's constitution and by-laws were not approved and ratified until 1973. The Wichita and Affiliated Tribes continued to operate with an unwritten constitution; its governing rules were approved by resolution and adopted by the tribe in 1961.[24]

Dealings with each tribal organization concerning recognition and issues of mutual interest were confused by the federal policy reversals during the middle decades of the twentieth century. Anglo cultural assumptions, values, and attitudes created a conceptual overlay that the negotiators included in these policies and recognition agreements. Adversarial argument served the U.S. government as an effective means of decisionmaking in the modern era. Permissible assumptions were based upon the principle of contradiction—true/false, us/them, friend/enemy, civilized/barbaric, either/or—in making policy decisions. These mutually exclusive categories were deliberately established to force restricted choices. This creation of dichotomies has been essential for Anglo and Western European logic throughout the modern era, and it imposed a rigid perception in the search for acceptable working relations between the tribes and the United States. An adversarial style of dialogue prevailed and was carried out in terms of unnecessary conflict. There was a position to be established and defended that the United States sought to achieve; it entailed having wards whose positions could be altered and reformed. If the termination policy of the 1950s had been successful, the tribes could have been eliminated according to this logic. The conception of negotiations and the way they were carried out remained grounded in the knowledge and experience of Western game theory. The metaphor of conflict and war was not only applied in Indian policy relations but extended into the future through the U.S. War on Poverty of the 1960s and the War on Drugs of the 1980s. Such an approach was grounded in the logic and reason underlying the cultural experience of Anglo-America and, in turn, it influenced continuing experiences and actions.

Arapaho Ghost Dance, painting detail. (Private collection)

Arapaho Ghost Dance, painting detail. (Private collection)

Arapaho Ghost Dance, painting detail. (Private collection)

Hide painting of the Arapaho Ghost Dance. (Private collection)

Introduction Ceremony of Satanta (a Kiowa) into the American Indian Hall of Fame. (Cookson Institute)

Sherman Coolidge (Arapaho), priest at Whirlwind Mission. (Oklahoma Episcopal Archives)

Painted tipis at the American Indian Exposition, Anadarko, Okla. (Cookson Institute)

Young Cheyenne people who are part of the Circle Keepers of the Cheyenne Cultural Center. (Private collection)

Opening ceremonies at the Oakerhater Honor Dance, Cheyenne. (Private collection)

Kiowa Gourd Clan dancing in 1969. (Archives and Manuscripts Division of the Oklahoma Historical Society)

Caddo singers during Turkey Dance. (Cookson Institute)

Young Caddo girl in traditional clothes learning the Turkey Dance. (Cookson Institute)

Caddo Turkey Dance, All-Caddo Dance, 1993. (Cookson Institute)

Doc Tate Nevaquaya, a Comanche, internationally famous flute player and artist. (Cookson Institute)

Caddo Women's Dance, All-Caddo Dance, 1993. (Cookson Institute)

Southern Plains Fancy Dancer. (Red Earth)

Women's Buckskin Dancer.
(Red Earth)

Women's Cloth Dancer.
(Red Earth)

Cheyenne singers commemorating the dead from the Battle of Washita. (Carrie Goeringer)

Scaffold constructed to commemorate the Cheyenne dead killed at the Battle of the Washita. (Carrie Goeringer)

Mildred Cleghorn, chair of the Fort Sill Apache, receives special recognition in 1989. (Cookson Institute)

The Reverend Bob Pinezaddleby, Kiowa, minister of the Mt. Scott United Methodist Comanche Mission. (Cookson Institute)

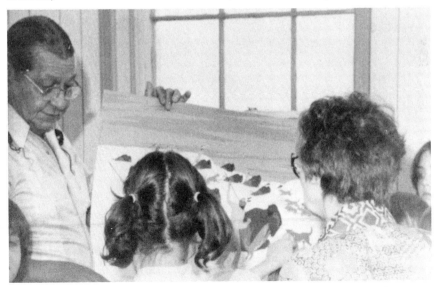

Dick West, a Cheyenne, long-time head of the Indian Art Department of Bacone College, an agency of the American Baptist Church. (Private collection)

University of Science and Arts of Oklahoma Seminar, left to right: *Lavonne Youngblood (Kiowa), Vickie Boettger (Kiowa), Mike Wetselline (Plains Apache). (Private collection)*

Southern Plains tribal administrators and staff at the Anadarko Adult Education Center. (Private collection)

Cheyenne-Arapaho Tribal Complex. (Private collection)

Tribal business owned by the Apache of Oklahoma Tribe. (Private collection)

Wichita and Affiliated Tribes Administration and Museum Building. (Private collection)

Delaware of Western Oklahoma Tribal Complex. (Private collection)

Kiowa Housing Authority, Anadarko, Okla. (Private collection)

13

SELF-DETERMINATION

Throughout the 1960s tribal demand for self-determination in matters of education, economics, and spirituality rose steadily. But during the eight years of the Democratic administrations of John Kennedy and Lyndon Johnson, the Bureau of Indian Affairs remained largely indifferent to the trends among American Indian tribal governments. The tribes did find alternative responses in the Office of Economic Opportunity's antipoverty programs, a central feature of the War on Poverty and the one area in which the recipients of the programs had a place in the planning of those programs. Tribes initiated their own programs without the involvement of the Bureau of Indian Affairs. Tribal people began to demonstrate openly for treaty rights, including hunting and fishing rights as well as religious freedom. Meanwhile, no significant change occurred either in policy or practical affairs in the relationship between the bureau and the tribes.

The real direction of Indian policy remained in the hands of Congress, through the committees for Interior and Insular Affairs and in the Bureau of the Budget. The congressional policymakers demanded Anglo-American solutions for Indian "problems." Yet tribal communities in American society by this time had reached a point where decisive change could occur. The American Indian Policy Review Commission was created by Congress, with a large number of American Indian members and staff. The commission conducted a series of studies of principal issues covering trust responsibilities and the federal Indian relationship, including treaty-review concerns; tribal government; federal administration and structure of Indian affairs; and management at the Bureau of Indian Affairs.[1] These studies continued to serve as the basis for reform into the 1990s. The section by Task Force One on federal trust obligations to the tribes in Oklahoma was strongly worded, concluding that:

> there has been a great failure on the part of the United States toward Oklahoma tribes. By rights, there should be no State of Oklahoma. But, there is. And, it is the responsibility of the United States to insure that the existence of this state does not lead to the death of the people who gave so much.[2]

Additional jurisdictional issues were covered by Task Force Four and Task Force Ten as they examined federal, state, and tribal jurisdiction as well as terminated and nonfederally recognized Indians.[3] Their conclusions reinforced those of Task Force One:

> Three things clearly emerged from the hearings and documentation accumulated from and about the situation [in Oklahoma].
> 1. There is a definite need to clarify jurisdictional relationships of the tribes which includes a clear recognition that Oklahoma tribes do enjoy "reservation status."
> 2. The exclusion of those tribes from the full extension of the Indian Reorganization Act of 1934 has had a deleterious and demoralizing effect on the people and the tribes.
> 3. There is an overwhelming need for a separately authorized congressional study to develop a rational and beneficial policy for the Indian tribes of Oklahoma.[4]

Other American Indian Policy Review Commission task forces dealt with social and economic concerns such as Indian education, health, reservation and resource development and protection, urban and rural nonreservation Indians, and alcohol and drug abuse.[5] Each report described fragmented, often contradictory approaches to social and economic issues. For example, the report of the Task Force on Indian Education revealed the adversarial relationship between biculturalism and acculturation that had paralyzed effective reform in American Indian education, noting the lack of follow-up on sixty recommendations contained in the Kennedy Report on Indian Education of 1969.[6] Still, this adversarial approach was continued in the

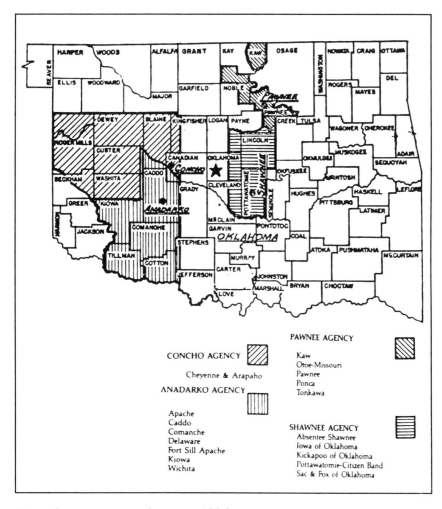

U.S. Indian Agency jurisdiction in Oklahoma
(U.S. Department of the Interior)

recommendations made by the BIA and the White House Conference on Indian Education in the late 1980s and early 1990s.[7]

Anglo-American sociological and historical interpretations of
the lasting effects of the American Indian Policy Review Commission's efforts were largely negative. Prof. Stephen Cornell indicated

that the recommendations were generally ignored because of the problem-solving approach taken by U.S. policymakers.[8] Prof. Francis Paul Prucha indicated that the outcomes of the task forces provided: "no overarching plan and no solution to the inherent problems arising from the tension between self-determination of the Indian tribes and the continuing trust responsibility of the federal government."[9] Kirke Kickingbird, a Kiowa who served as general counsel for the American Indian Policy Review Commission and as executive director of the Institute for the Development of Indian Law, defined the purpose and success of the task forces through his perspective on the Southern Plains:

> Forty-seven years have gone by since the last comprehensive study of Indian affairs was conducted. In the intervening years, the original intent of the reform policies of the 1930s has been compromised and distorted through administrative ignorance and neglect. The urgency of American Indian problems and the confusion as to Indian goals and methods of attaining them have led to the creation of the American Indian Policy Review Commission.[10]

Kickingbird provided the needed overview: the bureaucracy had grown step by step until the purpose for which it was established had become poorly served.

Layers of overriding systems that were supposed to hone decisions made it almost impossible to obtain a decision at all. The adversarial nature of U.S. governmental institutions and legal systems operated on the principle of contradiction and imposed a rigid falsity on perception in the search for a constructed certainty. Self-determination was a radical patterning system that attempted to break the hold of the constrictive bureaucracy. The repression of the traditional self-organizing models that the tribes had established on the Southern Plains in a centering position made it increasingly difficult for the tribes to move in positive or natural directions. Kickingbird offered the perception that grew from this self-organizing system, but it was lost on the Anglo-American officials and academics; his understanding had an impact on the peoples of the Southern Plains and on tribes throughout the United States, however, in their perception of the defects inherent in

Anglo-American ways of thinking. In turn, this perspective allowed a look at thought processes of the tribal societies and of their institutions as well as those of the larger national and global societies. The polarizing, distorting, and conflict-generating aspects of argument were too limiting for the processes of the tribal societies.

The implementation of Public Law 93-638, the Indian Self-Determination and Education Assistance Act of 1975, provided for much-needed change in that it was

> to provide maximum Indian participation in the Government and education of the Indian people; to provide for the full participation of the Indian tribes in programs and services conducted by the Federal Government for Indians and to encourage the development of human resources of the Indian people; to establish a program of assistance to upgrade Indian education; to support the right of Indian citizens to control their own educational activities.[11]

New measures offered the tribal governments the means for creating patterned responses to provide for the general welfare of the tribes. Grants enabled tribal governments to prepare for planning and for contracting and allowed for monitoring of programs. Provisions made for contracting all or part of federal programs and for the redesigning of programs to meet actual needs fell short of expectations, however. Although some redesigning of existing programs without the assumption of administration occurred, only spotty implementation took place. Although federal personnel were available to carry out tribal programs, many of these people did not have the expertise to bring about needed reform.[12] The act did provide for oversight committees involving American Indian people in the schools to see that funds provided for Indian education were used in that manner; previously the Johnson-O'Malley funds designated for Indian students had always gone into the general budget so that often little money was used to assist the Indian young people directly.[13]

Another important piece of reform legislation was the Indian Child Welfare Act of 1978, which recognized the best interests of Indian children by providing for their care within the tribal community. So many Indian children had been placed for adoption with Anglo-American families by the Anglo-dominated human-services agencies that the future of the children and the tribes was imperiled. The act mandated that preference be given to the child's extended family, thus preventing the destructive process of stripping Indian children of their culture.[14]

In anticipation of these renewed responsibilities, the Southern Plains tribes began to provide for reform in their constitutional and secular laws. The constitution of the Apache Tribe of Oklahoma was ratified in 1972. The Tribal Council was established by the adult members of the tribe, consisting of a continuing committee of a chairperson, vice-chairperson, secretary-treasurer, and two committee members, who are elected for two-year concurrent terms. The Caddo Tribe amended its constitution in 1976, and the Cheyenne and Arapaho tribes amended theirs in 1975. The Comanche Tribe had adopted its constitution and by-laws in 1966; the secretary of the interior approved it in 1967. The Delaware Tribe of Western Oklahoma had its constitution and by-laws approved and ratified in 1973. Its Executive Committee consists of its president, vice-president, secretary, treasurer, and two committee members, who are elected to no more than two consecutive four-year terms; elections are staggered. The Fort Sill Apache ratified their constitution, which was approved by the secretary of the interior in 1976. The Kiowa Tribe adopted its constitution in 1970, which provided for a Tribal Business Committee consisting of a chairperson, vice-chairperson, secretary, treasurer, and four committee members; elections are staggered and members are limited to two consecutive two-year terms. The Wichita and Affiliated Tribes continue to operate with an unwritten constitution.[15]

The process of developing a continuing system of tribal governance involved three essential elements. First, the role of people who simply buffered the tribal members from the bureaucratic efforts of the Bureau of Indian Affairs had to be transformed by setting up a regularly instituted and permanent entity within the tribe as a policymaking body for the tribal membership. The election of leaders superseded the appointed leadership. The executive committee, or Tribal Business Committee, became a permanent institution, and then the tribes emerged to gain a degree of self-determining status. Among the Caddo Tribe and the Cheyenne and

Arapaho tribes this move had taken place as early as the late 1930s, but even these tribes took on new life in the 1970s. Indeed by the 1970s such measures for self-determination were developing among all the Southern Plains tribes.[16]

The second element in the process of shaping tribal government was the gradual replacement of federal authority by tribal authority as the most important jurisdictional power within the tribe. Changes in this area were set in motion through the contracting provisions of the Self-Determination and Educational Assistance Act of 1975 (PL 93-638). In the late 1970s and throughout the 1980s increasing numbers of programs were contracted for by the tribes, but not without controversy. Still, the trend was clear: Bureau of Indian Affairs offices were being reduced as the tribes took responsibility for the various programs in higher education, health, housing, and other areas. As the United States moved into deeper debt with its global commitments and concerns, the government was inclined to favor terms with tribes even if the tribal leaders deviated from accepted processes in the scheme of things. Hence de facto gains by the tribes tended to secure de jure acceptance as the United States attempted to deal with the muddled reality of international affairs.

The third element in the formation of tribal republics—the acquisition of rights outside the reservations and the development of relations with the state of Oklahoma—was closely interwoven with the second element.[17] This third process involved the formation of new institutions and conferred on the tribes an awareness of their identity within a new context. Although relations between the state and the Southern Plains tribes continue to be affected by mistrust, misunderstanding, fear, anger, and frustration, the tribes, the state, and the United States can cooperate in implementing programs of common interest. Jurisdictional disputes usually delay or destroy developmental efforts to use human, natural, and capital resources effectively.

State leadership in Oklahoma has come to recognize that by working with tribes, it can use tribal expertise and thus coordinate efforts with tribes that are gaining resources to engage in cooperative program planning. Economic development can proceed only after jurisdictional disharmony is addressed through cooperative efforts between the state of Oklahoma and the Southern Plains tribes. Successful cooperation between Oklahoma officials and tribal leadership must rest upon the state's recognition of tribal sovereignty, mutual respect, government-to-government relationship, interaction between the appropriate levels of government, and an understanding of how each government—tribal, state, and federal—works. Dialogue leading to better understanding of governmental infrastructures must remain open so that conflicts over local, state, and tribal jurisdictional regulations can be worked on through cooperative agreements. Oklahoma has emerged as a leader among the western states in developing progressive relationships with the tribes because of the state's recognition of each tribe's ability to function as an interdependent entity, an awareness that creates opportunities for clear role definition and cooperative interaction. After eight years of work, the state legislature passed the Oklahoma Tribal Act in 1989, which served three primary purposes: it acknowledged the existence of the federally recognized Indian tribes within the state's boundaries; it authorized agreements between the state and its political subdivisions and the tribes; and it established a joint legislative state-tribal relations committee.[18]

As the Southern Plains tribes attempted to work out new relationships with the state of Oklahoma, each tribe tried to strengthen its own republican institutions. Notions of voting and majorities ran against the centrist traditions of the tribes; the idea of a republican form of governance based on the selection of a person entrusted to represent views and values was a difficult one. The concept that argument and discussion would thoroughly explore needs, possibilities, and solutions was inadequate in comparison to a consensual design, and it was particularly hard to accept a simple headcount that could polarize the tribal membership. Such "popular" institutions engendered insuperable tensions in many instances.

The striking characteristic of the government and administration of the Southern Plains tribes is the extent to which community responsibility is undertaken by the tribal members themselves in the time left free from work and other preoccupations. Factions divided internal affairs among the tribes although formal alliances remained from the traditional structures of the tribes, such as the extended family, the dance societies, the boarding school and college associations based on intellectual bonds. Self-appointed counterweights and adversaries formed against the elected government to create loyal oppositions within the tribes, which at times were used by the bureaucrats in Indian Affairs to justify their own positions. The controversies arising from issues of control and mutual social aid did polarize tribes, however. Elders played a much-reduced role compared to their traditional participation in tribal governance because of external forces that kept them out of the public eye on many issues. For example, the presence of the Christian missionaries and church members in active roles frequently prevented any mention of traditional tribal spiritual concerns in public discussion. Nevertheless, despite the issues that divide the tribal members, the people dream of concord and of rule in the interest of the community.

Republican institutions among the tribes are having difficulty in achieving stability. In particular the negative strength of factionalism, both social and political, prevents routine compromises, conventions, and agreements. Both division within the tribes, even among the smallest ones, and the pressure of external forces bring about incessant crises. Republicanism has made it difficult to move with any speed in reaching decisions so that even in business dealings and economic development, indecisiveness, unpredictability, and a lack of confidentiality are widespread.

Lack of continuity in elected leadership created difficulties as the tribes were expected to assume more responsibility. Examples of leadership did appear: Newton Lamar served for several terms as president of the Wichita and Affiliated Tribes in the 1970s and the 1980s. He was born at Gracemont, within the reservation boundaries or tribal jurisdictional area. He was Waco in heritage and was raised by his grandparents, who taught him to speak Wichita; he was also taught Wichita and Waco tradition and customs. After graduating from Riverside Indian School, north of Anadarko, he served in the U.S. Army Air Corps and then in the U.S. Air Force. On leaving the service, he took college-level courses and then worked in law enforcement and public relations in the West.

Lamar's goal, however, was to return to Oklahoma to work with the Wichita; he felt his tribe had been overlooked and forgotten by the U.S. government. In 1971 he moved to Anadarko with his wife, Catherine, and his family and concentrated on tribal business. He was elected vice-president of the Wichita and Affiliated Tribe in 1972, and in 1974 he was elected president and then reelected for four-year terms in 1976, in 1980, and in 1984. During that time, he provided stability in governance and growth in economic development, through the Wichita-Caddo-Delaware Enterprise Corporation, and through his broad-based efforts in housing, intergovernmental planning, and health. In the 1980s Lamar served as chairman of the National Tribal Chairmen's Association, playing a major role in intertribal economic development planning.[19]

Another elected leader who provided continuity of leadership for her tribe was Mildred Cleghorn of the Fort Sill Apache Tribe. She has been the only elected tribal chairperson since the tribe's reorganization in 1976, with one short exception. Born a prisoner of war in 1910 at the Fort Sill Military Reservation, she was the first Fort Sill Apache to earn a college degree, studying at Haskell Institute and Oklahoma State University. She worked in the Southern Plains as an extension agent and as a home economics teacher at Riverside Indian School. Cleghorn has created a collection of tribal dolls in traditional dress that has been shown throughout the United States and abroad.[20]

Mildred Cleghorn's accomplishments within the tribe are based on her ability to center the tribe in order to bring about a continuing effort from its members. In administration she has worked to create a centered General Council and a working Business Committee to plan effectively for the future. During her administration the tribe has acquired tribal lands within the reserve boundaries and tribal investments have grown. Health and human services programs have been developed in cooperation with the Bureau of Indian Affairs, including the institution of community health representatives and the creation of the only tribally controlled youth shelter in the Southern Plains. The tribe has initiated housing and water projects and has created a daycare center at the tribal complex near Apache.[21]

Edgar French served as president of the Delaware Tribe of Western Oklahoma from 1976 through 1989. French, like all traditional leaders of the Delaware, was a member of the Turtle Clan. He understood that the tribe had to be more than a corporate entity, so he supported social welfare programs as well as language and heritage projects headed by the internationally known Delaware scholar, Linda Poolaw. He also backed programs for child welfare, community-health outreach, and housing improvement. The Delaware attempted to create the first tribal enterprise zone within the United States, fostering technological development of space-age refrigeration. However, French was voted out of office at a critical juncture, and the project was abandoned.[22]

The Delaware Tribe has never been totally integrated internally so that its government could be truly monolithic; it rarely acted as a collective arm to carry out the will of the whole tribe. People's needs are diverse, and what they think they need and want is even more diverse. Given the slant of the established programs, satisfying the needs of one person may have denied satisfaction to others, a process that resulted in an inescapable factionalism that divided both social and economic efforts within the tribe. Because control of governmental action was the constant object of intense political competition, consensus was rarely achieved, given the rapid pace of activity in tribal affairs.[23]

Tribal efforts at stabilization and development were made more difficult by the economic crash and depression of the 1980s in the Southern Plains oil patch. The reservation areas were particularly hard hit as they faced widespread chronic poverty, obsolete methods of production, and contradictory overlays of organization. An unusually complex set of economic and social conditions was tied into this situation. The per capita industrial investment per worker is low, and food consumption is barely over the minimum necessary to sustain a healthy life. Energy levels are low, and health care is generally poor or missing entirely in parts of this rural area. Traditional tribal medicine is still repressed by existing health agencies dominated by Anglo health professionals. Life expectancy averages less than elsewhere in the United States. Functional illiteracy rates are high in English and in tribal languages; skilled labor is limited as the brighter young people are forced to seek employment in more productive regions distant from tribal homelands.[24]

Underdevelopment in reservation areas or tribal jurisdictional statistical areas is striking when compared to economically developed regions in the United States. In Oklahoma in the Southern Plains, the 1990 census showed a population of 252,420. Approximately one-half of the Indian population lived in urban concentrations while the remainder lived in the rural sections of the reservation areas or tribal jurisdictional statistical areas (see Table 13.1).[25]

Of the three reservations that were retained by the Southern Plains tribes, the population figures for 1990 in the tribal jurisdiction statistical areas were Kiowa-Comanche-Apache-Fort Sill Apache, 13,108; Cheyenne-Arapaho, 6,719; and Wichita-Caddo-Delaware, 545.[26]

According to the 1990 census, for every $100 U.S. families received, an Indian family received $69. The median income of Indian married-couple families was $16,500, or 76 percent of the $21,640 for all married-couple families. About one-fourth of all American Indian families were maintained by female householders with no husband present; the median income for these families was $7,200, about 72 percent of the median income of $9,960 of all families maintained by women without husbands. The census does not reflect the same numbers as that of tribal membership roles because the federal counting process does not require that the person be part of a federally recognized tribe.[27]

The United States continues to deal unilaterally with the tribes, whose summary numbers reflect the underdeveloped nature of their populations and reservations. The Wichita and Affiliated Tribes had an enrollment of 1,539 in 1989 but released no statistics on their population. The largest concentration of Wichita people resided in Caddo County in Oklahoma. The Caddo Tribe had a membership of 3,067 in 1989; of that total, 1,218 resided in the

Table 13.1. Counties with Largest Number of American Indian Populations

County	Reserve Area	Population
Tulsa	(Muscogee/Creek)	25,401
Oklahoma	(Unassigned Lands)	24,313
Cherokee	(Cherokee)	11,380
Muscogee	(Muskogee/Creek)	9,049
Cleveland	(Unassigned Lands)	8,959
Adair	(Cherokee)	8,065
Roger Mills	(Cheyenne-Arapaho)	7,117
Delaware	(Cherokee)	7,096
Sequoyah	(Cherokee)	7,000
Pottawatomie	(Potawatomie and Shawnee)	6,848

immediate area, primarily in Caddo County. Their unemployment rate at that time was 31 percent. Almost all the Caddo children attended public schools in their communities, and in the mid-1980s about sixty-four tribal members were attending colleges and universities with federal grant assistance. The estimated average education level of adult Caddo tribal members was 11.5 years. The tribal enrollment for the Comanche Tribe in 1989 was 8,469; Comanche residents in the area totaled 3,642 and were concentrated in Caddo, Comanche, Cotton, and Kiowa counties of Oklahoma. Their unemployment rate was 46 percent. Most Comanche children attended area public schools, and in the mid-1980s, 123 tribal members were in higher education with assistance from the tribe. The Kiowa Tribe had a 1989 enrollment of 9,104, with 3,999 people living in the immediate area, principally in Caddo, Comanche, Cotton, and Kiowa counties. Their unemployment rate was 47 percent. The Plains Apache or the Apache Tribe of Oklahoma had an enrollment of 1,186 members and local residents in the area totaled 485, living primarily in Caddo, Comanche, Cotton, and Kiowa counties. Their rate of unemployment was 53 percent in 1989. The Delaware Tribe of Western Oklahoma had a 1989 population of 1,058, with 393 in the area, primarily in Caddo County and an unemployment rate of 45 percent. Almost all Delaware children attended public schools; in the mid-1980s, eighteen tribal members had grants to attend colleges and universities. Figures are not kept separately for the Cheyenne and Arapaho tribes; their combined population totaled 9,340, with 5,220 living primarily in Blaine, Canadian, Custer, Dewey, Kingfisher, Roger Mills, and Washita counties in 1989. Their unemployment rate is the highest among the Southern Plains tribes at 62 percent. Most students attended public schools, although a significant number attend the Riverside Boarding School. In the mid-1980s, 130 Cheyenne and Arapaho students were engaged in higher education with grant assistance. The population of the Fort Sill Apache totals 335, and 70 of that number live in the area, primarily in Caddo and Comanche counties. Their unemployment rate was 47 percent in 1989. The unemployment figures of the tribal populations remain at extremely high levels, levels that would be considered unacceptable by the U.S. population at large.[28]

Furthermore, the situation is deteriorating among the Southern Plains tribes as the gap between the lower-income families and middle-class Americans in the region widens. Poverty is not evenly distributed, however, which makes the problem of development even more complicated. Sustainable development within the scope of the global economic system is an increasing problem. Relative strengths are difficult to identify given existing measurement systems and lack of direct communication with decisionmakers. Moreover, the tribal jurisdictional areas in the Southern Plains are unusually susceptible to circumstances over which people have little control.[29]

The relatively small tribes of the Southern Plains are increasingly active in their self-determination efforts. Yet pluralistic decision-making is suspended within the bilateral relations between the U.S. government and the individual tribal governments; only the United States has heavily influenced or imposed its will on the others. Mutual efforts have been dictated by policymakers in Washington rather than by leaders from the Southern Plains.

The consequence of pluralism in intertribal affairs is that there is great diversity among the sources of political action. American Indian people and their representative governments have been encouraged with both assistance and threats to exercise independent judgment in determining their interests and how best to pursue them. But given the conditions of interdependence, such diversity has unavoidably resulted in the actions of one group impinging on the interests of others. It is impossible to satisfy most human needs within the confines of each tribal entity today just as it was before the presence of the United States on the Southern Plains. What may have started as a modest, seemingly local concern causes ever-widening repercussions that affect other tribes and nations.

This competition in intertribal affairs sets the stage for conflict when people strive for contradictory ends. Yet it has also renewed intertribal and international awareness of the need for cooperation and mutual assistance. Varying levels of conflict and cooperation represent alternative methods for satisfying needs. The choices exist on an either/or basis within the Anglo-American point of view but are perceived as a range of alternatives within Southern Plains tribal frames of reference. The decisions may be determined by what the people expect or by what they imagine the result might be. Different cultural views compound the cross-purposes of many of the tribes and the United States.

Kirke and Lynn Kickingbird introduced a planning-change model at the Tribal Peacemaking Conference in Tulsa in May 1993, which accommodates many of the needs of the Southern Plains tribes as well as the needs of tribes throughout the western United States. Their model poses a number of questions based on traditional knowledge and logic expressed in terms other than Western European ones. It begins with the question of tribal and community identity, including history and culture, demographics, strengths, weaknesses, and internal and external environments. This is followed by questions about what needs to be done, when, and where to do it that in turn lead to the questions of what can be reasonably accomplished. Once this goal is defined, the questions center on what is needed to accomplish it in terms of priorities, operation plans, and implementation.[30]

The choices to be made in intertribal efforts to satisfy tribal needs are influenced only in part by rational calculation. The interplay of tradition, ethnocentrism, realistic and distorted images, and ideas with expressed good intention play a major part in decisionmaking. Attitudes of suspicion and trust, fear and assurance, as well as long-term loyalties, affect the decisionmaking processes. Cumulative evidence points to the need for renewed development of integrative processes among the tribes in their relations with the United States as a foundation for supportive societies and for the survival of American Indian tribal communities.

14

SELF-SUFFICIENCY

In the last decades of the twentieth century Southern Plains tribes attempted to renew their efforts towards self-governance amid the confusion of transition occurring in their socioeconomic context. Tribal people had long known that the world was the subject of immense suffering, that it exhibited acute symptoms by means of which it defended itself against collapse. They increasingly understood what was being projected onto them by the colonial institutions as well as what they projected toward the dominant society. The realization that all things show images was critical to their understanding of the patterns of existence. The earth held not only forms to be read for meaning but a configuration or expression to be faced.

The American Indian peoples discovered that the element most resistant to change was the Bureau of Indian Affairs, the arm of the government charged with facilitating self-determination reforms. The good work of a bureaucracy is taken for granted and seldom noticed; its purpose is to avoid mistakes, which are points of concern. In the principal study for self-determination policy reform, the concern was clearly stated:

> We identify a problem regarding the implementation of PL 93-638 [Indian Self-Determination and Education Assistance Act]: there are significant differences between the intent of the law and the way it is interpreted and implemented in the field. We attribute this problem to two primary causes:
> • the rigid adherence to Subchapter M of 25 Code of Federal Regulations by Bureau officials; and
> • the fact that Bureau personnel are not driven by a broad, overriding mission to make self-determination a reality.[1]

The constraints of the bureau's rules, regulations, contracts, and monitors as well as personal animosity in some cases were inconsistent with the tribes' images of themselves as sovereign entities. In Pres. Ronald Reagan's Indian Policy statement of January 24, 1983, he noted that "excessive regulation and self-perpetuating bureaucracy have stifled local decision-making, thwarted Indian control of Indian resources, and promoted dependency rather than self-sufficiency."[2] This sense of being either dependent or self-sufficient was interpreted as mutually exclusive in scholarly treatment as well as in government policymaking:

> Thus the issue of Indian self-determination versus federal paternalism is joined. Historians will have to follow this basic inconsistency, which now seems to lie at the very heart of developing Indian policy. Indian demands that the government continue its trust responsibility will inescapably perpetuate paternalism. It is impossible to expand trust responsibility without expanding paternalism, however devoutly the Indians and their spokesmen in government wish it were not so.[3]

This statement reflects Anglo-American logic and thought processes. By means of argument that states matters in terms of contradiction, one or another is shown to be false. The emphasis upon either/or forms of logic and the use of linear cause-and-effect relations in hindsight provide a limited foundation for creative thought within the American Indian traditions of the Southern Plains. The principle of contradiction applies only if the two proposed categories are truly mutually exclusive. In practice such categories are very difficult to find so that these positions have to be deliberately established. In the instance of self-determination and trust relations, traditional Western logic imposes the rigidity that is reflected in the Bureau of Indian Affairs' handling of policy issues. Within tribal affairs, adversarial positions work to the disadvantage of the centering processes of tribal traditions. In November 1984 the Presidential Commission on Indian Reservation Economies, chaired by Ross Swimmer, then Principal Chief of the Cherokee Nation, noted this either/or approach in its final report to the president of the United States:

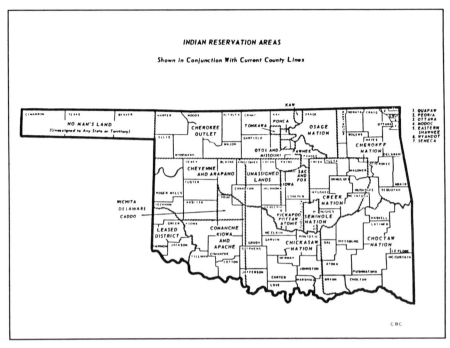

Tribal jurisdictional areas shown in conjunction with Oklahoma county boundary lines.

This policy is an extension and an expansion of the 1970 national Indian policy of self-determination for Indian tribes set forth by President [Richard] Nixon. The concept of self-determination was a major departure from past American Indian policy. For nearly 200 years national policy had wavered on the one hand towards the goal of removal, or separation from the rest of society, and on the other hand towards the goal of assimilation or absorption of the Indian culture into the dominant culture.[4]

Economic development was seen as a means of strengthening tribal foundations within their reservation bases, but sustainable development on tribal reserve areas in the Southern Plains was unusually susceptible to circumstances over which the tribes had little control.[5] The central question for tribal development strategists was where to break the cycle of conditions that resulted in chronic proverty. Gradually a general strategy took shape that offered broad guidelines for the allocation of resources by government and intertribal institutions, including increasing the availability of capital for investment, increasing the base of operations for service industry, increasing industrialization/commercialization, expanding output of agriculture and aquaculture, expanding the power resources of the tribe, opening markets, providing technical information, educating people, strengthening the competence of government administration, improving health conditions, and gauging social reaction. The strategy emphasized balanced growth. The expected effect was to provide for a more lasting impact from governmental assistance and steadier progress toward improved general welfare.

The preponderance of development planning and action has been undertaken by tribal governments in the Southern Plains and is generally true throughout the western states. During the last quarter of the twentieth century, as strapped as they are, these tribes have carried on their own development activity, generating amounts of about 90 percent of the capital investment and virtually all of the human effort involved.

However, these resources from within the tribes have not been enough in most cases to put them on the road to fully self-sustained growth, a situation that has led to the adoption of significant programs of intergovernmental assistance. U.S. policymakers recognized that a dominant segment of society could not live securely on a continent where significant numbers of people felt denied the essentials of subsistence.[6] Thus different layers of government and private economic organizations have responded in a variety of ways to provide technical assistance; preinvestment projects; supplies for child welfare assistance; efforts for prevention of disease; coordination of economic development workshops; temporary placement of senior executive and managerial staff; loans for public and private "self-liquidating" projects; equity investments in private enterprise; loans of long-term, minimum interest for agricultural and educational projects; short-term financial assistance to help overcome temporary cash-flow problems; grants to finance social institutions, including clinics, teaching and research institutions; coordination of central economic policies, including direction of investment trading; and capital subscriptions and supplementary contributions.

By far the greatest amount of economic assistance reflected the preferences of government planners to control major capital resources needed for development. U.S. agency heads wanted to make their own decisions about whom to aid, how, and under what circumstances. Central planning remained highly constrictive as to tribal initiatives. Much of this effort carried political overtones: "cooperative" tribes were often favored in allocation of resources. The problem remained that reciprocity was the prime instrument of U.S. policy. Recipients were prepared to pay some political price for procuring the boost they needed for development. Some tribal leaders were of course only too eager to pay their benefactors in loyalty because the flow of aid helped keep them in power.

Design-based discussions of bilateral and multilateral responsibility have had little practical effect. Any attempt by a consortia of Southern Plains tribes to seek development assistance, rather than being solely dependent upon unilateral aid, has never been successful. The Bureau of Indian Affairs has determined whether there should be multilateral participation and has also decided on the purposes to which the money should be applied and on what terms.

Lack of coordination is one of the major impediments to effective organization of development efforts. In the absence of adequate procedures for joint planning and clearance, programs overlap and leave significant gaps. Tribal economic development efforts have been badly fragmented. Consequently, resources are wasted and political influences continually intrude in shaping and direction of efforts.[7]

Many of the problems associated with tribal attempts at development arose from the very nature of the undertaking. There was a shortage of competent personnel willing to spend time on various projects, but in increasing numbers of cases, the tribal administration and staff have a greater knowledge of the subject at hand than the support staff offered through the Bureau of Indian Affairs. The uncertain impact of planned projects on a tribe's ultimate development was another concern. The federal bureaucracy and the tribal populations resisted changing long-established social and economic habits despite the need for change. Inadequate financial support, cumbersome and overlapping administration, and motivational suspicions caused further delay and waste.[8] Moreover, the key to effective technical assistance lay in finding persons with knowledge adapted to a specific tribal need and with the ability to communicate it in a particular situation. This requirement called for patience, tact, deep human empathy, and a real sense of humility, personal attributes that have been sacrificed all too often in the scramble for expertise.

Planning effective programs was difficult and was complicated by several factors. First, since 1975 tribal governments were expected to take the initiative in proposing projects. Many tribes, especially smaller ones, lacked the means to communicate effectively to U.S. officials which elements would contribute most to their development. Second, responsibility for approving projects was scattered among many agencies and departments competing for program funds. Third, experts often disagreed on the appropriate strategy for economic and social development, arriving at different priorities. Fourth, statistical data for the reservation jurisdictions and communities was unreliable and inadequate and was largely uncollected in any meaningful way until the 1990 U.S. Census.

Economic and social development could not occur unless capital was joined with informed activity. Stated in material terms, the issue was to stimulate a flow of capital large enough that the resulting increase in production would outrun the growth of population and thus launch a process of cumulative expansion and then to acquire a sufficient balance of exchange to provide the basic needs for the economic structure. The major source of development capital must be from the people of the tribes themselves; their savings and taxes should add up to at least 80 percent of the amount invested. This process is hampered by current tax policies that penalize personal savings. Taken as a whole, the tribes by some means have to move their economies to support the annual rate of gross capital formation to more than 15 percent of their Gross Tribal Product (GTP). The investment of private capital thus remains a priority development target.

The gap between the wealthier segments of the United States and the rural reservation areas of the Southern Plains is widening. The tribal response to the challenges of a weakening U.S. economy, with its continuing debt burden, and to the lack of dynamic economies of their own is critical for the long-term health of the tribes and of the Southern Plains. It is unrealistic to continue to act as if the United States or any other single nation remains responsible for the welfare of all.

Self-sufficiency demanded tribal initiative but forced issues of intertribal concerns and mutual assistance. Where the tribal populations are small, intertribal planning and action were critical in providing for effective development. Only elemental steps have been made toward intertribal activity in the twentieth century. In the Southern Plains the principal modern intertribal organizations included the Seven Tribes of Southwest Oklahoma—Apache of Oklahoma, Caddo, Comanche, Delaware of Western Oklahoma, Fort Sill Apache, Kiowa, and Wichita and Affiliated Tribes; the Wichita-Delaware-Caddo Enterprises, Caddo, Delaware of Western Oklahoma, and Wichita and Affiliated Tribes; the Kiowa-Comanche-Apache Enterprises—Apache of Oklahoma, Comanche, and Kiowa; and the special-project consortia, which decides on chemical-abuse prevention and labor policies and involves the Apache of Oklahoma, the Delaware of Western Oklahoma, the Fort Sill Apache, and the Wichita and Affiliated Tribes.

Only the Cheyenne and Arapaho tribes, the Comanche Tribe, the Delaware of Western Oklahoma Tribe and the Fort Sill Apache Tribe belonged to the National Congress of American Indians. The organizations' primary purpose was to coordinate the actions of the tribes in their attainment of common ends. Each sovereign entity was responsible for carrying out its own initiatives. Although consultation and conference were the dominant activities of these intertribal structures, the tribes depended upon voluntary cooperation to accomplish their ends. They sought reconciliation of differing frames of reference through continued discussion and debate.

The Southern Plains intertribal organizations have acquired identities of their own as well as a degree of autonomy in representing the common interests of the several tribes. Even so the organizations were best described as institutional systems of coexistence. The successful operation of an intertribal system has depended upon the development of procedures peculiarly adapted to the function of securing collaboration among tribes. This process remained true even though each tribe differs in its form of government, its economic and social conditions, and its relative power. For example, the Seven Tribes Council needs a shared statement of goals through which the tribes can assess their relative positions in a cooperative manner. Intertribal activity had involved the acceptance of basic contradictions between formal structure and actual practices: there was respect for the principle of tribal sovereignty and at the same time the attempt to reach pragmatic courses of action. When operating successfully these processes blended negotiation and tactics; negotiation would weave the network of intergovernmental consent needed to sanction action; appropriate tactics could provide the information needed to realize what should be done and how to do it. The use of both components was largely the responsibility of the tribal governments, but there should be an intertribal staff whose loyalty is to the organization as a whole. Such a system has never existed except in the work of the Bureau of Indian Affairs staff, and it had U.S. policy as its primary concern. A staff that operated for the Seven Tribes could provide the initiative, the selective intermediaries, the information base, and the creative imagination needed to articulate issues and to persuade governments to act.

Membership in intertribal organizations is open only to tribes of American Indians on the Southern Plains recognized as sovereign by the U.S. government. The effect of the membership and representation provisions of the intertribal organization ensures that participation corresponds to the governing authority of the associated tribes. The Seven Tribes of Southwest Oklahoma Council operates without a written constitution, which is an acceptable foundation for the participating tribes, perhaps even necessary to prevent undue outside interference. The apparent need is not a written constitution but agreed-upon goals and objectives.

The authority of intertribal organizations is clearly limited. For example, the Seven Tribes of Southwest Oklahoma Council lack legislative or executive powers. This organization does not require a mandatory action from its tribal members. The council and the economic development organizations are directly prohibited from interfering in matters that are considered to be the internal affairs of a tribe. There is a substantial reminder that the boundaries of intertribal action are circumscribed by the tribes in relationship with the United States. The council can recommend but cannot dictate to governments. It can study, discuss, plan, and propose action but does not legislate. In the council, the representation is based upon one tribe—one vote. The effect of the demand for sovereign equality is revealed in the pattern of organization, which is conciliar rather than hierarchical. The conciliar pattern ensures that all important decisions are made by consultation and agreement among members.

A peculiarly difficult problem for the council is to determine a satisfactory method of reaching decisions. If full regard is maintained for the sovereignty of each tribe, any action taken by the council requires the unanimous consent of the members and then only with the consent of the tribal organizations. The "unanimity rule" remains as the characteristic voting procedure. Planning, however, is never done on a regional intertribal basis but always within a tribal sphere of influence or jurisdiction.[9]

The procedures of the council are almost universally designed to ensure the practice of open deliberations; meetings of the main body are usually public. Yet there is little effort to acquaint students, educators, and private organizations with the activities of most intertribal affairs. Much of the work of the intertribal organizations, including the council and the economic enterprise corporations, is known by only a small number of people.

The problem of financing the council remains twofold: First, U.S. funding channeled through the Bureau of Indian Affairs or through individual tribes places limits on a real and continuing effort toward intertribal activity. Second, voluntary responses from tribal governments have been sporadic and difficult to obtain. Yet as the Southern Plains tribes enter into negotiations observing government-to-government policy reforms, the need for intertribal coordination is imperative. The U.S. government maintains unilateral relations with the result that intertribal alliances, although needed, remain relatively ineffective. Self-sufficiency thus provided a challenge that the tribes could not meet in the decade of the 1980s on the Southern Plains.

15

POLICY REFORM

Debate continues over the implementation of self-determination and self-sufficiency policies. Nevertheless, the U.S. government has proposed to accept even greater self-governance by the tribes on the Southern Plains and throughout the nation but they must determine the nature of those efforts. Pres. George Bush described the new relationship on June 14, 1991:

This government-to-government relationship is the result of sovereign and independent tribal governments being incorporated into the fabric of our Nation. . . . Over the years the relationship has flourished, grown, and evolved into a vibrant partnership in which over 500 tribal governments stand shoulder to shoulder with the other governmental units that form our Republic.

This is now a relationship in which tribal governments may choose to assume the administration of numerous Federal programs pursuant to the 1975 Indian Self-Determination and Education Assistance Act [PL 93-638].

This is a partnership in which an Office of Self-Governance has been established in the Department of the Interior and given the responsibility of working with tribes to craft creative ways of transferring decision-making powers over tribal government functions from the Department to tribal governments.

An Office of American Indian Trust will be established in the Department of the Interior and given the responsibility of overseeing the trust responsibility of the Department and of insuring that no Departmental action will be taken that will adversely affect or destroy those physical assets that the Federal Government holds in trust for the tribes.[1]

There is every indication that the administration of Pres. Bill Clinton supports this government-to-government policy initiative. New guidelines issued by President Clinton offer an expansion of tribal authority over federal programs.[2]

A major policy difference has provided a means to move away from the contracting for programs under PL 93-638. On December 4, 1991, President Bush signed PL 100-472, the Self-Governance Demonstration Project Act that allowed the tribes to take control of budgeted funds and to allocate them according to needs and priorities determined by the elected government rather than by the Bureau of Indian Affairs. The project extends through 1996 and provides for different strategies in determining budgets. Self-determination contracting had called for program amounts to be determined by contract with the Bureau of Indian Affairs; allocations were then determined by the Indian Priority System and by the congressional appropriations process.

In the "self-governance" process, program amounts are determined by tribal council according to staff presentations, tribal priorities, and community needs. Funding under the self-determination procedure is made in payments by cost-reimbursement through the Bureau of Indian Affairs funding processes. Payments and prepaid amounts are negotiated in the self-goverance project and are made on a quarterly basis or to the best advantage of the tribe as allowed by the law.[3]

Established programs are contracted with the Bureau of Indian Affairs or designated under the Indian Priority System. In the self-governance process, the tribes have the flexibility to create new programs or to modify, consolidate, or abolish Bureau of Indian Affairs programs. An Office of Self-Governance has been established in the Department of the Interior and given the responsibility of working with tribes to craft creative ways of transferring decisionmaking to them. In competitive grants, such as economic development and Indian child welfare, the contracting process allows grants to be awarded by a process of application review. In their self-governance efforts, tribes contend that these competitive grants should be incorporated into the projects, or compacts, to include all activities desired by the tribes. Bureau of Indian Affairs' program-carryovers to the new fiscal year remain within the program's specific budgets in the contracting process, under the new system carryover and savings are to be expended according to tribal council decisions.[4]

The management's method of decisionmaking emphasizes the difference between the two processes. Accountability in contracting shifts from the bureau to the respective tribal council in the self-governance process. Federal laws, rules, and regulations for managing programs may be replaced with the tribal laws and management guidelines made in cooperation with the secretary of the interior. In compact agreements, tribal staff reports on program performance according to tribal council requirements, submitting two reports to Congress on progress and problems according to a negotiated baseline measure.

The negotiation process, in theory, begins with the sharing of factual materials. This approach has been tested during the first seven tribal-compacts negotiations by the Absentee Shawnee Tribe, Cherokee Nation, Hoopa Valley Tribe, Jamestown S'Klallam Tribe, Lummi Nation, Mille Lake Band of Chippewa, and Quinault Nation. Once figures are agreed upon they become issues for negotiation in that they are defined as the complete budgets for all levels of the Bureau of Indian Affairs. These budgets are presented to the tribes, and the BIA and the tribal council then propose budget figures for justification and negotiation. These figures have to represent more than the bureau's estimates for each tribe. Tribal populations, reserve acreage, and historic contract amounts also must be agreed upon by the federal negotiators and the tribes.

The budget negotiations for multitribal agencies, such as the Anadarko Agency and the area offices on the Southern Plains, are expected to be very difficult because of the unilateral negotiating stance taken by the United States. Agency and area program budgets are seriously underfunded, but negotiations by law cannot have a negative impact upon neighboring tribal governments or tribal-organization contractors. Division of programs for partial transfer involving one or two federal personnel is not considered practical by the U.S. government, but more flexibility is necessary in regard to the Southern Plains. Negotiations should not be based upon the bureau's justification because it does not provide the detail that the internal area office and the agency office budgets provide. The Bureau of Indian Affairs is not flexible enough to reorganize structurally so that it can accommodate self-governance compacting.

In preparation for negotiations, tribes should establish a checklist that would include all issues and objectives to be incorporated into the compact and the annual funding agreement, including a precise definition of which programs the tribes intend to assume. Their list should include complete identification of current PL 93-638 contracts by program and amount, complete budget information from the area and agency offices, and a review of Bureau of Indian Affairs' justifications. The model compact of self-governance designed by federal officials must be reviewed and modified to meet specific tribal needs. Tribal policymakers, technical budget staff, and tribal lawyers and accountants should be present at the negotiations. Tribal authorities should oversee the creation of detailed records kept on the proceedings, and copies should be given to U.S. authorities. Congressional offices also must be apprised of the negotiation's developments.

Internal reorganization must be established to serve the particular needs of the individual tribe, provided for in the tribe's constitution, code of laws, policies, and procedures. Also important to consider are the Self-Governance Compact and Annual Agreement as well as the requirements set forth in the Office of Management and Budget's circular A-87. Particularly important to the tribe is the development of procedures for budgeting, internal monitoring, and evaluating performance and internal compliance systems. The common thread of these procedures weaves together valuable information for the tribal council as it serves the needs of the tribal members.[5]

Major considerations in tribal reorganization are identifying methods for timely decisionmaking, communicating policy decisions to tribal members, developing cost-effective program operations, and centering the tribal community. Combined effectiveness and cost efficiency will determine the opportunities the tribe will have to redesign programs, reallocate funds, and improve services to people. This reorganization process must proceed from the people through the council to its elected leaders.[6] Goals to be reached through internal tribal reorganization include tribal control and flexibility; tribal accountability and responsibility; responsiveness to tribal concerns and conditions; effectiveness of tribal operations; documentation of tribal organization, processes, and procedures; foundations for tribal stability; satisfaction of legislative and compact requirements; greater involvement and participation by tribal membership; and effective information delivery to facilitate tribal decisionmaking. Such goals are broad-based in order to fit comfortably within traditional tribal patterns.

Tribes emphasizing continuing education for members in regard to activities taking place within tribal government will gain knowledge and skills necessary to function on more than one level. The more tribal members understand about native and English languages, tribal traditions, and self-governance, the more likely they will be to achieve an effective consensus to support tribal operations. Education and communication continue to be essential for self-governance.[7]

Divisive issues arise because of controversy over the distribution of limited resources under a Bureau of Indian Affairs program that provides services to a number of tribes in a multitribal agency and area, as is the case on the Southern Plains. The judgment over perceived or real negative effects is complex but negotiable. The bureau is prone to protect its programs by claiming a negative effect and must be held to a high level of scrutiny before permitting it to claim that the division of resources will adversely impact other tribes. It is in this circumstance that intertribal communication and planning play a critical role.[8]

Distribution of resources can be based upon various criteria, including the number of tribes served by the agency or area offices; tribal enrollment relative to enrollment of all tribes served by the agency and area offices; reservation land and tribal jurisdiction acreage relative to land acreage of all tribes served by the agency and area offices; number of tribal students relative to students from all tribes served by the agency and area offices; number of transactions for a tribe relative to transactions of all tribes served by the agency and area offices; and historic funding levels of self-determination contracts.

The difficulties with division of resources are particularly acute in multitribal agencies concerning those programs and services with relatively small budgets and staffing levels, as is the case in the Southern Plains. Here again intertribal alliance can serve as viable means of replacing bureau employees funded by multiple-

element components within the agency budget. Effective intertribal alliances could prevent negotiated resource transfer from
having an adverse impact on other tribes being served by the agency.

Intertribal alliance planning can go a long way toward eliminat-
ing the problem of division of resources in a program that supports
a one- or two-person bureau staff used to serve a number of tribes.
Prior to negotiations each of the tribes needs to understand the
BIA's decisionmaking process for multiple-source funding. Clearly
the underlying concerns are to avoid adverse impacts on other
tribes. Multiple-source funding of bureau employees should not
increase for small programs when intertribal alliance planning has
anticipated reorganization and consolidation.

Two critically important elements in self-governance relations
between the Southern Plains tribes and the United States, the trust
responsibility and the compacts of self-governance, must be linked
in the negotiations. The trust relationship is generally defined as
the obligation of the United States to manage and preserve American Indian properties, which include land, money and other liquid
assets, and resources such as water, fish, timber, and minerals. The
United States holds legal title to this property, and the Native
American tribes, bands, villages, and people hold what is known as
beneficial title; thereby the income from trust assets is exempt
from state and local taxes. The obligations of the United States in
managing the American Indian properties are similar to those of a
private trust. Underlying treaties and statutes determine the extent
of the responsibility of the government with respect to a particular
tribe or type of resource. In each case the United States is held to
the highest fiduciary standards of prudent fiscal management.

In terms of the self-governance compacts, the key issues include
maintaining the positive aspects of the trust relationship, guaran-
teeing sufficient U.S. involvement in and technical control of the
management of tribal property and assets to meet existing standards for financial liability, and providing for maximum control by
and involvement of the tribes over their own property and assets.
The issues should be defined in the compact of self-governance
negotiated with representatives of the U.S. government. The difficulty arises from negotiations that are patterned on making and
defending a position. The defense of a position can involve excellent logic and ingenuity, but it can also involve deliberate

perceptual blindness. The United States should specifically pledge its trust responsibility to each individual tribe to protect and conserve those resources. The negotiations to achieve greater self-governance among the tribes of the Southern Plains provide a realistic means to end the most oppressive elements of paternalism. Self-governing tribes with a measure of homerule will benefit not only the United States and the state of Oklahoma but also themselves.[9]

The reworking of the notions of tribal government on the Southern Plains must be done with careful attention to traditional Native American patterns of existence as well as to the Anglo-American concepts of materialism, secularism, nominalism, positivism, and behaviorism. Classification, chains of explanation, and presenting facts to bring about planned outcomes are important elements in the negotiation process, but they are only part of the necessary skills. The process also should include acknowledgment of decisions, priorities, other people's views, problem solving methods, conflicts, guessing, emotional biases, and prejudices. There should be no pretence that negotiations consist only of pure information and that they proceed on a rational basis. Rather, they should be oriented toward a cosmological vision, an attempt at soul-making or making medicine that goes beyond measures of expediency.

Each tribal tradition includes material objects, beliefs, images of persons and events, practices, and patterned institutions that must serve the synergistic whole. The received images of the past provide constellations of symbols that are modified in relation to one another as tribes move into the future. The transmitted theme of mutual support among the tribes of the Southern Plains provides the means to work within existing systems. For example, Gary McAdams, president of the Wichita and Affiliated Tribes, emphasizes that the Wichita people must know who they are in the contemporary world; they have the continuing need to understand traditional tribal patterns to maintain stability in the present and into the future. Problems occur with the loss of institutional patterns because such loss rends the social fabric. At times it seems that the only thing the tribe still has in common is money that came from the claims against the U.S. government. Tribal purpose has to be more than sharing material wealth; it must be concerned with the social and spiritual aspects of being Wichita. The Wichita were an interactive people on the Southern Plains for centuries and are still competent today to work in alliance with the other Southern Plains tribes and the United States.[10]

Intertribal activity is always collaborative in nature. Its purpose is to provide for a joint course of action, with each tribe being responsible for implementing its own part of the activity. Consultation and conference are the dominant activities of intertribal organizations. As the alliances depend upon voluntary cooperation to accomplish their tasks, intertribal forums must seek through continued discussion and debate the reconciliation of differing tribal frames of reference.

The successful outcome of the self-governance policy depends upon the development of procedures peculiarly adapted to securing collaboration even in times of apparent crisis or when there is pressure for immediate change without consultation. Such development involves the acceptance of basic contradictions between the informal structure and the actual practices of the Seven Tribes of Southwest Oklahoma, or a similar organization. Common action by the tribes implies the recognition of at least two layers of activity: a respect for the principle of tribal sovereignty and a focus on the patterned needs and images of the Southern Plains in Native American terminology. Emphasizing the importance of both layers is largely the responsibility of the tribal governments, who at times are assisted by facilitators immersed in the logical activity of achieving tribal consensus based upon information and creative imagination. These efforts may seem general, nonspecific, or vague to objective observers outside the sphere of activity.

Elected leadership must be chosen with the same careful criteria that applied in the selection of traditional leadership. Reciprocity must be a focal point in tribal affairs so that honor and responsibility are expressed values. Although personal qualifications of a particular representative are taken into account, first consideration is given to what tribe he or she represents. In this period of negotiation and change, the chairpersons of the tribes are particularly important. Prestige is at stake rather than mere authority. The chairperson is responsible for seeing that every tribe has a voice in council. Under no circumstances can the chair presume to act for the organization unless explicitly instructed to do so. The demand for sovereign equality results in a pattern of organization that is conciliar, one that is in harmony with the patterns and images of the sustainable systems of the Southern Plains.

The procedures of intertribal organization must be almost universally designed to ensure the practice of open diplomacy. Verbatim records of primary sessions should be kept as well as summaries of committee meetings, and the summaries should be published in native languages and in English. Meetings of the main body and even of committees usually should be public. Every effort should be made to acquaint students, educators, private organizations, and tribal members with the work of the organization. These procedures can permit tribal representatives the means to explore differences and similarities so they can design bases of agreement without having to calculate during every moment of the meetings.[11]

As of 1994 no self-governance compact negotiations have been initiated by the Southern Plains tribes. Before this process starts each tribe must be in active communication with all the others; thus the compacts will provide effective bridges to join the tribal governments and the U.S. government. Given the patterns of alliances on the Southern Plains, tradition offers a considerable body of knowledge and skills to draw upon. Sovereignty must serve as an enabling principle rather than as a restrictive element in tribal efforts.

16

CONCLUSION

The tribes of the Southern Plains will respond to the self-governance policy-reform measures in ways that reveal how they have been shaped by modern America and through patterns that stem from their tribal traditions. Spirituality remains as a dynamic force in their community life; the vital changes in tribal efforts are linked largely with changes in spiritual beliefs and concepts. The secularization of a tribal society involves the devitalization of that society. On another level, each sovereign entity must effectively plan and negotiate in a concerted manner with the other tribes of the region as well as with the United States. Use of Western forms of analysis, adequate information, and skilled argument are not enough to succeed in this process of negotiation and implementation of the government-to-government policy reforms. Traditional patterns of design are necessary for the recreation of tribal mutual assistance and self-sufficiency.

The issue of rebuilding a sustainable basis for self-governance cannot be resolved through analysis in the Western style alone; the need exists to design a way forward into the future. Design uses information and logic, but it also must apply measurable patterns of existence in order to put forward concepts and to change existing perceptions. Traditional design seeks to bring long-term patterns into sympathetic harmony with present realities. No amount of analysis can reveal a pattern unless it already exists on earth, but design often seeks to perceive a relationship that is not known to have existed previously. Some designs will be better than others in all respects; others will be better in some respects.

In the self-governance negotiation process that exists, the parties start at extreme positions, understanding that they should gradually bargain and struggle their way to a compromise position. A great deal of time, effort, and expense is involved. However, an alternative method might be that the negotiating parties never meet. Each party designs the most workable solution, trying their utmost to design acceptable outcomes. The effort that previously had gone into adversarial conflict instead goes into design. If both parties do a good job of designing a workable outcome, then it probably does not matter much which is chosen; the important point is that the emphasis is placed on design instead of on argument. Thus the parties are not polarized but are in a position to reach consensus.

The stated purpose of allowing the formally recognized tribes to function as sovereign entities fails to recognize the fact that many of the tribes are too small to operate in ways that ensure appropriate action. Designs must be made carefully to guarantee the welfare of the smallest tribes along with the well-being of the Southern Plains itself.

U.S. Indian policy has reversed itself to the detriment of the tribes on several occasions. Instead of clarity and decisiveness, policy has too often resulted in turmoil. The Constitution did not create a government of "separated powers" but one of separated institutions sharing power. The executive branch is clearly part of the legislative process; almost all major bills are drafted and put forward by the executive offices. The courts, too, legislate. And Congress is equally involved in administration, especially in Indian affairs, in both its investigative function and in its appropriation of funds and oversight of spending. To the Southern Plains tribes, Congress, with its power to reward and punish, is as much a boss as is the president or the secretary of the interior. Different institutions sharing powers and getting involved in one another's business provide the checks and balances as well as many other benefits. But they also contribute to the turbulence and confusion.

Still another dimension of this turmoil stems from the fact that many people are involved in the process of policy reform and implementation, not just those who hold official positions. The print and electronic media play a role in the process of government, carrying out functions that are a necessary part of the process and performing them with uneven quality. There are also lobbyists, the spokespersons of special interests of every kind, from oil and gas producers and gaming backers to "friends of the Indians." Their activities in Washington, D.C., Oklahoma City, and throughout the Southern Plains are influential but sometimes counterproductive. Moreover, the world of academics and research influences the processes. Quasi-governmental organizations such as the Brookings Institution and the RAND Corporation in Santa Monica, California, compile and analyze information according to Western perceptions for the government. The tribes in turn must manage significant elements from their own research and information gathered through creative thought to balance their design efforts.

The issues are real and sometimes dangerous for the tribes of the Southern Plains and for the United States as well. With the end of the cold war, the United States is facing real financial disaster, unable to control spending through balanced budgets. As knowledgeable a figure as William Fulbright, longtime chairperson of the Senate Foreign Relations Committee, has sounded the nature of the crisis: "The trouble is that, in driving the Soviets towards bankruptcy, we have made alarming progress in that direction ourselves."[1] No longer can the tribes expect the United States alone to be responsible for their well-being.

But the problems cannot be expressed in monetary terms alone. Another dimension of the confusion and turbulence of policymaking lies in the complexity of the issues confronting the tribes. Inadequate knowledge of the workings of tribal social and economic affairs and a limited capacity to foresee developments that compound problems and to anticipate consequences further complicate federal decisionmaking. Adequate quantified information about reservation areas has become available for the first time with the 1990 U.S. Census summaries. Better understanding may not always lead to solutions, but it can make the process of getting there more intelligible.

Tribal traditions offer patterns that provide elements important to decisionmaking in the present. For example, the seal of the Comanche Tribe depicts symbols of moving again within traditional patterns, emphasizing traditional values. The Comanche people use these symbols in seeking harmony in education, in prioritizing and budgeting, in determining paths of action, and in improving social welfare.[2] Each tribe draws upon elements that remain important to decisionmaking, including the village crier and official interpreters, which must be seen in the light of the contemporary period. Values that emphasize elimination of waste, living in community, awareness of future generations, and spirituality expressed in the form of religion are chief among the centering activities. Each value among the Southern Plains tribes must be enunciated in intelligible terms to the larger community.

These values provide interpretive keys to overcoming obstacles that may arise in the government-to-government policymaking process. Such hindrances may be in the form of separate institutions sharing powers; media, experts, and others who influence policy without holding formal power; interest groups that exert ill-defined pressures; tribal influence in power sharing; and differences and complexities in analysis, synthesis, and design. With concerted tribal planning and action as well as meaningful application of power, the problems do not have to be insurmountable. The tribal leaders must require that creative alternatives be established so that continuing programs may be altered as to quality, cost-cutting, and continuous improvement. In addition there must be space for creative design according to traditional understanding and imagination to provide for a broader range of alternative solutions. Tradition as well as reason must play their roles; policy faces inward as much as outward. Seeking to reconcile conflicting goals, to adjust aspirations to available means, and to accommodate the different advocates of these elements one to another is possible where there is mutual respect.

The tribal leaders have to take the initiative to bring lasting change that will benefit the common welfare of the Southern Plains tribes. The notion of the common good of the tribal membership implies that this common good contains the answers to the policy questions. If there is competition for political leadership among the people, tribal governance, in order to decide directly upon issues, requires traditional models. For example, even though the United States repressed the Kiowa Sun Dance, or Skaw-tow, the Sun Dance camp circle provides a measure for the present through the memory of spiritual centering rather than through a system based upon personality.[3] There are a number of advantages to this sense of tribal governance: it provides a practical test for policy ends, and it leaves room for the role of tribal leadership as well as for the tribal community's welfare. Finally, it provides for centering within the tribal community. The tribal membership can influence policy during its government's term by the threat of throwing the government out if it strays from traditional understandings of patterned relations. The relationship between elected tribal governance and complete freedom means that if in principle everyone is free to compete for political leadership, then in most cases freedom of discussion for all will prevail. With adequate leadership, accommodation can be found among the factions of the tribe, given traditional patterns of existence.

Intertribal politics has a mixture of conflict and accommodation similar to that in tribal politics. As a consequence, the business between tribes, like that within tribes, requires skills of negotiation and design. One tribe's gain is not always another's loss. As a general rule, people in the United States have been taught that politics is concerned with power, given the adversarial relations within the dominant society. In its broadest meaning, politics concerns the activities and relationships of groups of peoples with interrelated governmental bodies as a perceived whole.

Making group decisions depends upon a procedure by which a tribal population can act in concert with other tribes where commonly known patterns and images should be sought along with the means of achieving them. For example, the peacemaking patterns of existence among the Delaware are critical to intertribal cooperation on the Southern Plains. Moreover, tribes must agree on how they should divide among themselves those benefits already available. In each instance, the traditional models provide the means through which tribal groups can act for their common benefit.

Knowledge can and should be increased and made available at all levels of participation among the tribal publics. Policy is made in a political process involving conversation among factions and among tribes before a variety of constituencies. The wisest course is probably to concentrate on attempting to maximize the strengths of the overall system as changes are made. The best way to improve policy is to conduct it with a highly discriminating eye to the realities of the traditional tribal processes. Vast increases in knowledge that strengthen the capacity to predict the consequences of intertribal and international policy actions will greatly improve the effectiveness of policy. The U.S. bureaucracy must not be rewarded for maneuvering around opposition but rather for reconciling different views.

Traditional tribal governance was open in the sense that there were avenues for participation. This system is still observed where traditional government operates alongside elected government, as with the Cheyenne Forty-four Chiefs and the Cheyenne and Arapaho tribes. It also operates in modified form among the Wichita, where the elders have advisory responsibilities to the elected officials. The tribes still respect their elders for their collective wisdom and their sense of patterns of existence to a greater degree than Anglo-American society respects theirs. And creative singers and dancers have important roles to play in the discernment of images.

These traditional institutional forms provide three effective criteria for decisionmaking in terms of existing policy and proposed policy changes: usefulness, i.e., the ability to provide meaningful solutions for problems; conceptual elaboration, i.e., the appropriateness of concepts (or the lack of them) in defining the issues to be confronted; explanatory power, i.e., the impact of existing policy and of natural self-organizing models on pattern-making and pattern-using systems. Tribes have long used the divergent thoughts and feelings of individuals and communities as a first cut in approaching policymaking, recognizing that most leaders did not face clearly defined alternatives. The outcome of their choices was seldom the result of simultaneous decisions. Southern Plains tribal politics has been crisis politics for the past 150 years as the United States has exerted its power in the region and as the Native American peoples have been ravaged by diseases to which they had little or no resistance.

The application of force is a costly way to achieve objectives, even as warfare has turned to politics. Shifting conceptual boundaries have proved to be confusing. The strength of the United States has not resulted from the logical neatness of rules and higher principles but from the authoritative establishment of paternalistic control and the forced acceptance of regulated practices. The crucial variable in the Southern Plains has been institutionalization.

The importance of tribal values in intertribal actions must extend beyond the particular institution imposed by rules. Values and traditional images are important in overcoming any weaknesses of will because they stress the importance of character and reputation in tribal society. In addition there must be insistence on the importance of social solidarity and the spirit of shared sacrifice. Although tribes of the Southern Plains differ in the extent to which they stress accommodation and communal values, there is common ground in the present, just as there was in the past.

Southern Plains tribal social patterns must seek harmony and common ground, including the earth and the soul of the earth. The source of tribal endurance in the face of U.S. policies of war and peace has been borne by the power to resolve conflict and to promote community action. Clearly, some peoples have governed themselves in more realistic ways than others. Ingeniously, coherently, the tribal societies resisted the alienation of the individual from the springs of community. Their patterns of self-rule supposed an ever-present awareness of exactly where the lines of power ran, through whose hands, and for precisely what purposes. Their politics was and continues to be intimate, immediate, always close at hand, not faceless and remote. In these tribal systems spirituality and a closeness to the earth served as more than a mere comfort or a useful function in traditional structures. These patterns and images remain the basis for creative thought, providing a focus of moral order integrated with natural order.[4]

Tribal communities and peoples need to continue to emphasize their inner being, but they can no longer ignore their outer countenance. The tribes are integrated into the mythic whole of existence; myth lives with and in the tribe. Spirituality is part of the civic life and is felt in it. Intertribal purpose provides the mutual support necessary for the spiritual presence among the specific tribes of the Southern Plains—Apache of Oklahoma, Caddo, Cheyenne and Arapaho, Comanche, Delaware of Western Oklahoma, Fort Sill Apache, Kiowa, and Wichita and Affiliated Tribes. Their collective presence extends beyond the great symbols, beyond the repercussions of ancestral heritage.

The tribes of the Southern Plains give the earth a respectful status of its own. This attitude remains as a major point of difference from U.S. policymakers' belief that the earth is primarily an economic resource. For the tribes, planning and development must locate human life at the center of sacred space. This orientation provides an orderly sense of the environment based on the harmony of the pattern of the ecosystem.

In the Southern Plains the continuing tribal renaissance in the arts, sciences, and spirituality has provided added energy as the variant patterns of classical civilizations grow in power and definition. One of the more powerful voices is Edgar Heap of Birds, a Cheyenne, trained in art at Temple University and the Tyler School of Art in Philadelphia and at the Royal College of Art in London. Heap of Birds also knows Cheyenne tradition. As a member of the Dog Soldier Society it is his responsibility to attend the funerals of the Cheyenne people; as he says, too many of these are for young people. His works are expressed in a broad range of media, including paintings, prints, and "word constructs" expressed on posters, billboards, and digital electronic signs. He asks for "deeds, not demands."5

The challenge from Heap of Birds is important within the multicultural environment as is the writing of the Pulitzer-Prize-winning Kiowa author, N. Scott Momaday. He describes the Southern Plains in *The Ancient Child: A Novel:*

The Washita River ran, bearing sediment and drift and leaves of trees and petals of wildflowers. The earth was fresh and fragrant, and the air clear and warm. The Great Plains had become intricate with color. The ruins of the old school at Rainy Mountain, holding against the weather of hundreds of seasons, stood out in the prairie like prehistoric cairns. The tall yellow grass sounded with the drone of bees and the crackle of grasshoppers. Birds drew lines on the sky, and terrapins crept along the creeks.

Above all, in the withering heat that shimmered in the noon and afternoon, the land was endless. It was the continental reach, beyond maps and geography, beyond the accounts of the voyageurs, almost beyond the distance of dreams. It was the middle and immeasurable meadow of North America. It was the destination and destiny of ancients who, coming with dogs and travois, followed herds of huge, lumbering animals down the long, cold cordilla, following the visions of their shamans, who rattled Arctic bones and cried in the voices of their owls and eagles and whose prayers were the lowing of thousand-mile winds. It was the sun's range. Nowhere on earth was there a more perfect equation of freedom and space. Those earliest inhabitants must have beheld the Plains, and each man must have said to himself, "From this time on, I shall belong to this land, for it is truly worthy of my strength, my dreams, my life and death. Here I am. Here, *I am.*" There was an abundance of game and water and grass, and an air full of brilliance to sustain the breathing of warriors and comely women and strong, beautiful children, of grandmothers and grandfathers, of holy people. Here, for those wanderers, was the center of the world, the sacred ground of sacred grounds.[6]

It is this sacred place and these extraordinary people that these negotiations are about and of whom deeds are required.

Issues of cooperation, motivation, apparent hostility, and symmetry center on the ecological systems of the Southern Plains. Intertribal and international systems must first seek a sustainable design in relation to the earth, one that is particularly interested in discovering isomorphic patterns and themes that repeat in varying forms at different levels. Mutually supportive designs established to affect the ecosystem may then be directed toward such a pattern at one level and thus have a reverberating effect throughout the larger system. Recognition of such isomorphism can lead to cooperative designs that are effective within the tribe, between the tribe and the larger systems, and within the larger systems.

In focusing on isomorphic patterns and themes tribal leaders should take particular care not to design means that replicate what already exists in the system. Interconnective design in the tribal–larger-systems network should be presented in language and tone that communicate a sense of appreciation of the various participants in the macrosystem. Cooperative arrangements that have worked can be singled out and confirmed. It is tempting when larger systems are criticizing a tribe to criticize the larger system in turn. Most often this response simply adds rigidity—and no new information—to the system. The use of affirmation by tribes and by larger systems often casts new light on preexisting relationships; this is especially true if bureaucrats have highlighted only deficits in the tribe and tribal members have seen only the negative aspects of the officials in the larger system, whether it is intertribal or international.

Any planning within the macrosystem in establishing effective self-governance or intertribal patterns of actions should meet certain criteria: (1) the plan should target the macrosystem, not a specific person or a subsystem; (2) it should use isomorphic patterns and themes in effective ways; (3) it should avoid replicating rigid patterns; (4) it should use affirmation, highlight preexisting resources, and make use of the unexpected; (5) it should be given in context. Tribes will be required to interact with larger systems over significant periods of time. Subsystems within the federal system have a view of their work that conceptualizes issues about tribes and complex systems; for example, health and educational agencies generally view their mandates as being in behalf of individuals. Most ceremonial expressions central to Southern Plains tribal traditions focus on these systems. Thus interaction with tribes may be required under the government-to-government relationship as it has rarely been before and then necessarily on a community basis. The welfare system in the United States, while ostensibly organized to support families, in fact frequently fragments them through practices and policies that lack appreciation of diverse family relationships and of the impact of such intervention on family systems.

Several dimensions contribute to the assessment of intrasystem issues. The first involves the definition of issues and asks, who in the system is defining an issue? what are the elements of the issue? for whom is this an issue? for whom is this not an issue? who first identified the issue? what lines of communication exist concerning the issue? how has the larger system resolved similar issues? how would things be different if this issue were resolved?

A second dimension involves examining the system's cherished beliefs and terms. The way a system views itself may be incongruent with interactional realities, possibly resulting in a distorted perception of participation. For instance, a tribe or an agency may insist that it is a nonhierachical organization when in fact key decisions are being made by a small group that excludes other tribal or agency members. It is then useful to ask, what is most important about this tribe or agency? how are decisions made or policies changed? how does a tribe or agency understand its mandate? As answers are verbalized, they can be matched to the system's actual operations. A third dimension involves determining the system's use or nonuse of blame when there are difficulties. How does the system explain what is happening? What does the tribe or agency see as necessary to change?

Bureaucracy, whether tribal, intertribal, state, or federal, was never designed as a mechanism for change but as a means of implementation. Unfortunately change in the instance of self-governance policy reform has to go through bureaucracies. Enterprising visionaries are likely to grow frustrated in a bureaucracy; when change requires such talents but must also pass through a bureaucracy, outcomes are likely to be negative. Therefore assessment of an intrasystem's dimensions has to be a continuing process, particularly in a period of reform.

The government-to-government policy changes are being made in a crisis period, and only significant structural development can now complete the work of transition. In the late 1980s the reform concept of self-determination was already in trouble because of bureaucratic inability to foster change through program contracting and because of inaccuracies in management's accounting of differences. The policy for the building and maintenance of the tribal entities on the Southern Plains that corresponded to models satisfactory to the United States had begun to wreck itself: it took far too little account of the ethnic differences among the tribes and failed to see that the tribes were too small and too poor materially to be viable as separate entities in the free enterprise system of the late twentieth century.

Manifestly intertribal federation was an alternative that basically went untried. But the tribes of the Southern Plains provide instructive avenues to understand the processes and designs that are established. The Wichita and Affiliated Tribes represent a long-standing union that existed for centuries across the plains in the Arkansas, Red, Trinity, and Brazos river systems. The federal recognition system has not allowed this union to proceed through official systems, but the self-identification and informal patterns remain. The Wichita, Waco, Tawakoni, and Keechi village and tribal alliances, further strengthened by the alliance with the Comanche bands, also provided involvement, and the bands of the Kiowa and the Plains Apache enhanced the bonds of the intertribal patterns of relations. Use of native languages provided significant keys, for individuals spoke four and five tribal languages. They also respected differences in spiritual expression and maintained sustainable material production and exchange systems that provided a significant foundation for all the peoples' efforts.

The highly defined and racist "blood-quantum"-based tribal membership requirements served to limit U.S. responsibility in the late nineteenth and early twentieth centuries. The policy interrupted these self-organizing systems as the United States attempted to suppress the patterns through institutions and procedures. Because the Anglo-American policymakers were committed to assimilation, they never fully understood the processes of change or design that were operative within the Southern Plains intertribal patterns of interaction among peoples and between the people and the ecosystem.

The hegemony and the resulting alliance systems imposed by the United States through its use of force excluded the American Indian peoples form increased prosperity in the nineteenth and early twentieth centuries. A colonial system imposed on the Southern Plains tribes channeled material wealth to the Midwest and to the Northeast to be redistributed as elected leaders in Washington desired. The United States consistently worked with the tribes on a unilateral basis, imposing the knowledge of Western civilization and material alternatives on tribal policy with ever-decreasing input from the tribes. It was a matter of basing all judgments upon the notion of right or wrong, upon the abstract processes of Western logic and critical thinking rather than upon the principles of systematic patterns of conditions and the flow of dynamic situations.

Rebuilding self-governing interdependent entities in tribal jurisdictional areas of the Southern Plains makes more sense than previous U.S. policies of removal, assimilation, relocation, and termination. Although enhancing homerule for tribal memberships is positive, hard-and-fast separation of the Southern Plains tribes one from another is less understandable. Economic interdependence based upon traditional patterns of the Southern Plains tribes can make possible a transfer of sovereignty from tribal entities to a flexible intertribal effort in which all tribes have a part. Such a move will facilitate the economic development of the tribes. If this restructuring is allowed in the tribes' traditional geographic region—the area that includes the present-day states of Kansas, Louisiana, New Mexico, Oklahoma, and Texas and the northern states of the Republic of Mexico—it will have reasonable prospects for success. In coordination with these states and the federal government as well as with private interests, this intertribal effort can contribute to the well-being of every element within the region.

It becomes a matter of transforming the old methods of representation so that they correspond to traditional patterns of effort. Moreover, it is a matter of devising structures of economic participation that will energize the peoples to work and to sacrifice intensively enough to bring about worthwhile change for the future. Finally, it is a matter of learning to perceive American Indian tribal economic development in terms of global commerce.

In this process of transformation it is important to know how the indigenous civilizations of the Southern Plains can be allowed to develop opportunities that will enhance the prospects of all who live in the region. The Southern Plains tribes sorely need their efforts to be recognized and felt in the coming century. Theirs is a profound and far-reaching creative stimulus that can unleash fresh energies from all concerned, including the Anglo, African, Asian, and Latino populations. With a renewed freedom of expression, the world experiences rather than its history may help. But the structures that the tribes need are those gained from centuries of experience in the Southern Plains. It is through these structures that the renewed perception of the patterns and images will be nourished by the vigor and resilience of native genius, the heritage of self-respect, and the confidence that has carried the Southern Plains tribal communities through the past and into the present.

NOTES

CHAPTER 1. INTRODUCTION

1. Henrietta Whiteman, "White Buffalo Woman," in *The American Indian and the Problem of History*, ed. Calvin Martin (New York: Oxford University Press, 1987), p. 170.

CHAPTER 2. SOUTHERN PLAINS ENVIRONMENTS

1. W. D. Johnson, "The High Plains and Their Utilization," in U.S. Geological Survey, *21st Annual Report*, pt. 4 (Washington, D.C.: U.S. Government Printing Office, 1900), pp. 601–741; Charles N. Gould, L. L. Hutchinson, and Gaylord Nelson, *Preliminary Report of the Mineral Resources of Oklahoma*, Oklahoma Geological Survey Bulletin no. 1 (Norman, 1908); V. T. Holiday and B. L. Allen, "Geology and Soils," in *Lubbock Lake: Late Quaternary Studies*, ed. E. Johnson (College Station: Texas A&M University Press, 1987), pp. 14–21; J. R. Walker, *Geomorphic Evolution of the Southern High Plains*, Baylor Geological Studies Bulletin no. 35 (Waco, Tex., 1978); Walter Prescott Webb, *The Great Plains* (Boston: Ginn and Company, 1931), p. 506; and Dan Flores, *Caprock Canyonlands* (Austin: University of Texas Press, 1990), p. 7.

2. J. R. Borchert, "The Climate of the Central North American Grassland," *Annals of the Association of American Geographers* 40 (1950): 1–39; Paul Bonnifield, *The Dust Bowl: Men, Dirt, and Depression* (Albuquerque: University of New Mexico Press, 1979), pp. 10–12; Donald Worster, *Dust Bowl; The Southern Plains in the 1930s* (New York: Oxford University Press, 1979), pp. 67–74; and Marion Clawson, "Natural Resources of the Great Plains in Historical Perspective," in *The Great Plains: Perspectives and Prospects*, ed. Merlin P. Lawson and M. E. Baker (Lincoln, Nebr.: Center for Great Plains Studies, 1981), pp. 3–10.

3. S. G. Archer and C. E. Bunch, *The American Grass Book: A Manual of Pasture and Range Practices* (Norman: University of Oklahoma Press, 1953); F. W. Gould, *Common Texas Grasses: An Illustrated Guide* (College Station: Texas A&M University Press, 1978); Doyle McCoy, *Roadside Trees and Shrubs*

of Oklahoma (Norman: University of Oklahoma Press, 1981); and J. E. Weaver and F. W. Albertson, *Grasslands of the Great Plains: Their Names and Use* (Lincoln, Nebr.: Johnson Publishing Company, 1956).

4. Fred Wendorf and J. J. Hester, eds., *Late Pleistocene Environments of the Southern High Plains*, Publications of the Fort Burgwin Research Center, no. 9 (Dallas: Southern Methodist University Press, 1975), pp. 1–9, and W. Eugene Hollon, *The Southwest: Old and New* (New York: Alfred A. Knopf, 1961), pp. 23–24.

5. Jack Hofman, "Land of Sun, Wind, and Grass," in *From Clovis to Comanchero: Archeological Overview of the Southern Great Plains*, ed. Jack Hofman et al. (Fayetteville: Arkansas Archeological Survey, 1989), pp. 5–14, and L. E. Albert and Don Wyckoff, "Oklahoma Environments: Past and Present," in *Prehistory of Oklahoma*, ed. Robert Bell (Orlando, Fla.: Academic Press, 1984), pp. 1–43.

6. Adrian Anderson, "The Cooperton Mammoth: An Early Bone Quarry," *Great Plains Journal* 14 (1975): 130–173.

7. Frank Leonhardy, "Domebo: A Paleo-Indian Mammoth Kill Site in the Prairie Plains," *Contributions of the Museum of the Great Plains* 1 (Lawton, Okla.: 1966), pp. 1–43.

8. Albert and Wyckoff, "Oklahoma Environments: Past and Present," p. 36.

9. N. Scott Momaday, "Native American Attitudes to the Environment," in *Seeing with a Native Eye: Essays on Native American Religion*, ed. Walter Capps (New York: Harper and Row, 1976), pp. 79–85.

CHAPTER 3. ORIGINS

1. In fall 1991 Wichita elders validated the published materials concerning tribal tradition and history; the group included Vivian McCurdy (Wichita), Wanda Bowman (Wichita), Louisa Riffel (Wichita), Drucilla Picard (Wichita), Cecelia Conner (Wichita), Faye Owings (Wichita), Mary Woosypitti (Wichita), and Margaret Bell (Wichita) (taped sessions, August–December 1991, Wichita Tribal Archives and Library, Wichita Tribal Complex, Wichita Reserve); conversation with Gene Watkins (Wichita), September 14, 1990; conversation with Gary McAdams (Wichita), October 12, 1990; see also George A. Dorsey, *The Mythology of the Wichita* (Washington, D.C.: Carnegie Institution of Washington, 1904), pp. 25–29.

2. Presentation by Gary McAdams (Wichita) at the University of Science and Arts of Oklahoma, Chickasha, October 12, 1990, and presentation by Vanessa Vance (Wichita) at the University of Science and Arts of Oklahoma, Chickasha, January 17, 1992.

3. Leslie Spier, "Wichita and Caddo Relationship Terms," *American Anthropologist* 26 (April–June 1924): 258–263; Karl Schmitt and Iva Osanai Schmitt, *Wichita Kinship: Past and Present* (Norman, Okla.: University Book Exchange, 1952); conversation with Margaret Bell (Wichita), September 17, 1991; conversation with Vivian McCurdy (Wichita), October 29, 1991; presenta-

tion by Virgil Swift (Wichita) at the Annual Meeting of the Oklahoma Historical Society, Elk City, March 24, 1992.

4. Conversation with Miriam Kebow (Wichita), October 1, 1991; conversa-
tion with Virgil Swift (Wichita), October 1, 1991; Dorsey, *Mythology of the
Wichita*, pp. 25–29; see also George Dorsey, Introduction (Wichita Reserve:
Wichita Cultural Society, c. 1990).

5. Conversation with Wanda Bowman (Wichita), September 24, 1990; E. B.
Townsend to commissioner of Indian Affairs, Wichita Agency, May 19, 1883,
Kiowa Agency Records, Wichita and Affiliated Bands, Microcopy, KA-50, In-
dian Archives, Oklahoma Historical Society, Oklahoma City.

6. "Testimony of Don Juan de Onate, December 14, 1601," in *Don Juan de
Onate, Colonizer of New Mexico, 1595–1628*, ed. George Hammond and
Agapito Rey, 2 vols. (Albuquerque: University of New Mexico Press, 1953),
2:754, and conversation with Wanda Bowman (Wichita), September 24, 1990.

7. Presentation by Virgil Swift (Wichita), at the Wichita Tribal Complex,
September 3, 1991.

8. Dorsey, *Mythology of the Wichita*, pp. 27–29.

9. Schmitt and Schmitt, *Wichita, Kinship*, pp. 33–35.

10. Presentations by Stuart Owings (Wichita), who served as traditional
chief of the Wichita-Pawnee Visitations for two decades, at the University of
Science and Arts of Oklahoma, Chickasha, September 30, 1988, and at the Red
Earth Writers Conference, June 11, 1988; Martha Royce Blaine, "The Pawnee-
Wichita Visitation Cycle: Historic Manifestations of an Ancient Friendship,"
in *Pathways to Plains Prehistory: Anthropological Perspectives of Plains
Natives and Their Pasts*, ed. D. G. Wyckoff and J. L. Hofman, Oklahoma
Anthropological Society Memoir no. 3 (1982): 113–134.

11. Presentation by Stuart Owings (Wichita), September 24, 1991, at the
Wichita Tribal Complex and presentation by Alex Matthews (Pawnee), September 24, 1991, at the Wichita Tribal Complex.

12. Statements by Edgar "Yogi" Delaware (Wichita) and Carol Lewis (Comanche), April 15, 1986; conversation with Wanda Bowman (Wichita), February
17, 1988.

13. Timothy G. Baugh, "Ecology and Exchange: The Dynamics of Plains-
Pueblo Interaction," in *Farmers, Hunters, and Colonists: Interaction between
the Southwest and the Southern Plains*, ed. Katherine Spielmann (Tucson:
University of Arizona Press, 1991), pp. 107–127.

14. Conversation with Berdena Holder (Wichita), September 3, 1991; conversation with Cleta Adair (Wichita), September 10, 1991; see also Preston Holder,
*The Hoe and the Horse on the Plains: A Study of Cultural Development
among North American Indians* (Lincoln: University of Nebraska Press, 1970);
Preston Holder, "The Role of Caddoan Horticulturists in the Cultural History
of the Great Plains" (Ph.D. diss., Columbia University, 1951); Earl Elam, "The
History of the Wichita Confederacy to 1868" (Ph.D. diss., Texas Tech University, 1971); W. W. Newcomb, *The People Called Wichita* (Phoenix, Ariz.: Indian
Tribal Series, 1976); Mildred Wedel, "The Wichita Indians in the Arkansas River Basin," in *Plains Indian Studies: A Collection of Essays in Honor of*

John C. Ewers and Waldo R. Wedel, ed. Douglas Ubelaker and Herman Viola, Smithsonian Contributions to Anthropology no. 30 (Washington, D.C.: Smithsonian Institution Press, 1982), pp. 118–134; Robert Bell, "Wichita Indians and the French Trade on the Oklahoma Frontier," *Bulletin of the Oklahoma Anthropological Society* 30 (1981): 11–18; Elizabeth A. H. John, "Portrait of a Wichita Village, 1808," *Chronicles of Oklahoma* 60 (Winter 1982–1983): 412–437.

CHAPTER 4. COMMERCE

1. For more detail, see Vynola Newkumet and Howard Meredith, *Hasinai: A Traditional History of the Caddo Confederacy* (College Station: Texas A&M University Press, 1988), pp. 6–12; Timothy K. Perttula, *"The Caddo Nation": Archaeological and Ethnohistorical Perspectives* (Austin: University of Texas Press, 1992), pp. 230–242; see also George A. Dorsey, *Traditions of the Caddo* (Washington, D.C.: Carnegie Institution of Washington, 1905), and John R. Swanton, *Source Material on the History and Ethnology of the Caddo Indians,* Bureau of American Ethnology Bulletin 132 (Washington, D.C.: U.S. Government Printing Office, 1942).

2. Conversation with Frank Whitebead (Caddo), August 12, 1978, and conversations with Vynola Newkumet (Caddo), August 12, 1978, September 3, 1978, December 4, 1980, January 12, 1981, January 14, 1981, September 4, 1981, June 19, 1982, and July 23–27, 1982.

3. See Newkumet and Meredith, *Hasinai,* pp. 29–34; Timothy Baugh, "Ecology and Exchange: The Dynamics of Plains-Pueblo Interaction," in *Farmers, Hunters, and Colonists,* ed. Katherine A. Spielmann (Tucson: University of Arizona Press, 1991), pp. 107–127, and Dennis A. Peterson et al., *An Archeological Survey of the Spiro Vicinity, Le Flore County, Oklahoma,* Oklahoma Archeological Survey, Archeological Resource Survey Report no. 37 (April 1993): 1–7.

4. For examples of village sites in the Caddoan area, see Robert J. Mallouf, *Archeological Investigations at Proposed Big Pine Lake, 1974–1975, Lamar and Red River Counties* (Austin: Texas Historical Commission, 1976); James Briscoe, *The Plantation Site: An Early Caddoan Settlement in Eastern Oklahoma* (Oklahoma City: Oklahoma Department of Transportation, 1977); Guy Muto, *The Habiukut of Eastern Oklahoma: Parris Mound* (Oklahoma City: Oklahoma Historical Society, 1978); Dee Ann Story, ed. *The Deshazo Site: Nacogdoches County, Texas* (Austin: Texas Antiquities Committee, 1982); Peterson et al., *Archeological Survey of the Spiro Vicinity.*

5. Robert Bell, "Arkansas Valley Caddoan: The Harlan Phase," and James Brown, "Arkansas Valley Caddoan: The Spiro Phase," *Prehistory of Oklahoma,* ed. Robert Bell (Orlando, Fla.: Academic Press, 1984), pp. 221–263; see also James Brown and Robert Bell, *First Annual Report of Caddoan Archeology Spiro Focus Research* (Norman: University of Oklahoma Research Institute, 1964), and Dee Ann Story, ed., *Archeological Investigations at the*

George C. Davis Site, Cherokee County, Texas: Summers of 1979 and 1980, Occasional Papers no. 1 (Austin: Texas Archeological Research Laboratory, University of Texas, 1981).

6. Phil Newkumet, "Works Progress Administration Archaeological Project Quarterly Report [Spiro Mound]," December 1938–April 1939, Western History Collections, University of Oklahoma, Norman; Robert Bell, "Trade Materials at Spiro Mound as Indicated by Artifacts," *American Antiquity* 12 (1947): 181–184; Henry Hamilton, "The Spiro Mound," *Missouri Archaeologist* 14 (1952): 1–276; James Brown, *Spiro Studies,* 2 vol. (Norman: University of Oklahoma Research Institute, 1966); Daniel Rogers et al., *Spiro Archaeology: 1979 Excavations* (Norman: Oklahoma Archaeological Survey, 1980); Daniel Rogers, *Spiro Archaeology: 1980 Research* (Norman: Oklahoma Archaeological Survey, 1982); Daniel Rogers, *Spiro Archaeology: The Plaza* (Norman: Oklahoma Archaeological Survey, 1982).

7. See Philip Phillips and James Brown, *Pre-Columbian Shell Engravings from the Craig Mound at Spiro, Oklahoma,* 6 vol., 2pts. (Cambridge: Peabody Museum Press, Harvard University, 1978–1984).

CHAPTER 5. HORSE CULTURE

1. Conversation with Sam Devaney (Comanche), September 21, 1987; conversation with Hammond Motah (Comanche), October 5, 1990; report of E. L. Clark quoting Straight Feather (Comanche), May 18, 1881, Kiowa, Comanche, and Wichita Agency Files, sec. C, case 6, drawer A, Indian Archives, Oklahoma Historical Society, Oklahoma City; Ernest Wallace and Adamson Hoebel, *The Comanches: Lords of the Southern Plains* (Norman: University of Oklahoma Press, 1976), pp. 22–26; Elizabeth John, *Storms Brewed in Other Men's Worlds* (College Station: Texas A&M University Press, 1975), pp. 307–308; Willard H. Rollings, *The Comanche* (New York: Chelsea House Publishers, 1989), pp. 24–26.

2. William Brown, Jr., "Comancheria Demography, 1805–1830," *Panhandle-Plains Historical Review* 59 (1986): 1–17, and Elizabeth John, "Nurturing the Peace: Spanish and Comanche Cooperation in the Early Nineteenth Century," *New Mexico Historical Review* 59 (1984): 346–366.

3. Conversation with Iola Haden (Comanche), August 6, 1986; conversation with Doc Tate Nevaquaya (Comanche), November 8, 1989; Adamson Hoebel, *The Political Organization and Law-ways of the Comanche Indians,* in *Memoirs* of the American Anthropological Association no. 54 (1940).

4. Galen M. Buller, "Comanche Oral Narratives" (Ph.D. diss., University of Nebraska, 1977), pp. 6–28, including conversations with Lillie Asee (Comanche), Edith Gordon (Comanche), Dorothy Martinez (Comanche), and Ella Pewardy (Comanche).

5. Jodye Lynn Dickson Schilz and Thomas Schilz, *Buffalo Hump and the Penateka Comanches,* University of Texas at El Paso Southern Studies Series no. 88 (El Paso: Texas Western Press, 1989), p. 21.

6. Conversations with Vynola Newkumet (Caddo), April 13, 1982, and April 20, 1982; presentation by Gary McAdams (Wichita), University of Science and Arts of Oklahoma, Chickasha, February 14, 1991; Katherine Spielmann, "Coercion or Cooperation? Plains-Pueblo Interaction in the Protohistoric Period," and Frances Levine, "Economic Perspectives on the Comanchero Trade," in *Farmers, Hunters, and Colonists*, ed. Katherine Spielmann (Tucson: University of Arizona Press, 1991), pp. 36–50, 155–169.

CHAPTER 6. RELIGION

1. Erminie Voegelin, "Kiowa-Crow Mythological Affiliations," *American Anthropologist* 35 (1933): 470–474.

2. An excellent traditional account of the Kiowa migration story is expressed in N. Scott Momaday, *The Way to Rainy Mountain* (Albuquerque: University of New Mexico Press, 1969; for context, see George Hyde, *Indians of the High Plains: From the Prehistoric Period to the Coming of Europeans* (Norman: University of Oklahoma Press, 1959); Preston Holder, *The Hoe and the Horse on the Plains* (Lincoln: University of Nebraska Press, 1970); and Rodney Frey, *The World of the Crow Indians: As Driftwood Lodges* (Norman: University of Oklahoma Press, 1987).

3. See James Mooney, *Calendar History of the Kiowa Indians* (Washington, D.C.: Smithsonian Institution Press, 1979); Maurice Boyd with Linn Pauahty, *Kiowa Voices*, 2 vols. (Fort Worth: Texas Christian University Press, 1981–1983); Ernest Wallace, "The Habitat and Range of the Comanche, Kiowa, and Kiowa-Apache Indians, 1719–1874," manuscript 1984, pp. 3–4, Wichita Tribal Archives, Wichita and Affiliated Tribes Complex, Wichita Reserve; Paul Vestal and Richard Schultes, *An Economic Botany of the Kiowa Indians as It Relates to the History of the Tribe* (Cambridge, Mass.: Botanical Museum, 1939), pp. 11–110.

4. Mooney, *Calendar History of the Kiowa*, p. 234.

5. Presentation by David Paddlety (Kiowa), American Indian Studies, University of Science and Arts of Oklahoma, Chickasha, January 20, 1992; George Hunt (Kiowa) to Wilbur Nye, "The Annual Sun Dance of the Kiowa Indians," *Chronicles of Oklahoma* 12 (September 1934): 340–358; see also John Ewers, *Murals in the Round: Painted Tepees of the Kiowa and Kiowa Apache Indians* (Washington, D.C.: Smithsonian Institution Press, 1978).

6. Conversation with Vickie Boettger (Kiowa), September 18, 1989, and conversation with Kathy Toehay (Kiowa), March 30, 1990.

7. Boyd with Pauahty, *Kiowa Voices*, 1:8; see also Alice Marriott, *The Ten Grandmothers* (Norman: University of Oklahoma Press, 1945).

8. Jane Richardson, *Law and Status among the Kiowa Indians*, Monographs of the American Ethnological Society (New York: J. J. Augustin, 1940); see also John P. Harrington, *Vocabulary of the Kiowa Language*, Bureau of American Ethnology Bulletin 84 (Washington, D.C.: U.S. Government Printing Office, 1928); Laurel J. Watkins with Parker McKenzie, *A Grammar of Kiowa* (Lincoln:

University of Nebraska Press, 1984); Parker McKenzie and John Harrington, *Popular Account of the Kiowa Indian Language,* Monographs of the School of American Research no. 12 (Santa Fe: School of American Research and Museum of New Mexico, 1948); Edith Trager, "The Kiowa Language: A Grammatical Study" (Ph.D. diss., University of Pennsylvania, 1960).

9. Conversation with Kathy Toehay (Kiowa), March 30, 1990; see also Francis Levine, "Economic Perspective on the Comanchero Trade," in *Farmers, Hunters, and Colonists,* ed. K. Spielmann (Tucson: University of Arizona Press, 1991), pp. 155–169; Waldo Wedel, "Notes on Plains-Southwestern Contacts in the Light of Archeology," in *For the Dean: Essays in Anthropology,* ed. Erik Reed and Dale King (n.p., 1950), pp. 99–116; Waldo Wedel, "Further Notes on Puebloan–Central Plains Contacts in Light of Archaeology," in *Pathways to Plains Prehistory,* ed. Don Wyckoff and Jack Hofman, Oklahoma Anthropological Society *Memoir* 3 (1982): 145–152; Jack Hofman, "Protohistoric Culture History on the Southern Great Plains," in *From Clovis to Comanchero,* ed. Jack Hofman et al. (Fayetteville: Arkansas Archeological Society, 1989), pp. 91–100.

10. Conversation with Martin Bitzeedey (Apache of Oklahoma), April 9, 1988; conversation with Mike Wetselline (Apache of Oklahoma), February 19, 1991; John Upton Terrell, *The Plains Apache* (New York: Thomas Y. Crowell Company, 1975), pp. 24–25; Mooney, *Calendar History of the Kiowa,* p. 247; Charles Brant, "Kiowa Apache Culture History: Some Further Observations," *Southwestern Journal of Anthropology* 9 (1953): 195–202.

11. See Gilbert McAlister, "Kiowa-Apache Social Organization," in *Social Anthropology of North American Tribes,* ed. F. Eggans (Chicago: University of Chicago Press, 1955), pp. 99–172.

12. Charles Brant, ed. *Jim Whitewolf: The Life of a Kiowa Apache Indian* (New York: Dover Publications, 1969), p. 3; see also McAllister, "Kiowa-Apache Social Organization," and Charles Brant, "The Kiowa Apache Indians: A Study in Ethnology and Acculturation" (Ph.D. diss., Cornell University, 1951).

13. Brant, ed., Whitewolf, pp. 5–6, 31, and "Kiowa Apache Culture History," pp. 195–202.

14. William Bittle, "The Manatidie: A Focus for Kiowa-Apache Tribal Identity," *Plains Anthropologist* 7 (1962): 152–163, and John Beatty, *Kiowa-Apache Music and Dance,* Ethnology Series no. 31 (Greeley: Museum of Anthropology, University of Northern Colorado, 1974), pp. 26–34.

CHAPTER 7. TRADITIONAL ALLIANCES

1. Mildred Mott Wedel, "The Wichita Indians in the Arkansas River Basin," *Plains Indian Studies: A Collection of Essays in Honor of John C. Ewers and Waldo R. Wedel,* ed. Douglas Weelaker and Herman Viola, Smithsonian Contributions to Anthropology no. 30 (Washington, D.C.: Smithsonian Institution Press, 1982), pp. 118–134; Frank Watt, "The Waco Indian Village and Its People," *Central Texas Archeologist* 9 (1968): 3–48; Leroy Johnson, Jr., and Edward Jelks,

"The Tawakoni-Yscani Village, 1760: A Study in Archaeological Site Identification," *Texas Journal of Science* 10 (December 1958): 405–422; John Ewers, "The Influence of Epidemics on the Indian Populations and Cultures of Texas," *Plains Anthropologist* 18 (1973): 104–115; Russell Thornton, *American Indian Holocaust and Survival: A Population History since 1492* (Norman: University of Oklahoma Press, 1987), pp. 128–131.

2. See Joseph Thoburn, "The Prehistoric Cultures of Oklahoma," *Archaeology of the Arkansas River Valley,* ed. Warren Moorehead et al. (New Haven, Conn.: Yale University Press, 1931), p. 78, and Robert Bell et al., "A Pilot Study of Wichita Indian Archeology and Ethnology," in *Final Report,* National Science Foundation (n.p., 1967), pp. 119–120.

3. David Rood, "Wichita Grammar: A Generative Semantic Sketch" (Ph.D. diss., University of California, Berkeley, 1969), pp. 32–99; see also David Rood, *Wichita Grammar* (New York: Garland Publishing Company, 1976); David Rood and Doris Lamar, *Wichita Language Lessons: A Manual to Accompany Tape Recordings and Audio Tapes* (Wichita Reserve: Wichita and Affiliated Tribes, 1992); David Rood, "Wichita Texts," in *Caddoan Texts,* ed. Douglas Parks, Native American Texts Series 2 (1977), pp. 91–129; Wallace Chafe, *The Caddoan, Iroquoian, and Siouan Languages* (The Hague: Mouton, 1976), pp. 11–13, 55–82; Wallace Chafe, "Caddo Texts," in Parks, ed., *Caddoan Texts,* pp. 27–43.

4. Karl Schmitt and Iva Osanai Schmitt, *Wichita Kinship: Past and Present* (Norman, Okla.: University Book Exchange, 1952), pp. 11–22; see also Leslie Spier, "The Wichita and Caddo Relationship Terms," *American Anthropologist* 26 (April–June 1924): 258–263.

5. John Speth, "Some Unexplored Aspects of Mutualistic Plains-Pueblo Food Exchange," in *Farmers, Hunters, and Colonists,* ed. Katherine Spielmann (Tucson: University of Arizona Press, 1991), pp. 18–35, and Douglas Hurt, *Indian Agriculture in America: Prehistory to the Present* (Lawrence: University Press of Kansas, 1987), pp. 1–26.

6. George Dorsey, *The Mythology of the Wichita* (Washington, D.C.: Carnegie Institution of Washington, 1904), pp. 1–29.

7. Presentation by Stuart Owings (Wichita), Wichita Tribal Complex, September 25, 1991; presentation by Alex Matthews (Pawnee), Wichita Tribal Complex, September 25, 1991; Martha Royce Blaine, "The Pawnee-Wichita Visitation Cycle: Historic Manifestations of an Ancient Friendship," in *Pathways to Plains Prehistory,* ed. Don Wyckoff and Jack Hofman, Oklahoma Anthropological Society Memoir 3 (1982): 113–134.

8. George Dorsey, "Wichita Tales," *Journal of American Folklore* 15 (October–December 1902): 229–232; Dorsey, *Mythology of the Wichita,* pp. 25–29; Albert Gatchet, ed., "Migration of the Wichita Indians," *American Antiquarian* 13 (September 1891): 249–250; see also "Statement by Uts-tuts-kins," *Senate Executive Document* no. 13, 48th Cong., 1st sess., 1884, 1:36.

9. Vynola Newkumet and Howard Meredith, *Hasinai: A Traditional History of the Caddo Confederacy* (College Station: Texas A&M University Press, 1988), pp. 46–50; Don Wyckoff and Timothy Baugh, "Early Historic Hasinai

Elites: A Model for the Material of Governing Elites," *Mid-Continent Journal of Archaeology* 6 (1980): 225–228; Clarence Webb and Hiram Gregory, *The Caddo of Louisiana*, Anthropological Study no. 2 (Baton Rouge: Department of Culture, Recreation, and Tourism, Louisiana Archaeological Survey and Antiquities Commission, 1978); Timothy Perttula, *"The Caddo Nation"* (Austin: University of Texas Press, 1992), pp. 3–10.

10. See "Legal History of the Kiowa," *Kiowa Indian News: Gyady-Gkoot Pigh'gyah*, September 1990.

11. Ralph Smith, "The Tawehash in French, Spanish, English, and American Imperial Affairs," *West Texas Historical Association Yearbook* 28 (October 1952): 18–49; Elizabeth Ann Harper [John], "The Taovayas Indians in Frontier Trade and Diplomacy, 1719–1768," *Chronicles of Oklahoma* 31 (Autumn 1953): 268–289; idem, "The Taovayas Indians in Frontier Trade and Diplomacy, 1769–1779," *Southwestern Historical Quarterly* 57 (October 1953): 181–201; idem, "The Taovayas Indians in Frontier Trade and Diplomacy, 1779–1835," *Panhandle-Plains Historical Review* 26 (1953): 40–72.

12. See Rupert Richardson, *The Comanche Barrier to South Plains Settlement* (Glendale, Calif.: Arthur H. Clark Company, 1933); William Leckie, *The Military Conquest of the Southern Plains* (Norman: University of Oklahoma Press, 1963); James Haley, *The Buffalo War: The History of the Red River Indian Uprising of 1874* (Norman: University of Oklahoma Press, 1976); Stan Hoig, *Tribal Wars of the Southern Plains* (Norman: University of Oklahoma Press, 1993).

13. Conversation with Evelyn Kianute (Caddo), March 24, 1989, and presentation by Marilyn Tiger (Comanche), American Indian Studies, University of Science and Arts of Oklahoma, Chickasha, March 14, 1990.

14. Mary Haas, *Language, Culture, and History: Essays by Mary R. Haas* (Stanford, Calif.: Stanford University Press, 1978), pp. 110–163; Winfred Lehmann, *Historical Linguistics: An Introduction*, 2d ed. (New York: Holt, Rinehart, and Winston, 1973), pp. 131–144; conversation with Charles Van Tuyl (Cherokee), July 11, 1990.

15. Conversation with Vickie Boettger (Kiowa), September 18, 1989, and Laurel Watkins with Parker McKenzie, *A Grammar of Kiowa* (Lincoln: University of Nebraska Press, 1984), pp. 204–243.

16. Rood, "Wichita Grammar," pp. 32–99; Wallace Chafe, "Caddoan," in *Languages of Native America: Historical and Comparative Assessment*, ed. Lyle Campbell and Marianne Mithun (Austin: University of Texas Press, 1979), pp. 213–235; Newkumet and Meredith, *Hasinai*, pp. 84–89; Comanche (Nu-mu-nuh) Language Preservation, manuscript, Comanche Tribe, Lawton, Okla.; Watkins with McKenzie, *Grammar of Kiowa*, pp. 134–194.

17. W. P. Clark, *The Indian Sign Language* (Lincoln: University of Nebraska Press, 1982), pp. 16–17.

CHAPTER 8. EXTERNAL DEMANDS

1. Felix Cohen, *Handbook of Federal Indian Law* (Albuquerque: University of New Mexico Press, 1970), pp. 188–194; Francis Paul Prucha, *The Great Father: The United States Government and the American Indians*, 2 vols. (Lincoln: University of Nebraska Press, 1984), 2:609–758; Imre Sutton, ed., *Irredeemable America: The Indians' Estate and Land Claims* (Albuquerque: University of New Mexico Press, 1985), pp. 71–82.

2. Seymour Connor and Odie Faulk, *North America Divided: The Mexican War, 1846–1848* (New York: Oxford University Press, 1971), p. 167; Jack Bauer, *The Mexican War, 1846–1848* (New York: Macmillan Publishing Company, 1974), pp. 384–388; Richard Griswold del Castillo, *The Treaty of Guadalupe Hidalgo: A Legacy of Conflict* (Norman: University of Oklahoma Press, 1990), pp. 101–103, 148–150; Thomas Hall, *Social Change in the Southwest, 1350–1880* (Lawrence: University Press of Kansas, 1989), pp. 167–236; Ralph Smith, "The Comanche Bridge between Oklahoma and Mexico, 1842–1844," *Chronicles of Oklahoma* 34 (Spring 1961): 54–69.

3. *Treaties and Agreements of the Indian Tribes of the Southwest including Western Oklahoma* (Washington, D.C.: Institute for the Development of Indian Law, 1973), pp. 3–11, 60–62, 118–126; Charles Kappler, ed., *Laws and Treaties*, 2 vols. (Washington, D.C.: U.S. Government Printing Office, 1904), 2:385, 435, 977–982; Craig Miner, *Tribal Sovereignty and Industrial Civilization in Indian Territory, 1865–1907* (Norman: University of Oklahoma Press, 1988), pp. 42–54.

4. Douglas Green and Thomas Tonnesen, *American Indians: Social Justice and Public Policy* (Madison: University of Wisconsin System, Institute on Race and Ethnicity, 1991), pp. 8–31; James Mooney, *Calendar History of the Kiowa Indians* (Washington, D.C.: Smithsonian Institution Press, 1979), pp. 199–213; John Terrell, *The Plains Apache* (New York: Thomas Y. Crowell Company, 1975), pp. 25–26; James Mooney, *The Ghost Dance Religion* (Chicago: University of Chicago Press, 1973), pp. 141–177; Russell Thornton, *We Shall Live Again: The 1870 and 1890 Ghost Dance Movements as Demographic Revitalization* (Cambridge: Cambridge University Press, 1986), pp. 46–48; Virginia Allen, "Stress and Death in the Settlement of Indian Territory," *Chronicles of Oklahoma* 54 (Fall 1976): 352–359.

5. U.S. Senate, U.S. Commission on Industrial Relations, "The Land Question in the Southwest," *Final Report*, 9, S. Doc. 415, 64th Cong., 1st sess., 1916, pp. 8955, 9052–9053; U.S. Bureau of the Census, *Twelfth Census of the United States, 1900*, Agriculture, 6, pp. 228–256; H. Henrietta Stockel, *Survival of the Spirit: Chiricahua Apaches in Captivity* (Reno: University of Nevada Press, 1993), pp. 185–235; John Anthony Turcheneske, "The Apache Prisoners of War at Fort Sill, 1894–1914" (Ph. D. diss., University of New Mexico, 1978), pp. 114–116.

6. Arrell Morgan Gibson, *The West in the Life of the Nation* (Lexington, Ky.: D. C. Heath and Company, 1976), pp. 508–514, and Frederick Hoxie, "End

of the Savage: The Indian Policy in the United States Senate, 1880–1890," *Chronicles of Oklahoma* 55 (Summer 1977): 157–179.

7. Douglas Hale, "European Immigrants in Oklahoma," *Chronicles of Oklahoma* 53 (Summer 1975): 179–203; Green and Tonnesen, ed., *American Indians*, pp. 8–31; Lloyd Burton, *American Indian Water Rights and the Limits of the Law* (Lawrence: University Press of Kansas, 1991), pp. 12–20.

8. Patricia Nelson Limerick, *The Legacy of Conquest: The Unbroken Past of the American West* (New York: W. W. Norton and Company, 1987), pp. 55–73; Richard White, *"It's Your Misfortune and None of My Own": A History of the American West* (Norman: University of Oklahoma Press, 1991), pp. 236–237; Forrest D. Monahan, "Kiowa-Comanche Reservation in the 1890s," *Chronicles of Oklahoma* 45 (Winter 1967–1968): 451–463.

9. *Yearbook of the United States Department of Agriculture* (Washington, D.C.: U.S. Government Printing Office, 1903), p. 777.

10. As quoted in Arrell Morgan Gibson, *The American Indian: Prehistory to the Present* (Lexington, Ky.: D. C. Heath and Company, 1980), p. 520.

CHAPTER 9. PEACEMAKING

1. *Walam Olum or Red Score: The Migration Legend of the Lenni Lenape or Delaware Indians* (Indianapolis: Indiana Historical Society, 1954), pp. 9–50; *The Red Record: The Walam Olum, The Oldest Native North American History*, trans. David McCutchen (Garden City Park, N.J.: Avery Publishing Group, 1993), pp. 52–65.

2. *Walam Olum*, p. 512.

3. James Mooney, "Passing of the Delaware Nation," *Proceedings of the Mississippi Valley Historical Association*, ed. B. F. Shambaugh (Cedar Rapids, Iowa: Torch Press, 1911), pp. 329–340, and Russell Thornton, *American Indian Holocaust and Survival* (Norman: University of Oklahoma Press, 1987), p. 70.

4. H. Craig Miner and William E. Unrau, *The End of Indian Kansas: A Study of Cultural Revolution, 1854–1871* (Lawrence: University Press of Kansas, 1978), pp. 34–43; see also Joseph B. Herring, *The Enduring Indians of Kansas: A Century and a Half of Acculturation* (Lawrence: University Press of Kansas, 1990).

5. Sadie Bedoka interview, Indian-Pioneer Papers, Indian Archives, Oklahoma Historical Society, Oklahoma City.

6. Treaty of Bird's Fort, September 29, 1843, *Texas Indian Papers*, ed. James Day, 3 vols. (Austin: Texas State Library, 1969), 1:241–245; minutes of the Indian Council at Tehuacani Creek, March 28, 1843, *Texas Indian Papers*, 1:160; Kenneth Neighbours, "Robert S. Neighbors and the Founding of Texas Indian Reservations," *West Texas Historical Association Year Book* 31 (October 1955): 65–74; Berlin Chapman, "Establishment of the Wichita Reservation," *Chronicles of Oklahoma* 11 (December 1933): 1044–1055; William Parker, *Notes Taken during the Expedition through Unexplored Texas* (Philadelphia:

Hayes and Zell, 1856), pp. 83–84; Duane Hale, *Peacemakers on the Frontier: A History of the Delaware Tribe of Western Oklahoma* (Anadarko: Delaware Tribe of Western Oklahoma Press, 1987), pp. 33–65; *Cooley's Traditional Stories of the Delaware*, ed. Duane Hale (Anadarko: Delaware Tribe of Western Oklahoma Press, 1984), pp. 49–50.

7. See Duane Hale, ed. *Turtle Tales: Oral Traditions of the Delaware of Western Oklahoma* (Anadarko: Delaware Tribe of Western Oklahoma Press, 1984).

8. Presentation with Art Thomas (Delaware), November 2, 1989, American Indian Studies, University of Science and Arts of Oklahoma, Anadarko.

9. Presentation by Linda Poolaw (Delaware), March 7, 1988, American Indian Studies, University of Science and Arts of Oklahoma, Chickasha.

CHAPTER 10. RESERVATION SYSTEM

1. Vine Deloria, Jr., and Clifford Lytle, *The Nations Within: The Past and Future of American Indian Sovereignty* (New York: Pantheon Books, 1984), pp. 28–36; Vine Deloria, Jr., and Clifford Lytle, *American Indians, American Justice* (Austin: University of Texas Press, 1983), pp. 6–8; Francis Paul Prucha, *The Great Father*, 2 vols. (Lincoln: University of Nebraska Press, 1984), 2:631–658; Robert Utley, *The Indian Frontier of the American West, 1846–1890* (Albuquerque: University of New Mexico Press, 1984), pp. 99–127.

2. James Mooney, *The Cheyenne Indians*, in *Memoirs of the American Anthropological Society* 1 (September 1907): 361–370; Donald Berthrong, *The Southern Cheyenne* (Norman: University of Oklahoma Press, 1963), pp. 3–26; Alfred Kroeber, *The Arapaho* (Lincoln: University of Nebraska Press, 1983), pp. 3–8; see also Lawrence Hart, comp., *The Cheyenne Way of Peace* (Clinton, Okla.: Cheyenne Cultural Center, 1978).

3. Conversation with Dick West (Cheyenne), January 27, 1980.

4. Conversation with Dee Ann Lamebull (Cheyenne), August 4, 1993; conversation with Pauline Harjo (Arapaho), May 13, 1989; Augusta Custer interview, September 15, 1937, Indian-Pioneer Papers.

5. Berthrong, *Southern Cheyenne*, pp. 59–67; George Dorsey, *The Cheyenne: Ceremonial Organization*, Field Museum Publication 99, 4 (1905); George Dorsey, *The Cheyenne: The Sun Dance*, Field Museum Publication no. 103 (1905); Peter Powell, *Sweet Medicine: The Continuing Role of the Sacred Arrows, the Sun Dance, and the Sacred Buffalo Hat in North Cheyenne History*, 2 vols. (Norman: University of Oklahoma Press, 1969), 2:467–471; Peter Powell, *People of the Sacred Mountain: A History of the North Cheyenne Chiefs and Warrior Societies, 1830–1879*, 2 vols. (San Francisco: Harper and Row, 1981), 1:6–7.

6. Hart, *Cheyenne Way of Peace*, pp. 23–25; K. N. Llewellyn and Adamson Hoebel, *The Cheyenne Way: Conflict and Case Law in Primitive Jurisprudence* (Norman: University of Oklahoma Press, 1941), pp. 67–98; Berthrong, *Southern Cheyennes*, pp. 56–62; Stan Hoig, *The Peace Chiefs of the Cheyennes* (Nor-

man: University of Oklahoma Press, 1980), pp. 3–14; John Stands in Timber and Margot Liberty, *Cheyenne Memories* (Lincoln: University of Nebraska Press, 1972), pp. 35–39; Powell, *Sweet Medicine*, pp. 460–466; George Dorsey, "How the Pawnee Captured the Cheyenne Medicine Arrows," *American Anthropologist* 8 (1903): 1–15.

7. Kroeber, *Arapaho*, pp. 359–363.

8. Charles Kappler, ed., *Indian Treaties, 1778–1883* (New York: Interland Publishing, 1972), pp. 594, 807, 887, 984; Cheyenne and Arapaho, Treaty of Medicine Lodge, Cheyenne and Arapaho—Federal Relations, August 25, 1868, Indian Archives, Oklahoma Historical Society, Oklahoma City; Description of Reservation Agreed upon by the Arapaho, Cheyenne and Arapaho—Federal Relations, October 26, 1872; Cheyenne and Arapaho Reservation, Executive Order Setting Aside, August 25, 1888, p. 47, Cheyenne and Arapaho vol. 27, Indian Archives, Oklahoma Historical Society; Berthrong, *Southern Cheyenne*, pp. 345–371; Donald Berthrong, *The Cheyenne and Arapaho Ordeal: Reservation and Agency Life in the Indian Territory, 1875–1907* (Norman: University of Oklahoma Press, 1976), pp. 49–90; Margaret Coel, *Chief Left Hand, Southern Arapaho* (Norman: University of Oklahoma Press, 1981), pp. 292–317; for a perspective on the Anglo-American acculturation process, see John Seger, *Early Days among the Cheyenne and Arapahoe Indians* (Norman: University of Oklahoma Press, 1979); see also a Marxist interpretation in John Moore, *The Cheyenne Nation: A Social and Demographic History* (Lincoln: University of Nebraska Press, 1987).

9. W. S. Nye, *Carbine and Lance: The Story of Old Fort Sill* (Norman: University of Oklahoma Press, 1943), pp. 187–239; James Mooney, *Calendar History of the Kiowa Indians* (Washington, D.C.: Smithsonian Institution Press, 1979), pp. 338–339; *Making Medicine: Ledger Drawing Art from Fort Marion* (Oklahoma City: Center of the American Indian, 1984).

10. D. S. Otis, *The Dawes Act and the Allotment of Indian Lands* (Norman: University of Oklahoma Press, 1973), pp. 3–22; Cheyenne and Arapaho—Liquor Traffic, Agent's Reports, Vices, February 15, 1873, through June 20, 1931, Indian Archives, Oklahoma Historical Society, Oklahoma City; Robert Berhofer, Jr., "Commentary," in *Indian-White Relations: A Persistent Paradox*, ed. Jane Smith and Robert Kvasnicka (Washington, D.C.: Howard University Press, 1976), p. 85; Frederick Hoxie, *A Final Promise: The Campaign to Assimilate the Indians, 1880–1920* (Lincoln: University of Nebraska Press, 1984), pp. 147–210.

11. James Mooney, *The Ghost Dance Religion* (Chicago: University of Chicago Press, 1973), pp. 206–207.

12. Ibid., pp. 201–331; see also Russell Thornton, *We Shall Live Again* (Cambridge: Cambridge University Press, 1986), pp. 46–48.

13. Arapaho Agriculture, International Council File, May 1875, p. 111, Indian Archives, Oklahoma Historical Society, Oklahoma City; Cheyenne and Arapaho Reservation—Telephone and telegraph, March 22, 1871, extension of the line, August 29, 1881, Indian Archives, Oklahoma Historical Society, Oklahoma City; Cheyenne and Arapaho Reservation—Timber, Cheyenne and

Arapaho, vol. 6, March 14, 1883, p. 194, and March 23, 1883, p. 223, Indian Archives, Oklahoma Historical Society, Oklahoma City; Berthrong, *Cheyenne and Arapaho Ordeal*, pp. 137–147.

14. Berthrong, *Cheyenne and Arapaho Ordeal*, p. 151.

15. Ibid., p. 161.

16. Cheyenne—Treaty of 1891, Cheyenne and Arapaho—Indian Council, February, 1906, Indian Archives, Oklahoma Historical Society, Oklahoma City; Cheyenne and Arapaho—Allotment, Cheyenne and Arapaho Allotments, June 30, 1991 (description of), July 21, 1903 (roll), Indian Archives, Oklahoma Historical Society, Oklahoma City; Donald Berthrong, "Struggle for Power: The Impact of Southern Cheyenne and Arapaho 'School Boys' on Tribal Politics," *American Indian Quarterly* 16 (Winter 1992): 1–24; Berthrong, *Southern Cheyenne*, p. 167.

17. Presentation by Lawrence Hart (Cheyenne), October 9, 1980, Bacone College, Muskogee, Oklahoma; Presentation by Edgar Heap of Birds (Cheyenne), November 6, 1985, American Indian Studies, University of Science and Arts of Oklahoma, Chickasha; presentation by Ruth Whiteskunk (Cheyenne), February 21, 1990, Cheyenne Curriculum Workshop, Southwestern Oklahoma State University, Weatherford.

18. Interview with Martha Hamilton-Jacobson, April 28, 1938, Indian-Pioneer Papers; Berthrong, *Cheyenne and Arapaho Ordeal*, pp. 297–338; see also William Hagan, *United States–Comanche Relations: The Reservation Years* (Norman: University of Oklahoma Press, 1990), pp. 286–294.

19. Kirke Kickingbird and Karen Ducheneaux, *One Hundred Million Acres* (New York: Macmillan Publishing Company, 1973), p. 131; Linda S. Parker, *Native American Estate: The Struggle over Indian and Hawaiian Lands* (Honolulu: University of Hawaii Press, 1989), pp. 52–53; see also Imre Sutton, *Indian Land Tenure: Bibliographic Essays and a Guide to the Literature* (New York: Clearwater Publishing Company, 1975), pp. 116–118.

CHAPTER 11. PRISONERS OF WAR

1. Mildred Cleghorn (Fort Sill Apache), "Traditional Indian Leadership," speech delivered to the National Tribal Chairmen's Association, Washington, D.C., June 24, 1986, typescript, Fort Sill Apache Tribal Offices, Apache, Oklahoma.

2. Presentation by Michael Darrow (Fort Sill Apache), January 13, 1987, American Indian Studies, University of Science and Arts of Oklahoma, Anadarko; Sam Haozous transcript, Western History Collections, University of Oklahoma, Norman; "The Fort Sill Apaches: Their Vital Statistics, Tribal Origins, Antecedents," comp. Gillett Griswold, typescript, U.S. Field Artillery and Fort Sill Museum (1885–1962); H. Henrietta Stockel, *Survival of the Spirit: Chiricahua Apaches in Captivity* (Reno: University of Nevada Press, 1993), pp. 185–192; Thomas Mails, *The People Called Apache* (Englewood Cliffs, N.J.: Ridge Press and Prentice-Hall, 1974), pp. 14–17; Morris Edward Opler, *An*

Apache Life-Way (Chicago: University of Chicago Press, 1965), pp. 1–2; Barbara Perlman, *Allan Houser* (Santa Fe, N. Mex.: Glenn Green Galleries, 1987), pp. 60–61; Angie Debo, *Geronimo: The Man, His Time, and His Place* (Norman: University of Oklahoma Press, 1977), pp. 439–454.

3. Geronimo, *Geronimo: Story of His Life*, trans. Asa Daklugie, ed. S. M. Barrett (Chickasha: American Indian Studies, University of Science and Arts of Oklahoma, 1986), pp. 3–11; Henrietta Stockel, *Women of the Apache Nation* (Reno: University of Nevada Press, 1991), pp. 3–6.

4. Debo, *Geronimo: The Man*, pp. 281–298; Jason Betzinez with Wilbur Nye, *I Fought with Geronimo* (Lincoln: University of Nebraska Press, 1987), pp. 132–140; C. L. Sonnichsen, ed., *Geronimo and the End of the Apache Wars* (Lincoln: University of Nebraska Press, 1986), pp. 72–88; Eve Ball, *In the Days of Victorio: Recollections of a Warm Springs Apache* (Tucson: University of Arizona Press, 1986), pp. 181–189; John Turcheneske, Jr., "The Apache Prisoners of War at Fort Sill, 1894–1914" (Ph.D. diss., University of New Mexico, 1978), pp. 7–8; see also D. C. Cole, *The Chiricahua Apache, 1846–1876: From War to Reservation* (Albuquerque: University of New Mexico Press, 1988), pp. 164–165.

5. See Max Moorhead, *The Apache Frontier: Jacobo Ugarte and the Spanish-Indian Relations in Northern New Spain, 1769–1791* (Norman: University of Oklahoma Press, 1968); Ralph Smith, "Apache Plunder Trails Southward, 1831–1840," *New Mexico Historical Review* 37 (January 1972): 20–42; Donald Worcester, *The Apaches: Eagles of the Southwest* (Norman: University of Oklahoma Press, 1970); Elizabeth John, *Storms Brewed in Other Men's Worlds* (College Station: Texas A&M University Press, 1975).

6. Conversation with Beverly Hicks (Kiowa), January 27, 1987; conversation with Mildred Cleghorn (Fort Sill Apache), August 29, 1988; conversation with Pat Regan (Fort SIll Apache), September 24, 1988.

7. Geronimo, *Geronimo: Story of His Life*, pp. 12–15, and Morris Opler and Harry Hoijer, "The Raid and War-Path Language of the Chiricahua Apache," *American Anthropologist* 42 (October–December 1940): 617–634.

8. Stockel, *Women of the Apache Nation*, pp. 10–11, 104–105; see also Mails, *People Called Apache*, pp. 313–319.

9. U.S. House of Representatives, *A Bill Authorizing the Secretary of War to Grant Freedom to Certain of the Apache Prisoners of War Now Being Held at Fort Sill, Oklahoma, and Giving Them Equal Status with Other Indians*, H.R. 16651, 62d Cong. 2d sess. 1912; U.S. House of Representatives, *A Bill Providing for the Allotment of Land to the Apache Indians Now under the Charge of the War Department at Fort Sill, Oklahoma, as Prisoners of War*, H.R. 25297, 61st Cong. 2d sess. 1910; U.S. Senate, *Apache Prisoners of War*, S. Doc. 266, 61st Cong. 2d sess. 1910.

10. Conversation with Mildred Cleghorn (Fort Sill Apache), September 24, 1988, and Benedict Jozhe, "A Brief History of the Fort Sill Apache Tribe," *Chronicles of Oklahoma* 39 (Winter 1961–1962): 427–432.

11. Geronimo, *Geronimo: Story of His Life*, pp. 213–214.

CHAPTER 12. CONTEMPORARY ALLIANCES

1. Edwin Wade, ed., *The Arts of the North American Indian: Native Traditions in Evolution* (New York: Hudson Hills Press in association with the Philbrook Art Center, Tulsa, Okla., 1986), pp. 45–53, 65–92, 157–158; Myles Libhart, ed., *Contemporary Southern Plains Indian Painting* (Anadarko: Oklahoma Indian Arts and Crafts Cooperative, 1972), pp. 7–22; *Contemporary Southern Plains Indian Metal Work* (Anadarko: Oklahoma Indian Arts and Crafts Cooperative, 1976), pp. 7–33; Jamake Highwater, *Song from the Earth: American Indian Painting* (Boston: New York Graphic Society, 1976), pp. 41–113; J J. Brody, *Indian Painters and White Patrons* (Albuquerque: University of New Mexico Press, 1971); Charles Waugaman, *Cheyenne Artist: The Story of Richard West* (New York: Friendship Press, 1970), pp. 36–38; *Allan Houser: A Life in Art* (Santa Fe; Museum of New Mexico, 1981), pp. 9–11; Barbara Perlman, *Allan Houser* (Santa Fe, N. Mex.: Glenn Green Galleries, 1987), pp. 15–17.

2. Marsden Hartley, "Red Man Ceremonials: An American Plea for American Esthetics," *Art and Archaeology* 9 (1920): 7–14; Marsden Hartley, "Tribal Esthetics," *Dial* 65 (1918): 399–401; Sharyn Rohlfsen Udall, *Modernist Painting in New Mexico, 1913–1935* (Albuquerque: University of New Mexico Press, 1984), pp. 44–45.

3. See John Ewers, *Plains Indian Painting* (Palo Alto, Calif.: Stanford University Press, 1939); Howard Meredith, "Native Response: Rural Indian People in Oklahoma, 1900–1939," in *Rural Oklahoma*, ed. Donald Green (Oklahoma City: Oklahoma Historical Society, 1977), pp. 74–83.

4. Conversation with Sharon Ahtone Harjo (Kiowa), September 6, 1974; conversation with Dick West (Cheyenne), January 27, 1980; conversation with Pauline Beaver Harjo (Arapaho), June 3, 1989; conversations with Doc Tate Nevaquaya (Comanche), April 22, 1990, and June 6, 1993.

5. Geary Hobson, ed., *The Remembered Earth: An Anthology of Contemporary Native American Literature* (Albuquerque: University of New Mexico Press, 1979), pp. 1–11; LaVonne Brown Ruoff, *American Indian Literatures: An Introduction, Bibliographic Review, and Selected Bibliography* (New York: Modern Language Association of America, 1990), pp. 67–75; see also Brian Swann, ed., *On Translation of Native American Literatures* (Washington, D.C.: Smithsonian Institution Press, 1992), and Arnold Krupat, *Ethnocriticism: Ethnography, History, Literature* (Berkeley: University of California Press, 1992).

6. Worcester v. Georgia, 31 U.S. 515 (1832), and William Lockhart et al., *The American Constitution* (St. Paul, Minn.: West Publishing Company, 1970), p. 76.

7. *U.S. Statutes at Large*, 48:984 and 49:1967; Vine Deloria, Jr., and Clifford Lytle, *American Indians, American Justice* (Austin: University of Texas Press, 1983), pp. 12–15.

8. Lewis Meriam et al., *The Problem of Indian Administration* (Baltimore: Institute for Government Research, 1928), and Randolph C. Downes, "A Crusade for Indian Reform, 1922–1934," *Mississippi Valley Historical Review* 23 (July 1945): 343–355.

9. Kenneth Philip, *John Collier's Crusade for Indian Reform, 1920–1954* (Tucson: University of Arizona Press, 1977), pp. 113–134, and Graham Taylor, *The New Deal and American Indian Tribalism: The Administration of the Indian Reorganization Act of 1934–1945* (Lincoln: University of Nebraska Press, 1980), pp. 17–38.

10. Commissioner of Indian Affairs, *Annual Report, 1934–1935* (Washington, D.C.: U.S. Government Printing Office, 1935), p. 114, and William Hagan, *American Indians*, rev. ed. (Chicago: University of Chicago Press, 1979), pp. 155–156.

11. "Meeting Held at Anadarko, Oklahoma," October 23, 1934, Elmer Thomas Papers, Western History Collections, University of Oklahoma, Norman, and U.S. House of Representatives, Committee on Indian Affairs, *Hearings on H.R. 6234, General Welfare of the Indians of Oklahoma*, 74th Cong. 1st sess. 1935, pp. 1–4.

12. U.S. Statutes at Large, 49:1967–1968.

13. Constitution and By-laws of the Caddo Indian Tribe of Oklahoma, ratified January 17, 1938; Corporate Charter of the Caddo Indian Tribe of Oklahoma, ratified November 15, 1938; *Daily Oklahoman* (Oklahoma City), January 19, 1938; Vynola Newkumet and Howard Meredith, *Hasinai: A Traditional History of the Caddo Confederacy* (College Station: Texas A&M University Press, 1988), pp. 77–78; Constitution and By-laws of the Cheyenne–Arapaho Tribes of Oklahoma, ratified September 18, 1937.

14. Lawrence Kelly, "The Indian Reorganization Act: Dream or Reality?" *Pacific Historical Review* 44 (1976): 291–312; see also Taylor, *New Deal and American Indian Tribalism*; William Brophy and Sophie Aberle, *The Indian: America's Unfinished Business* (Norman: University of Oklahoma Press, 1967); Vine Deloria, Jr., and Clifford Lytle, *The Nations Within* (New York: Pantheon Books, 1984).

15. Ben Dwight to J. B. Milam, Oklahoma City, November 4, 1944, Bartley Milam Papers, Manuscript Collections, University of Tulsa; National Congress of American Indians, Convention Summary, Denver, Colorado, November 15, 16, and 17, 1944; Constitution and By-laws of the National Congress of American Indians, adopted November 16, 1944; W. G. Stigler Collection, Western History Collections, University of Oklahoma, Norman; Hazel Hertzberg, *The Search for an American Indian Identity: Modern Pan-Indian Movements* (Syracuse, N.Y.: Syracuse University Press, 1971), pp. 208–209; Arrell Morgan Gibson, *The American Indian: Prehistory to the Present* (Lexington, Mass.: D. C. Heath, 1980), p. 549; N. B. Johnson, "The National Congress of American Indians," *Chronicles of Oklahoma* 30 (Summer 1952): 141.

16. A message from the president, National Congress of American Indians, October 5, 1946, W. G. Stigler Collection.

17. *U.S. Statutes at Large*, 60:1049.

18. Lyman Tyler, *Indian Affairs: A Study of the Changes in Policy of the United States towards Indians* (Provo, Utah: Institute of American Indian Studies, Brigham Young University, 1964), pp. 109–122; Lyman Tyler, *Indian Affairs: A Work Paper on Termination with an Attempt to Show Its Antece-*

dents (Provo, Utah: Institute of American Indian Studies, Brigham Young University, 1964), pp. 35–40; Donald Fixico, *Termination and Relocation: Federal Indian Policy, 1945–1960* (Albuquerque: University of New Mexico Press, 1986), pp. 63–69; see also Larry Burt, *Tribalism in Crisis: Federal Indian Policy, 1953–1961* (Albuquerque: University of New Mexico Press, 1982), pp. 5–7.

19. Charles Wilkinson and Eric Biggs, "The Evolution of the Termination Policy," *American Indian Law Review* 5 (1980): 139–194; Kenneth Philip, "Termination: A Legacy of the Indian New Deal," *Western Historical Quarterly* 14 (April 1983): 165–180; Blue Clark, "Bury My Heart in Smog: Urban Indians," in *The Native American Experience*, ed. Philip Weeks (Arlington Heights, Ill.: Harlan Davidson, 1988), pp. 278–291; see also Francis Paul Prucha, *The Great Father*, 2 vols. (Lincoln: University of Nebraska Press, 1984), 2:1079–1084.

20. Conversation with Hammond Motah (Comanche), November 8, 1989; conversation with Doc Tate Nevaquaya (Comanche), November 8, 1989; Dennis Zotigh, *Moving History: Evolution of the Powwow* (Oklahoma City: Center of the American Indian, 1991), pp. 1–2; Thomas Kavanaugh, "Southern Plains Dance Tradition and Dynamics," in *Native American Dance: Ceremonies and Social Traditions*, ed. Charlotte Heth (Washington, D.C.: National Museum of the American Indian, Smithsonian Institution with Starwood Publishing, 1992), pp. 105–123; Morris Foster, *Being Comanche: A Social History of an American Indian Community* (Tucson: University of Arizona Press, 1991), pp. 145–154.

21. Presentation by David Paddlety (Kiowa), January 20, 1992, American Indian Studies, University of Science and Arts of Oklahoma, Chickasha; presentation by Dava Kelly (Kiowa), February 7, 1992, American Indian Studies, University of Science and Arts of Oklahoma, Chickasha; presentation by Gina Pauahty (Kiowa), American Indian Studies, University of Science and Arts of Oklahoma, Chickasha; Maurice Boyd with Linn Pauahty, *Kiowa Voices: Ceremonial Dance, Ritual and Song*, 2 vols. (Fort Worth: Texas Christian University Press, 1981), 1:114–122; Robert Stahl, "Joe True: Convergent Needs and Assumed Identity," *Being and Becoming Indian: Biographical Studies of North American Frontiers*, ed. James Clifton (Chicago: Dorsey Press, 1989), pp. 276–289.

22. Conversation with Vynola Newkumet (Caddo), September 5, 1981; conversation with Reathia Cuzzen (Caddo), June 18, 1993; conversation with Mary Lou Davis (Caddo), January 23, 1993; conversation with Mildred Cleghorn (Fort Sill Apache), September 24, 1988; conversation with Pat Regan (Fort Sill Apache), September 24, 1988.

23. "Revival for a Rare Art," *Life International*, March 16, 1959; John Williams and Howard Meredith, *Bacone Indian University: A History* (Oklahoma City: Oklahoma Heritage Association with Western Heritage Books, 1980), pp. 92–98, 110–111; Libhart, ed., *Contemporary Southern Plains Indian Painting*, pp. 66–79; *Contemporary Southern Plains Indian Metalwork*, pp. 65–79.

24. Conversation with Newton Lamar (Wichita), February 13, 1985; conver-

sation with Henryetta Whiteman (Cheyenne), February 18, 1987; conversation with Vernon Hadden (Wichita), September 13, 1989; conversation with Art Thomas (Delaware), November 2, 1989; Constitution and By-laws of the Delaware Tribe of Western Oklahoma, ratified April 21, 1973; Wichita Governing Resolution, adopted by the Wichita and Affiliated Tribes, May 8, 1961.

CHAPTER 13. SELF-DETERMINATION

1. *Report on Trust Responsibilities and the Federal-Indian Relationship; Including Treaty Review, Final Report* (Washington, D.C.: U.S. Government Printing Office, 1976); *Report on Tribal Government, Final Report* (Washington, D.C.: U.S. Government Printing Office, 1976); *Report on Federal Administration and Structure of Indian Affairs, Final Report* (Washington, D.C.: U.S. Government Printing Office, 1976); *Bureau of Indian Affairs Management Study, Final Report* (Washington, D.C.: U.S. Government Printing Office, 1976).

2. *Report on Trust Responsibilities and the Federal-Indian Relationship*, p. 170.

3. *Report on Federal, State, and Tribal Jurisdiction, Final Report* (Washington, D.C.: U.S. Government Printing Office, 1976); *Report on Terminated and Nonfederally Recognized Indians, Final Report* (Washington, D.C.: U.S. Government Printing Office, 1976).

4. *Report on Federal, State, and Tribal Jurisdiction*, p. 120.

5. *Report on Education, Final Report* (Washington, D.C.: U.S. Government Printing Office, 1976); *Report on Indian Health, Final Report* (Washington, D.C.: U.S. Government Printing Office, 1976); *Report on Reservation and Resource Development and Protection, Final Report* (Washington, D.C.: U.S. Government Printing Office, 1976); *Report on Urban and Rural Non-Reservation Indians, Final Report* (Washington, D.C.: U.S. Government Printing Office, 1976); *Report on Alcohol and Drug Abuse, Final Report* (Washington, D.C.: U.S. Government Printing Office, 1976).

6. *Report on Indian Education*, pp. 84–85; see also U.S. Senate, *Indian Education: A National Tragedy—National Challenge*, Report no. 91-501, 91st Cong. 1st sess., 1969; *The Education of American Indians: A Survey of the Literature* (Washington, D.C.: U.S. Government Printing Office, 1969); Francis McKinley, Stephen Bayne, and Glen Nimnicht, *Who Should Control Indian Education?* (Berkeley, Calif.: Far West Laboratory and Educational Research and Development, 1970).

7. *Report on BIA Education: Excellence in Indian Education through the Effective Schools Process* (Washington, D.C.: Bureau of Indian Affairs, U.S. Department of the Interior, 1988), and *Indian Nations at Risk: An Educational Strategy for Action, Final Report of the Indian Nations at Risk Task Force* (Washington, D.C.: U.S. Department of Education, 1991).

8. Stephen Cornell, *The Return of the Native: American Indian Political Resurgence* (New York: Oxford University Press, 1988), p. 203.

9. Francis Paul Prucha, *The Great Father,* 2 vols. (Lincoln: University of Nebraska Press, 1984), 2:1170.

10. Kirke Kickingbird, "The American Indian Policy Review Commission: A Prospect for Future Change in Federal Indian Policy," *American Indian Law Review* 3 (1975): 243–253.

11. U.S. Statutes at Large, 92:3075–3078; U.S. Senate, *Implementation of Public Law 93-638, the Indian Self-Determination and Education Assistance Act,* 94th Cong. 1st sess., 1975 (Washington, D.C.: U.S. Government Printing Office, 1976), p. 3; see also U.S. Senate, *Indian Postsecondary Educational Assistance Act,* 94th Cong., 2d sess., 1976 (Washington, D.C.: U.S. Government Printing Office, 1976); U.S. Senate, *Indian Law Enforcement Improvement Act of 1975,* 2 parts, 94th Cong., 1st sess., 1975 (Washington, D.C.: U.S. Government Printing Office, 1975).

12. *Handbook for Decision Makers on Title I of the Indian Self-Determination and Education Assistance Act* (Washington, D.C.: Bureau of Indian Affairs, Department of the Interior, 1976); and *Code of Federal Regulations,* 25:271.

13. Senate, *Implementation of Public Law 93-638,* pp. 13–17.

14. *U.S. Statutes at Large,* 92:3069–3075, and Manuel Guerrero, "Indian Child Welfare Act of 1978: A Response to the Threat to Indian Culture Caused by Foster and Adoptive Placements of Indian Children," *American Indian Law Review* 7 (1979): 51–77.

15. Constitution of the Apache Tribe of Oklahoma, ratified February 5, 1972 and amended July 17, 1976; Constitution and By-laws of the Caddo Tribe, ratified June 26, 1976; Constitution and By-laws of the Cheyenne-Arapaho Tribes, ratified April 19, 1975; Constitution of the Comanche Tribe, ratified November 19, 1966; Constitution of the Comanche Tribe, approved January 9, 1967, and amended June 10, 1978; Constitution and By-laws of the Delaware Tribe of Western Oklahoma, ratified April 21, 1973, and amended March 6, 1976; Constitution and By-laws of the Fort Sill Apache Tribe, ratified October 30, 1976, and amended March 11, 1978; Constitution and By-laws of the Kiowa Tribe, ratified May 23, 1970, and amended June 3, 1978.

16. Vynola Newkumet and Howard Meredith, *Hasinai: A Traditional History of the Caddo Confederacy* (College Station: Texas A&M University Press, 1988), pp. 51–71; Howard Meredith and Vynola Newkumet, "Melford Williams: Caddo Leadership Patterns in the Twentieth Century," *Journal of the West* 23 (July 1984): 64–69; Stan Hoig, *People of the Sacred Arrows: The Southern Cheyenne Today* (Dutton: Cobblehill Books, 1992), pp. 107–108.

17. Robert H. Henry, attorney general, to E. Kelly Haney, state senator, Oklahoma City, March 1, 1991, Office of the U.S. Attorney, Western District of Oklahoma, Oklahoma City.

18. *Promoting Effective State-Tribal Relations: A Dialogue,* proceedings of a session held in Tulsa, Oklahoma, August 1989 (Denver: National Conference of State Legislatures, 1990), p. 19; see also Julie Wrend and Clay Smith, eds., *American Indian Law Deskbook: Conference of Western Attorneys General* (Niwot: University Press of Colorado, 1993), pp. 28–31, and John Moore, "The

Enduring Reservation of Oklahoma," in *State and Reservation: New Perspectives on Federal Indian Policy*, ed. George Castile and Robert Bee (Tucson: University of Arizona Press, 1992), pp. 92–109.

19. Conversation with Newton Lamar (Wichita), February 13, 1985.

20. Conversation with Mildred Cleghorn (Fort Sill Apache), March 19, 1992; *Daily Oklahoman* (Oklahoma City), November 27, 1988; *Anadarko Daily News*, December 6, 1988.

21. Fort Sill Chiricahua, Warm Springs Apache—Government Operations, manuscript, Office Files, Fort Sill Apache Tribal Complex.

22. Presentation by Linda Poolaw (Delaware), March 7, 1988, American Indian Studies, University of Science and Arts of Oklahoma, Chickasha, and Duane Hale, *Peacemakers of the Frontier* (Anadarko: Delaware Tribe of Western Oklahoma Press, 1987), pp. 157–158.

23. See *Delaware Tribe of Western Oklahoma: Needs Assessment Survey Results, 1983*, prepared by Kathy Murray (Anadarko: Delaware Tribe of Western Oklahoma, 1983), and *Delaware Tribe of Western Oklahoma: Tribal Specific Health Plan* (Anadarko: Delaware Tribe of Western Oklahoma, 1979).

24. "Federal Trust Responsibility at Issue in Oil and Gas Cases," *Native American Rights Fund Legal Review* 13 (Summer 1988): 1–5; "Government Urges Controls on Indian Gaming Industry," *New York Times*, December 19, 1993; see also Paul H. Stuart, "Financing Self-Determination: Federal Indian Expenditures, 1975–1988," *American Indian Culture and Research Journal* 14 (1990): 1–18.

25. *1990 Census of Population and Housing, Summary Population and Housing Characteristics*, CPH-1-38, Oklahoma Data Center, Oklahoma Dept. of Commerce, Oklahoma City.

26. Ibid.

27. U.S. Department of Commerce, *News*, November 18, 1992; and *Phoenix Sun*, November 22, 1992.

28. *Oklahoma Indian Tribal Governments Report* (Oklahoma City: Oklahoma Indian Affairs Commission, c. 1991), pp. 1–23.

29. Population by Detailed Race and American Indian Tribe, 1990, Census of Population and Housing, Oklahoma State Data Center, Oklahoma Department of Commerce, Oklahoma City.

30. *Tribal Peacemaking Conference, May 21–22, 1993, Tulsa, Oklahoma* (Oklahoma City: Tribal Court Training Program, Native American Legal Resource Center, Oklahoma City University Law School, 1993), p. IX–TPM–13.

CHAPTER 14. SELF-SUFFICIENCY

1. *Indian Self-Determination Study*, Contract K51C14201205 for the assistant secretary of the interior for Indian Affairs (May, 1984), pp. 1–2.

2. Statement by the president—Indian Policy, Office of the Press Secretary, January 24, 1983.

3. Francis Paul Prucha,"American Indian Policy in the Twentieth Century," *Western Historical Quarterly* 15 (January 1984): 5–18.

4. Presidential Commission on Indian Reservation Economies, *Report and Recommendations to the President of the United States* (Washington, D.C.: U.S. Government Printing Office, 1984), p. 3.

5. Hazel Hertzberg, "Reaganomics on the Reservation," *New Republic,* November 22, 1983, pp. 15–17; "Indians and Enterprise," *Sunday Oklahoman* (Oklahoma City), January 20, 1985; Henrietta Whiteman, "Employment Status of American Indian Women," *Conference on the Educational and Occupational Needs of American Indian Women* (Washington, D.C.: National Institute of Education, 1980), pp. 617–626; see also Sandra Cadwalader and Vine Deloria, Jr., *The Aggressions of Civilization: Federal Indian Policy since the 1880s* (Philadelphia: Temple University Press, 1984).

6. Daniel Israel, "The Re-emergence of Tribal Nationalism and Its Impact on Reservation Resource Development," *University of Colorado Law Review* 47 (1976): 617–626; Cardell Jacobson, "Internal Colonialism and Native Americans: Indian Labor in the United States from 1871 to World War II," *Social Science Quarterly* 65 (March 1984): 768–800; Norris Hundley, Jr., "The 'Winters' Decision and Indian Water Rights: A Mystery Re-examined," *Western Historical Quarterly* 13 (January 1982): 17–42; Michael Nelson and Bradley Brooke, "The Winters Doctrine: Seventy Years of Application of 'Reserved' Water Rights to Indian Reservations," *Arid Lands Resource Information Paper* no. 9 (Tucson: Center for Arid Land Studies, University of Arizona, 1977); "Federal Trust Responsibility at Issue in Oil and Gas Cases," *Native American Rights Fund Legal Review* 13 (Summer 1988): 1–6.

7. See Sar Levitan and Elizabeth Miller, *The Equivocal Prospects for Indian Reservation,* Occasional Paper no. 2 (Washington, D.C.: Center for Social Policy Studies, George Washington University, 1993), pp. 6–17.

8. *Report of the Task Force on Indian Economic Development,* July 1986, pp. 71–98; U.S. Senate, *Final Report and Legislative Recommendations,* 101st Cong., 1st sess., Report 101–216, 1989, pp. 69–87; Stephen Cornell and Joseph Kalt, "Reloading the Dice: Improving the Chances for Economic Development on American Indian Reservations," in *What Can Tribes Do? Strategies and Institutions in American Indian Economic Development,* ed. Stephen Cornell and Joseph Kalt, American Indian Manual and Handbook Series no. 4 (Los Angeles: American Indian Studies Center, University of California, 1992), pp. 6–7.

9. Presentation by Edgar French (Delaware), October 13, 1993, American Indian Studies, University of Science and Arts of Oklahoma, Chickasha.

CHAPTER 15. POLICY REFORM

1. Statements by the president, Office of the Press Secretary, Los Angeles, Calif., June 14, 1991.

2. *New York Times,* April 30, 1994.

3. "History of the Self-Governance Demonstration Project," *First Nations Development Institute Business Alert* 8 (September–October 1993): 9–11.

4. See Sharon O'Brien, *American Indian Tribal Governments* (Norman: University of Oklahoma Press, 1989), p. 293.

5. Presentation by Ted Lonewolf (Kiowa), American Indian Studies, University of Science and Arts of Oklahoma, Chickasha, October 29, 1993.

6. Presentation by Wallace Coffey (Comanche), American Indian Studies, University of Science and Arts of Oklahoma, Chickasha, December 3, 1993.

7. Ibid., and presentation by Edgar French (Delaware), American Indian Studies, University of Science and Arts of Oklahoma, Chickasha, October 13, 1993.

8. The standard is found in *Conference Report 100-498 Accompanying H. J. Resolution 395,* 100th Cong., 1st sess., December 22, 1987.

9. Robert Anderson, comp., *Tax Advantages for Economic Development of Oklahoma Indian Trust Properties* (Oklahoma City: Oklahoma State Department of Commerce, 1989); Functional Statements, Anadarko Agency; Anadarko Agency briefing paper, "Status of Indian Court System in Western Oklahoma," Anadarko Agency, November 20, 1990.

10. Conversations with Gary McAdams (Wichita), October 12, 1990, and November 1, 1990; presentation by Gary McAdams (Wichita), November 12, 1991, American Indian Studies, University of Science and Arts of Oklahoma, Wichita Tribal Complex; presentation by Vanessa Vance (Wichita), November 26, 1991, American Indian Studies, University of Science and Arts of Oklahoma, Wichita Tribal Complex; see also Rebecca Adamson, "Native Americans in the 21st Century and Philanthropy's Role," *First Nations Development Institute Business Alert* 8 (May/June 1993): 1–5; Patricia L. Parker, "Traditional Cultural Properties," *Cultural Resources Management* 16 (1993): 1–5; "Guidelines for Evaluating and Documenting Traditional Cultural Properties," *National Register Bulletin* no. 38, U.S. Department of the Interior, National Park Service, Interagency Resources Division (Washington, D.C.: U.S. Government Printing Office, 1992).

11. Further discussion on this topic is in Howard Meredith, *Modern American Indian Tribal Government and Politics* (Tsaile, Navajo Nation: Navajo Community College Press, 1993), pp. 147–154.

CHAPTER 16. CONCLUSION

1. William Fulbright with Seth Tillman, *The Price of Empire* (New York: Pantheon Books, 1989), p. 14.

2. Presentation by Kenneth Torralba (Comanche), American Indian Studies, University of Science and Arts of Oklahoma, Chickasha, November 17, 1993.

3. Presentation by Marland Toyekoyah (Kiowa), American Indian Studies, University of Science and Arts of Oklahoma, Chickasha, December 1, 1993.

4. For more extended discussion of this concern, see Howard Meredith,

Modern American Indian Tribal Government and Politics (Tsaile, Navajo Nation: Navajo Community College Press, 1993).

5. Edgar Heap of Birds, ed. *Makers* (Norman: Point Rider Press, 1988), p. 15.

6. N. Scott Momaday, *The Ancient Child: A Novel* (New York: Doubleday, 1989), pp. 243–244.

BIBLIOGRAPHY

ORAL TRADITION

Personal Contact (in the classroom, interviews, presentations)

Adair, Cleta (Wichita)
Bell, Margaret (Wichita)
Bitzeedey, Martin (Plains Apache)
Boettger, Vickie (Kiowa)
Bowman, Wanda (Wichita)
Cleghorn, Mildred (Chiricahua Apache)
Coffey, Wallace (Comanche)
Conner, Cecelia (Wichita)
Cuzzen, Reathia (Caddo)
Darrow, Michael (Chiricahua Apache)
Davis, Mary Lou (Caddo)
Delaware, Edgar (Wichita)
Devaney, Sam (Comanche)
Frank, Donnie (Caddo)
French, Edgar (Delaware)
Hadden, Vernon (Wichita)
Haden, Iola (Comanche)
Harjo, Pauline (Arapaho)
Harjo, Sharon Ahtone (Kiowa)
Hart, Lawrence (Cheyenne)
Heap of Birds, Edgar (Cheyenne)
Hicks, Beverly (Kiowa)
Holder, Berdena (Wichita)
Hunter, Vernon (Caddo)
Kassanavoid, Forrest (Comanche)
Kebow, Miriam (Wichita)
Kelly, Dava (Kiowa)
Kianute, Evelyn (Caddo)
Lamar, Newton (Wichita)
Lamebull, Dee Ann (Cheyenne)
Lewis, Carol (Comanche)

Lonewolf, Ted (Kiowa)
McAdams, Gary (Wichita)
McCurdy, Vivian (Wichita)
Matthews, Alex (Pawnee)
Moonlight, Clara (Wichita)
Motah, Hammond (Comanche)
Nevaquaya, Doc Tate (Comanche)
Newkumet, Vynola (Caddo)
Owings, Faye (Wichita)
Owings, Stuart (Wichita)
Paddlety, David (Kiowa)
Picard, Drucilla (Wichita)
Poolaw, Linda (Delaware)
Regan, Pat (Chiricahua Apache)
Riffel, Louisa (Wichita)
Sapahoodle, Cletus (Kiowa)
Stumblingbear, Elton (Plains Apache)
Swift, Virgil (Wichita)
Thomas, Art (Delaware)
Tiger, Marilyn (Comanche)
Toehay, Kathy (Kiowa)
Torralba, Kenneth (Comanche)
Toyekoyah, Marland (Kiowa)
Vance, Vanessa (Wichita)
Van Tuyl, Charles (Cherokee)
Watkins, Gene (Wichita)
Wetselline, Mike (Plains Apache)
Whitebead, Irving (Caddo)
Whiteman, Henryetta (Cheyenne)
Whiteskunk, Ruth (Cheyenne)
Woosypitti, Mary (Wichita)

Oral History Collections

Doris Duke Oral Indian History Collection. Western History Collections, University of Oklahoma, Norman.

Indian-Pioneer Papers. Indian Archives, Oklahoma Historical Society, Oklahoma City.

MANUSCRIPT COLLECTIONS AND DOCUMENTS

American Indian Policy Review Commission. *Bureau of Indian Affairs Management Study, Final Report.* (Washington, D.C.: U.S. Government Printing Office, 1976.

———. *Report on Alcohol and Drug Abuse, Final Report.* Washington, D.C.: U.S. Government Printing Office, 1976.

———. *Report on Education, Final Report.* Washington, D.C.: U.S. Government Printing Office, 1976.

———. *Report on Federal Administration and Structure of Indian Affairs, Final Report.* Washington, D.C.: U.S. Government Printing Office, 1976.

———. *Report on Federal, State, and Tribal Jurisdiction, Final Report.* Washington, D.C.: U.S. Government Printing Office, 1976.

———. *Report on Reservation and Resource Development and Protection, Final Report.* Washington, D.C.: U.S. Government Printing Office, 1976.

———. *Report on Terminated and Nonfederally Recognized Indians, Final Report.* Washington, D.C.: U.S. Government Printing Office, 1976.

———. *Report on Tribal Government, Final Report.* Washington, D.C.: U.S. Government Printing Office, 1976.

———. *Report on Trust Responsibilities and the Federal-Indian Relationship; Including Treaty Review, Final Report.* Washington, D.C.: U.S. Government Printing Office, 1976.

———. *Report on Urban and Rural Non-Reservation Indians, Final Report.* Washington, D.C.: U.S. Government Printing Office, 1976.

Anadarko Agency. Briefing Paper. Anadarko, Okla., 1990.

Anderson, Robert, comp. *Tax Advantages for Economic Development of Oklahoma Indian Trust Properties.* Oklahoma City: Oklahoma State Department of Commerce, 1989.

Arapaho Agriculture, International Council File. Indian Archives, Oklahoma Historical Society, Oklahoma City.

Briscoe, James. *The Plantation Site: An Early Caddoan Settlement in Eastern Oklahoma.* Oklahoma City: Oklahoma Department of Transportation, 1977.

Brown, James. *Spiro Studies.* 2 vols. Norman: University of Oklahoma Research Institute, 1966.

Brown, James, and Robert Bell. *First Annual Report of Caddoan Archeology Spiro Focus Research.* Norman: University of Oklahoma Research Institute, 1964.

Census of Population and Housing. 1990. Oklahoma Data Center, Oklahoma Department of Commerce, Oklahoma City.

Cheyenne and Arapaho—Agents' Reports. Indian Archives, Oklahoma Historical Society, Oklahoma City.

Cheyenne and Arapaho—Federal Relations. Indian Archives, Oklahoma Historical Society, Oklahoma City.

Cheyenne and Arapaho Reservation Files. Indian Archives, Oklahoma Historical Society, Oklahoma City.

Code of Federal Regulations. 25.

Commissioner of Indian Affairs. *Annual Report, 1934–1935.* Washington, D.C.: U.S. Government Printing Office, 1935.

Conference Report 100–498 Accompanying H.J. Resolution 395. 100th Cong., 1st sess., December 22, 1987.

Constitution of the Apache Tribe of Oklahoma. Ratified February 5, 1972. Amended July 17, 1976.

Constitution and By-laws of the Caddo Tribe. Ratified June 26, 1976.

Constitution and By-laws of the Caddo Indian Tribe of Oklahoma. Ratified January 17, 1938.

Constitution and By-laws of the Cheyenne-Arapaho Tribes. Ratified April 19, 1975.

Constitution and By-laws of the Cheyenne-Arapaho Tribes of Oklahoma. Ratified September 18, 1937.

Constitution of the Comanche Tribe. Ratified November 19, 1966. Amended June 10, 1978.

Constitution and By-laws of the Delaware Tribe of Western Oklahoma. Ratified April 21, 1973. Amended March 6, 1976.

Constitution and By-laws of the Fort Sill Apache Tribe. Ratified October 30, 1976. Amended March 11, 1978.

Constitution and By-laws of the Kiowa Tribe. Ratified May 23, 1970. Amended June 3, 1978.

Constitution and By-laws of the National Congress of American Indians. Adopted November 16, 1944.

Cornell, Stephen, and Joseph Kalt, eds. *What Can Tribes Do? Strategies and Institutions in American Indian Economic Development.* American Indian Manual and Handbook Series no. 4. Los Angeles: American Indian Studies Center, University of California, Los Angeles, 1992.

Corporate Charter of the Caddo Indian Tribe of Oklahoma. Ratified November 15, 1938.

Delaware Tribe of Western Oklahoma: Needs Assessment Survey Results, 1983. Prepared by Kathy Murray. Anadarko: Delaware Tribe of Western Oklahoma, 1983.

———. *Tribal Specific Health Plan.* Anadarko: Delaware Tribe of Western Oklahoma, 1979.

Dorsey, George. *The Cheyenne: Ceremonial Organization.* Field Museum Publication 99, 4 (1905).

———. *The Cheyenne: The Sun Dance.* Field Museum Publication 103 (1905).

———. *The Mythology of the Wichita.* Washington, D.C.: Carnegie Institution of Washington, 1904.

———. *Traditions of the Caddo.* Washington, D.C.: Carnegie Institution of Washington, 1905.

The Education of American Indians: A Survey of the Literature. Washington, D.C.: U.S. Government Printing Office, 1969.

"The Fort Sill Apaches: Their Vital Statistics, Tribal Origins, Antecedents." 1885–1962. Gillett Griswold, comp. U.S. Field Artillery and Fort Sill Museum.

Fort Sill Chiricahua and Warm Springs Apache—Government Operations. Office Files, Fort Sill Apache Tribal Complex, Fort Sill Apache Tribal Jurisdiction.

Gould, Charles N., L. L. Hutchinson, and Gaylord Nelson. *Preliminary Report of the Mineral Resources of Oklahoma.* Oklahoma Geological Survey Bulletin no. 1. Norman, 1908.

"Guidelines for Evaluating and Documenting Traditional Cultural Properties." *National Register Bulletin 38.* U.S. Department of the Interior, National Park Service, Interagency Resources Division. Washington, D.C.: U.S. Government Printing Office, 1992.

Haas, Mary. *Language, Culture, and History: Essays by Mary R. Haas.* Stanford, Calif.: Sanford University Press, 1978.

Handbook for Decision Makers on Title I of the Indian Self-Determination and Education Assistance Act. Washington, D.C.: Bureau of Indian Affairs, Department of the Interior, 1976.

Haozous, Sam. Transcript. Western History Collections, University of Oklahoma, Norman.

Harrington, John. *Vocabulary of the Kiowa Language.* Bureau of American Ethnology Bulletin 84. Washington, D.C.: U.S. Government Printing Office, 1928.

Henry, Robert H. Attorney General of Oklahoma. Opinion, Office of the U.S. Attorney, Western District of Oklahoma, Oklahoma City.

Holiday, V. T., and B. L. Allen. "Geology and Soils." In *Lubbock Lake: Late Quaternary Studies,* ed. E. Johnson, pp. 14–21. College Station: Texas A&M University Press, 1987.

Indian Nations at Risk: An Educational Strategy for Action, Final Report of the Indian Nations at Risk Task Force. Washington, D.C.: U.S. Department of Education, 1991.

Indian Self-determination Study. Contract K51C14201205 for the Assistant Secretary of the Interior for Indian Affairs. May 1984.

Johnson, W. D., "The High Plains and Their Utilization." U.S. Geological Survey, *21st Annual Report,* part 4. Washington, D.C.: U.S. Government Printing Office, 1900.

Kappler, Charles, ed. *Indian Treaties, 1778–1883.* New York: Interland, 1972.

Kiowa Agency Records. Wichita and Affiliated Bands. Indian Archives, Oklahoma Historical Society, Oklahoma City.

Kiowa, Comanche, and Wichita Agency Files. Indian Archives, Oklahoma Historical Society, Oklahoma City.

Lehmann, Winfred. *Historical Linguistics: An Introduction.* 2d ed. New York: Holt, Rinehart, and Winston, 1973.

Levitan, Sar, and Elizabeth Miller. *The Equivocal Prospects for Indian Reservation.* Occasional Paper no. 2. Washington, D.C.: Center for Social Policy Studies, George Washington University, 1993.

McKinley, Francis, Stephen Bayne, and Glen Nimnicht, *Who Should Control Indian Education?* Berkeley, Calif.: Far West Laboratory and Educational Research and Development, 1970.

Mallouf, Robert J. *Archeological Investigations at Proposed Big Pine Lake, 1974–1975, Lamar and Red River Counties.* Austin: Texas Historical Commission, 1976.

Meriam, Lewis, et al. *The Problem of Indian Administration.* Baltimore: Institute for Government Research, 1928.

Milam, Bartley. Papers. Manuscripts Collection, University of Tulsa, Tulsa, Okla.

Muto, Guy. *The Habiukeut of Eastern Oklahoma: Parris Mound.* Oklahoma City: Oklahoma Historical Society, 1978.

Newkumet, Phil. "Works Progress Administration Archaeological Project Quarterly Report [Spiro Mound]." December 1938–April 1939. Western History Collections, University of Oklahoma, Norman.

Oklahoma Department of Commerce. Population by Detailed Race and American Indian Tribe, 1990.

Oklahoma Indian Affairs Commission. *Oklahoma Indian Tribal Governments Report,* c. 1991.

Peterson, Dennis, et al. *An Archeological Survey of the Spiro Vicinity, Le Flore County, Oklahoma.* Oklahoma Archeological Survey, Archeological Resource Survey Report no. 37, April 1993.

Presidential Commission on Indian Reservation Economies. *Report and Recommendations to the President of the United States.* Washington, D.C.: U.S. Government Printing Office, 1984.

Promoting Effective State-Tribal Relations: A Dialogue. Proceedings of a Session Held in Tulsa, Oklahoma, August 1989. Denver: National Conference of State Legislatures, 1990.

Report on BIA Education: Excellence in Indian Education through the Effective Schools Process. Washington, D.C.: Bureau of Indian Affairs, U.S. Department of the Interior, 1988.

Report of the Task Force on Indian Economic Development. July 1986.

Rogers, Daniel. *Spiro Archaeology: 1980 Research.* Norman: Oklahoma Archaeological Survey, 1982.

———. *Spiro Archaeology: The Plaza.* Norman: Oklahoma Archaeological Survey, 1982.

Rogers, Daniel, et al. *Spiro Archaeology: 1979 Excavations.* Norman: Oklahoma Archaeological Survey, 1980.

Statement by the president. Office of the Press Secretary. June 14, 1991.

Statement by the president—Indian Policy. Office of the Press Secretary. January 24, 1983.

"Statement by Uts-tuts-kins." *Senate Executive Document* no. 13. 48th Cong., 1st sess. 1884.

Stigler, W. G. Papers. Western History Collections, University of Oklahoma, Norman.

Story, Dee Ann, ed. *Archaeological Investigations at the George C. Davis Site, Cherokee County, Texas: Summers of 1979 and 1980.* Occasional Papers no 1. Austin: Texas Archeological Research Laboratory, University of Texas, 1981.

———. *The Deshazo Site: Nacogdoches County, Texas.* Austin: Texas Antiquities Committee, 1982.

Swanton, John R. *Source Material on the History and Ethnology of the Caddo*

Indians. Bureau of American Ethnology Bulletin 132. Washington, D.C.: U.S. Government Printing Office, 1942.

"Testimony of Don Juan de Onate, December 14, 1601." In *Don Juan de Onate, Colonizer of New Mexico, 1595–1628.* Ed. George Hammond and Agapito Rey. 2 vols. Albuquerque: University of New Mexico Press, 1953.

Texas Indian Papers. Ed. James Day. 3 vols. Austin: Texas State Library, 1969.

Thomas, Elmer. Papers. Western History Collections, University of Oklahoma, Norman.

Treaties and Agreements of the Indian Tribes of the Southwest Including Western Oklahoma. Washington, D.C.: Institute for the Development of Indian Law, 1973.

Tyler, Lyman. *Indian Affairs: A Study of the Changes in Policy of the United States towards Indians.* Provo, Utah: Institute of American Indian Studies, Brigham Young University, 1964.

———. *Indian Affairs: A Work Paper on Termination with an Attempt to Show Its Antecedents.* Provo, Utah: Institute of American Indian Studies, Brigham Young University, 1964.

U.S. Bureau of the Census. *Twelfth Census of the United States, 1900.* Agriculture.

———. *1990 Census of Population and Housing, Summary Population and Housing Characteristics.* CPH-1-38. Okla.

U.S. Congress. House. *A Bill Authorizing the Secretary of War to Grant Freedom to Certain of the Apache Prisoners of War Now Being Held at Fort Sill, Oklahoma, and Giving Them Equal Status with Other Indians.* H.R. 16651, 62d Cong., 2d sess., 1912.

———. *A Bill Providing for the Allotment of Land to the Apache Indians Now under the Charge of the War Department at Fort Sill, Oklahoma, as Prisoners of War.* H.R. 25297, 61st Cong., 2d sess., 1910.

———. Committee on Indian Affairs. *Hearings on H.R. 6234, General Welfare of the Indians of Oklahoma.* 74th Cong. 1st sess., 1935.

U.S. Congress. Senate. *Apache Prisoners of War.* S. Doc. 266, 61st Cong., 2d sess., 1910.

———. *Final Report and Legislative Recommendations.* 101st Cong., 1st sess., 1989.

———. *Implementation of Public Law 93-638, the Indian Self-Determination and Education Assistance Act.* 94th Cong., 1st sess., 1975.

———. *Indian Education: A National Tragedy—National Challenge.* Report no. 91-501, 91st Cong., 1st sess., 1969.

———. *Indian Law Enforcement Improvement Act of 1975.* 2 parts. 94th Cong., 1st sess., 1975.

———. *Indian Postsecondary Educational Assistance Act.* 94th Cong., 2d sess., 1976.

———. U.S. Commission on Industrial Relations. "The Land Question in the Southwest." *Final Report,* 9 S. Doc. 415, 64th Cong., 1st sess., 1916.

U.S. Department of Commerce. *News.* November 18, 1992.

U.S. Statutes at Large. 48, 49, 60, 92.

Walker, J. R. *Geomorphic Evolution of the Southern High Plains.* Baylor Geological Studies Bulletin no. 35. Waco, Tex., 1978.

Webb, Clarence, and Hiram Gregory. *The Caddo of Louisiana.* Anthropological Study no. 2. Baton Rouge: Department of Culture, Recreation, and Tourism, Louisiana Archaeological Survey and Antiquities Commission, 1978.

Wendorf, Fred, and J. J. Hester, eds. *Late Pleistocene Environments of the Southern High Plains.* Publications of the Fort Burgwin Research Center no. 9. Dallas: Southern Methodist University Press, 1975.

Whiteman, Henrietta. "Employment Status of American Indian Women." *Conference on the Educational and Occupational Needs of American Indian Women.* Washington, D.C.: National Institute of Education, 1980.

Wichita Governing Resolution. Adopted by the Wichita and Affiliated Tribes, May 8, 1961.

Wichita Tribal Archives. Wichita and Affiliated Tribes Complex, Wichita Tribal Jurisdictional Area.

Wrend, Julie, and Clay Smith, eds. *American Indian Law Deskbook: Conference of Western Attorneys General.* Niwot: University Press of Colorado, 1993.

Yearbook of the United States Department of Agriculture. Washington, D.C.: U.S. Government Printing Office, 1903.

BOOKS

Allan Houser: A Life in Art. Santa Fe: Museum of New Mexico, 1981.

Archer, S. G., and C. E. Bunch. *The American Grass Book: A Manual of Pasture and Range Practices.* Norman: University of Oklahoma Press, 1953.

Ball, Eve. *In the Days of Victorio: Recollections of a Warm Springs Apache.* Tucson: University of Arizona Press, 1986.

Bauer, Jack. *The Mexican War, 1846–1848.* New York: Macmillan Publishing Company, 1974.

Beatty, John. *Kiowa-Apache Music and Dance.* Ethnology Series no. 31. Greeley: Museum of Anthropology, University of North Colorado, 1974.

Berthrong, Donald. *The Cheyenne and Arapaho Ordeal: Reservation and Agency Life in the Indian Territory, 1875–1907.* Norman: University of Oklahoma Press, 1976.

————. *The Southern Cheyenne.* Norman: University of Oklahoma Press, 1963.

Betzinez, Jason, with Wilbur Nye. *I Fought with Geronimo.* Lincoln: University of Nebraska Press, 1987.

Bonnifield, Paul. *The Dust Bowl: Men, Dirt, and Depression.* Albuquerque: University of New Mexico Press, 1979.

Boyd, Maurice, with Linn Pauahty. *Kiowa Voices: Ceremonial Dance, Ritual and Song.* 2 vols., Fort Worth: Texas Christian University Press, 1981–1983.

Brant, Charles, ed., *Jim Whitewolf: The Life of a Kiowa Apache Indian.* New York: Dover Publications, 1969.

Brody, J. J. *Indian Painters and White Patrons.* Albuquerque: University of New Mexico Press, 1971.

Brophy, William, and Sophie Aberle. *The Indian: America's Unfinished Business.* Norman: University of Oklahoma Press, 1967.

Burt, Larry. *Tribalism in Crisis: Federal Indian Policy, 1953–1961.* Albuquerque: University of New Mexico Press, 1982.

Burton, Lloyd. *American Indian Water Rights and the Limits of the Law.* Lawrence: University Press of Kansas, 1991.

Cadwalader, Sandra, and Vine Deloria, Jr. *The Aggressions of Civilization: Federal Indian Policy since the 1880s.* Philadelphia: Temple University Press, 1984.

Chafe, Wallace. *The Caddoan, Iroquoian, and Siouan Languages.* The Hague: Mouton, 1976.

Clark, W. P. *The Indian Sign Language.* Lincoln: University of Nebraska Press, 1982.

Coel, Margaret. *Chief Left Hand, Southern Arapaho.* Norman: University of Oklahoma Press, 1981.

Cohen, Felix. *Handbook of Federal Indian Law.* Albuquerque: University of New Mexico Press, 1970.

Cole, D. C. *The Chiricahua Apache, 1846–1876: From War to Reservation.* Albuquerque: University of New Mexico Press, 1988.

Conner, Seymour, and Odie Faulk. *North America Divided: The Mexican War, 1846–1848.* New York: Oxford University Press, 1971.

Contemporary Southern Plains Indian Metal Work. Anadarko: Oklahoma Indian Arts and Crafts Cooperative, 1976.

Cooley's Traditional Stories of the Delaware. Ed. Duane Hale. Anadarko: Delaware Tribe of Western Oklahoma Press, 1984.

Cornell, Stephen. *The Return of the Native: American Indian Political Resurgence.* New York: Oxford University Press, 1988.

Debo, Angie. *Geronimo: The Man, His Time, and His Place.* Norman: University of Oklahoma Press, 1977.

Deloria, Vine, Jr., and Clifford Lytle. *American Indians, American Justice.* Austin: University of Texas Press, 1983.

———. *The Nations Within: The Past and Future of American Indian Sovereignty.* New York: Pantheon Books, 1984.

Ewers, John. *Murals in the Round: Painted Tepees of the Kiowa and Kiowa Apache Indians.* Washington, D.C.: Smithsonian Institution Press, 1978.

———. *Plains Indian Painting.* Palo Alto, Calif.: Stanford University Press, 1939.

Fixico, Donald. *Termination and Relocation: Federal Indian Policy, 1945–1960.* Albuquerque: University of New Mexico Press, 1986.

Flores, Dan. *Caprock Canyonlands.* Austin: University of Texas Press, 1990.

Foster, Morris. *Being Comanche: A Social History of an American Indian Community.* Tucson: University of Arizona Press, 1991.

Frey, Rodney. *The World of the Crow Indians: As Driftwood Lodges.* Norman: University of Oklahoma Press, 1987.

Fulbright, William, with Seth Tillman. *The Price of Empire*. New York: Pantheon Books, 1989.

Geronimo. *Geronimo: Story of His Life*. Trans. Asa Daklugie, ed. S. M. Barrett. Chickasha: American Indian Studies, University of Science and Arts of Oklahoma, 1986.

Gibson, Arrell Morgan. *The American Indian: Prehistory to the Present*. Lexington, Mass.: D. C. Heath, 1980.

——. *The West in the Life of the Nation*. Lexington, Mass.: D. C. Heath and Company, 1976.

Gould, F. W. *Common Texas Grasses: An Illustrated Guide*. College Station: Texas A&M University Press, 1978.

Green, Douglas, and Thomas Tonnesen. *American Indians: Social Justice and Public Policy*. Madison: University of Wisconsin System, Institute on Race and Ethnicity, 1991.

Griswold del Castillo, Richard. *The Treaty of Guadalupe Hidalgo: A Legacy of Conflict*. Norman: University of Oklahoma Press, 1990.

Hagan, William. *American Indians*. Rev. ed. Chicago: University of Chicago Press, 1979.

——. *United States–Comanche Relations: The Reservation Years*. Norman: University of Oklahoma Press, 1990.

Hale, Duane. *Peacemakers on the Frontier: A History of the Delaware Tribe of Western Oklahoma*. Anadarko: Delaware Tribe of Western Oklahoma Press, 1987.

Haley, James. *The Buffalo War: The History of the Red River Indian Uprising of 1874*. Norman: University of Oklahoma Press, 1976.

Hall, Thomas. *Social Change in the Southwest, 1350–1880*. Lawrence: University Press of Kansas, 1989.

Hart, Lawrence, comp. *The Cheyenne Way of Peace*. Clinton, Okla.: Cheyenne Cultural Center, 1978.

Heap of Birds, Edgar, ed., *Makers*. Norman: Point Rider Press, 1988.

Herring, Joseph B. *The Enduring Indians of Kansas: A Century and a Half of Acculturation*. Lawrence: University Press of Kansas, 1990.

Hertzberg, Hazel. *The Search for an American Indian Identity: Modern Pan-Indian Movements*. Syracuse, N.Y.: Syracuse University Press, 1971.

Highwater, Jamake. *Song from the Earth: American Indian Painting*. Boston: New York Graphic Society, 1976.

Hobson, Geary, ed. *The Remembered Earth: An Anthology of Contemporary Native American Literature*. Albuquerque: University of New Mexico Press, 1979.

Hoebel, Adamson. *The Political Organization and Law-ways of the Comanche Indians*. In *Memoirs* of the American Anthropological Association no. 54, 1940.

Hoig, Stan. *The Peace Chiefs of the Cheyennes*. Norman: University of Oklahoma Press, 1980.

——. *People of the Sacred Arrows: The Southern Cheyenne Today*. Dutton: Cobblehill Books, 1992.

————. *Tribal Wars of the Southern Plains*. Norman: University of Oklahoma Press, 1993.

Holder, Preston. *The Hoe and the Horse on the Plains: A Study of Cultural Development among North American Indians*. Lincoln: University of Nebraska Press, 1970.

Hollon, W. Eugene. *The Southwest: Old and New*. New York: Alfred A. Knopf, 1961.

Hoxie, Frederick. *A Final Promise: The Campaign to Assimilate the Indians, 1880–1920*. Lincoln: University of Nebraska Press, 1984.

Hurt, Douglas. *Indian Agriculture in America: Prehistory to the Present*. Lawrence: University Press of Kansas, 1987.

Hyde, George. *Indians of the High Plains: From the Prehistoric Period to the Coming of Europeans*. Norman: University of Oklahoma Press, 1959.

John, Elizabeth. *Storm Brewed in Other Men's Worlds*. College Station: Texas A&M University Press, 1975.

Kickingbird, Kirke, and Karen Ducheneaux. *One Hundred Million Acres*. New York: Macmillan Publishing Company, 1973.

Kroeber, Alfred. *The Arapaho*. Lincoln: University of Nebraska Press, 1983.

Krupat, Arnold. *Ethnocriticism: Ethnology, History, Literature*. Berkeley: University of California Press, 1992.

Leckie, William. *The Military Conquest of the Southern Plains*. Norman: University of Oklahoma Press, 1963.

Libhart, Myles, ed. *Contemporary Southern Plains Indian Painting*. Anadarko: Oklahoma Indian Arts and Crafts Cooperative, 1972.

Limerick, Patricia Nelson. *The Legacy of Conquest: The Unbroken Past of the American West*. New York: W. W. Norton and Company, 1987.

Llewellyn, K. N., and Adamson Hoebel. *The Cheyenne Way: Conflict and Case Law in Primitive Jurisprudence*. Norman: University of Oklahoma Press, 1941.

Lockhart, William, et al. *The American Constitution*. St. Paul: West Publishing Company, 1970.

McCoy, Doyle. *Roadside Trees and Shrubs of Oklahoma*. Norman: University of Oklahoma Press, 1981.

McKenzie, Parker, and John Harrington. *Popular Account of the Kiowa Indian Language*. Monographs of the School of American Research no. 12. Santa Fe: Museum of New Mexico, 1948.

Mails, Thomas. *The People Called Apache*. Englewood Cliffs, N.J.: Prentice Hall, 1974.

Making Medicine: Ledger Drawing Art from Fort Marion. Oklahoma City: Center of the American Indian, 1984.

Marriott, Alice. *The Ten Grandmothers*. Norman: University of Oklahoma Press, 1945.

Meredith, Howard. *Modern American Indian Tribal Government and Politics*. Tsaile, Navajo Nation, Ariz.: Navajo Community College Press, 1993.

Miner, Craig. *Tribal Sovereignty and Industrial Civilization in Indian Territory, 1865–1907*. Norman: University of Oklahoma Press, 1988.

Miner, Craig, and William E. Unrau. *The End of Indian Kansas: A Study of Cultural Revolution, 1854–1871.* Lawrence: University Press of Kansas, 1978.

Momaday, N. Scott. *The Ancient Child: A Novel.* New York: Doubleday, 1989.

———. *The Way to Rainy Mountain.* Albuquerque: University of New Mexico Press, 1969.

Mooney, James. *Calendar History of the Kiowa Indians.* Washington, D.C.: Smithsonian Institution Press, 1979.

———. *The Cheyenne Indians.* In *Memoirs* of the American Anthropological Society 1 (September 1907).

———. *The Ghost Dance Religion.* Chicago: University of Chicago Press, 1973.

Moore, John. *The Cheyenne Nation: A Social and Demographic History.* Lincoln: University of Nebraska Press, 1987.

Moorhead, Max. *The Apache Frontier: Jacobo Ugarte and the Spanish-Indian Relations in Northern New Spain, 1769–1791.* Norman: University of Oklahoma Press, 1968.

Newcomb, W. W. *The People Called Wichita.* Phoenix, Ariz.: Indian Tribal Series, 1976.

Newkumet, Vynola, and Howard Meredith. *Hasinai: A Traditional History of the Caddo Confederacy.* College Station: Texas A&M University Press, 1988.

Nye, W. S. *Carbine and Lance: The Story of Old Fort Sill.* Norman: University of Oklahoma Press, 1943.

O'Brien, Sharon. *American Indian Tribal Governments.* Norman: University of Oklahoma Press, 1989.

Opler, Morris Edward. *An Apache Life-Way.* Chicago: University of Chicago Press, 1965.

Otis, D. S. *The Dawes Act and the Allotment of Indian Lands.* Norman: University of Oklahoma Press, 1973.

Parker, Linda S. *Native American Estate: The Struggle over Indian and Hawaiian Lands.* Honolulu: University of Hawaii Press, 1989.

Parker, William. *Notes Taken during the Expedition through Unexplored Texas.* Philadelphia: Hayes and Zell, 1856.

Perlman, Barbara. *Allan Houser.* Santa Fe, N. Mex.: Glenn Green Galleries, 1987.

Perttula, Timothy. *"The Caddo Nation": Archaeological and Ethnohistorical Perspectives.* Austin: University of Texas Press, 1992.

Philip, Kenneth. *John Collier's Crusade for Indian Reform, 1920–1954.* Tucson: University of Arizona Press, 1977.

Phillips, Philip, and James Brown. *Pre-Columbian Shell Engravings from the Craig Mound at Spiro, Oklahoma.* 6 vols., 2 parts. Cambridge: Peabody Museum Press, Harvard University, 1978–1984.

Powell, Peter. *People of the Sacred Mountain: A History of the North Cheyenne Chiefs and Warrior Societies, 1830–1879.* 2 vols. San Francisco: Harper and Row, 1981.

———. *Sweet Medicine: The Continuing Role of the Sacred Arrows, the Sun Dance, and the Sacred Buffalo Hat in North Cheyenne History.* 2 vols. Norman: University of Oklahoma Press, 1969.

Prucha, Francis Paul. *The Great Father: The United States Government and the American Indians.* 2 vols. Lincoln: University of Nebraska Press, 1984.

The Red Record: The Walam Olum, the Oldest Native North American History. Trans. David McCutchen. Garden City Park, N.J.: Avery Publishing Group, 1993.

Richardson, Jane. *Law and Status among the Kiowa Indians.* Monographs of the American Ethnological Society. New York: J. J. Augustin, 1940.

Richardson, Rupert. *The Comanche Barrier to South Plains Settlement.* Glendale, Calif.: Arthur H. Clark Company, 1933.

Rollings, Willard H. *The Comanche.* New York: Chelsea House Publishers, 1989.

Rood, David. *Wichita Grammar.* New York: Garland Publishing Company, 1976.

Rood, David, and Doris Lamar. *Wichita Language Lessons: A Manual to Accompany Tape Recordings and Audio Tapes.* Wichita Reserve: Wichita and Affiliated Tribes, 1992.

Ruoff, LaVonne Brown. *American Indian Literatures: An Introduction, Bibliographic Review, and Selected Bibliography.* New York: Modern Language Association of America, 1990.

Schilz, Jodye Lynn Dickson, and Thomas Schilz. *Buffalo Hump and the Penateka Comanches.* The University of Texas at El Paso Southwestern Studies Series no. 88. El Paso: Texas Western Press, 1989.

Schmitt, Karl, and Iva Osanai Schmitt. *Wichita Kinship: Past and Present.* Norman, Okla.: University Book Exchange, 1952.

Seger, John. *Early Days among the Cheyenne and Arapahoe Indians.* Norman: University of Oklahoma Press, 1979.

Sonnichsen, C. L. ed. *Geronimo and the End of the Apache Wars.* Lincoln: University of Nebraska Press, 1986.

Stands in Timber, John, and Margot Liberty. *Cheyenne Memories.* Lincoln: University of Nebraska Press, 1972.

Stockel, Henrietta. *Survival of the Spirit: Chiricahua Apaches in Captivity.* Reno: University of Nevada Press, 1993.

———. *Women of the Apache Nation: Voices of Truth.* Reno: University of Nevada Press, 1991.

Sutton, Imre. *Indian Land Tenure: Bibliographic Essays and a Guide to the Literature.* New York: Clearwater Publishing Company, 1975.

———, ed. *Irredeemable America: The Indians' Estate and Land Claims.* Albuquerque: University of New Mexico Press, 1985.

Swann, Brian, ed. *On Translation of Native American Literatures.* Washington, D.C.: Smithsonian Institution Press, 1992.

Taylor, Graham. *The New Deal and American Indian Tribalism: The Administration of the Indian Reorganization Act of 1934–1945.* Lincoln: University of Nebraska Press, 1980.

Terrell, John Upton. *The Plains Apache.* New York: Thomas Y. Crowell Company, 1975.

Thornton, Russell. *American Indian Holocaust and Survival: A Population History since 1492.* Norman: University of Oklahoma Press, 1987.

———. *We Shall Live Again: The 1870 and 1890 Ghost Dance Movements as Demographic Revitalization.* Cambridge: Cambridge University Press, 1986.

Turtle Tales: Oral Traditions of the Delaware of Western Oklahoma. Ed. Duane Hale. Anadarko: Delaware Tribe of Western Oklahoma Press, 1984.

Udall, Sharyn Rohlfsen. *Modernist Painting in New Mexico, 1913–1935.* Albuquerque: University of New Mexico Press, 1984.

Utley, Robert. *The Indian Frontier of the American West, 1846–1890.* Albuquerque: University of New Mexico Press, 1984.

Vestal, Paul, and Richard Schultes. *An Economic Botany of the Kiowa Indians as It Relates to the History of the Tribe.* Cambridge, Mass.: Botanical Museum, 1939.

Wade, Edwin, ed. *The Arts of the North American Indian: Native Traditions in Evolution.* New York: Hudson Hills Press in association with the Philbrook Art Center, Tulsa, Okla., 1986.

Walam Olum or Red Score: The Migration Legend of the Lenni Lenape or Delaware Indians. Indianapolis: Indiana Historical Society, 1954.

Wallace, Ernest, and Adamson Hoebel. *The Comanches: Lords of the Southern Plains.* Norman: University of Oklahoma Press, 1976.

Watkins, Laurel J., with Parker McKenzie. *A Grammar of Kiowa.* Lincoln: University of Nebraska Press, 1984.

Waugaman, Charles. *Cheyenne Artist: The Story of Richard West.* New York: Friendship Press, 1970.

Weaver, J. E., and F. W. Albertson. *Grasslands of the Great Plains: Their Names and Use.* Lincoln, Nebr.: Johnson Publishing Company, 1956.

Webb, Walter Prescott. *The Great Plains.* Boston: Ginn and Company, 1931.

White, Richard. *"It's Your Misfortune and None of My Own": A History of the American West.* Norman: University of Oklahoma Press, 1991.

Williams, John, and Howard Meredith. *Bacone Indian University: A History.* Oklahoma City: Oklahoma Heritage Association with Western Heritage Books, 1980.

Worcester, Donald. *The Apaches: Eagles of the Southwest.* Norman: University of Oklahoma Press, 1970.

———. *Dust Bowl: The Southern Plains in the 1930s.* New York: Oxford University Press, 1979.

Zotigh, Dennis. *Moving History: Evolution of the Powwow.* Oklahoma City: Center of the American Indian, 1991.

ARTICLES

Adamson, Rebecca. "Native Americans in the 21st Century and Philanthropy's Role." *First Nations Development Institute Business Alert* 8 (May/June, 1993): 1–5.

Albert, L. E., and Don Wyckoff. "Oklahoma Environments: Past and Present." In *Prehistory of Oklahoma*, ed. Robert Bell, pp. 1–43. Orlando, Fla.: Academic Press, 1984.

Allen, Virginia. "Stress and Death in the Settlement of Indian Territory." *Chronicles of Oklahoma* 54 (Fall 1976): 352–359.

Anderson, Adrian. "The Cooperton Mammoth: An Early Bone Quarry." *Great Plains Journal* 14 (1975): 130–173.

Baugh, Timothy G. "Ecology and Exchange: The Dynamics of Plains-Pueblo Interaction." In *Farmers, Hunters, and Colonists: Interaction between the Southwest and the Southern Plains*, ed. Katherine Spielmann, pp. 107–127. Tucson: University of Arizona Press, 1991.

Bell, Robert. "Arkansas Valley Caddoan: The Harlan Phase." In *Prehistory of Oklahoma*, ed. Robert Bell, pp. 221–240. Orlando: Academic Press, 1984.

———. "Trade Materials at Spiro Mound as Indicated by Artifacts." *American Antiquity* 12 (1947): 181–184.

———. "Wichita Indians and the French Trade on the Oklahoma Frontier." *Bulletin of the Oklahoma Anthropological Society* 30 (1981): 11–18.

Bell, Robert, et al. "A Pilot Study of Wichita Indian Archeology and Ethnology." *Final Report*, National Science Foundation (1967): 119–120.

Berhofer, Robert, Jr. "Commentary." In *Indian-White Relations: A Persistent Paradox*, ed. Jane Smith and Robert Kvasnicka, pp. 79–86. Washington, D.C.: Howard University Press, 1976.

Berthrong, Donald. "Struggle for Power: The Impact of Southern Cheyenne and Arapaho 'School Boys' on Tribal Politics." *American Indian Quarterly* 16 (Winter 1992): 1–24.

Bittle, William. "The Manatidie: A Focus for Kiowa-Apache Tribal Identity." *Plains Anthropologist* 7 (1962): 152–163.

Blaine, Martha Royce. "The Pawnee-Wichita Visitation Cycle: Historic Manifestations of an Ancient Friendship." In *Pathways to Plains Prehistory: Anthropological Perspectives of Plains Natives and Their Pasts*, ed. D. D. Wyckoff and J. L. Hofman, pp. 113–134. Oklahoma Anthropological Society *Memoir* no. 3 (1982).

Borchert, J. R. "The Climate of the Central North American Grassland." *Annals of the Association of American Geographers* 40 (1950): 1–39.

Brant, Charles. "Kiowa Apache Culture History: Some Further Observations." *Southwestern Journal of Anthropology* 9 (1953): 195–202.

Brown, James. "Arkansas Valley Caddoan: The Spiro Phase." In *Prehistory of Oklahoma*, ed. Robert Bell, pp. 241–263. Orlando: Academic Press, 1984.

Brown, William, Jr. "Comancheria Demography, 1805–1830." *Panhandle-Plains Historical Review* 59 (1986): 1–17.

Chafe, Wallace. "Caddo Texts." In *Caddoan Texts*, ed. Douglas Parks, Native American Texts Series 2 (1977): 27–43.

———. "Caddoan." In *Languages of Native America: Historical and Comparative Assessment*, ed. Lyle Campbell and Marianne Mithun, pp. 213–235. Austin: University of Texas Press, 1979.

Chapman, Berlin. "Establishment of the Wichita Reservation." *Chronicles of Oklahoma* 11 (December 1933): 1044–1055.

Clark, Blue. "Bury My Heart in Smog: Urban Indians." In *The Native American Experience*, ed. Philip Weeks, pp. 278–291. Arlington Heights, Ill.: Harlan Davidson, 1988.

Clawson, Marion. "Natural Resources of the Great Plains in Historical Perspective." In *The Great Plains: Perspectives and Prospects*, ed. Merlin Lawson and M. E. Baker, pp. 3–10. Lincoln Center for Great Plains Studies, 1981.

Dorsey, George. "How the Pawnee Captured the Cheyenne Medicine Arrows." *American Anthropologist* 8 (1903): 1–5.

———. "Wichita Tales." *Journal of American Folklore* 15 (October–December, 1902): 229–232.

Downes, Randolph C. "A Crusade for Indian Reform, 1922–1934." *Mississippi Valley Historical Review* 23 (July 1945): 343–355.

Ewers, John. "The Influence of Epidemics on the Indian Populations and Cultures of Texas." *Plains Anthropologist* 18 (1973): 104–115.

"Federal Trust Responsibility at Issue in Oil and Gas Cases." *Native American Rights Fund Legal Review* 13 (Summer 1988): 1–6.

Gatchet, Albert, ed. "Migration of the Wichita Indians." *American Antiquarian* 13 (September 1891): 249–250.

Guerrero, Manuel. "Indian Child Welfare Act of 1978: A Response to the Threat to Indian Culture Caused by Foster and Adoptive Placements of Indian Children." *American Indian Law Review* 7 (1979): 51–77.

Hale, Douglas. "European Immigrants in Oklahoma." *Chronicles of Oklahoma* 53 (Summer 1975): 179–203.

Hamilton, Henry. "The Spiro Mound." *Missouri Archaeologist* 14 (1952): 1–276.

Hartley, Marsden. "Red Man Ceremonials: An American Plea for American Esthetics." *Art and Archaeology* 9 (1920): 7–14.

———. "Tribal Esthetics." *Dial* 65 (1918): 399–401.

Hertzberg, Hazel. "Reaganomics on the Reservation." *New Republic*, November 22, 1983, pp. 15–17.

"History of the Self-Governance Demonstration Project." *First Nations Development Institute Business Alert* 8 (September/October): 9–11.

Hofman, Jack. "Land of Sun, Wind, and Grass." In *From Clovis to Comanchero: Archeological Overview of the Southern Great Plains*, ed. Jack Hofman et al., pp. 5–14. Fayetteville: Arkansas Archeological Survey, 1989.

———. "Protohistorical Culture History on the Southern Great Plains." In *From Clovis to Comanchero: Archeological Overview of the Southern Great Plains*, ed. Jack Hofman et al., pp. 91–100. Fayetteville: Arkansas Archeological Society, 1989.

Hoxie, Frederick. "End of the Savage; The Indian Policy in the United States Senate, 1880–1890." *Chronicles of Oklahoma* 55 (Summer 1977): 157–179.

Hundley, Norris, Jr. "The 'Winters' Decision and Indian Water Rights: A Mystery Re-examined." *Western Historical Quarterly* 13 (January 1982): 17–42.

Hunt, George, to Wilbur Nye. "The Annual Sun Dance of the Kiowa Indians." *Chronicles of Oklahoma* 12 (September 1934): 340–358.

Israel, Daniel. "The Re-emergence of Tribal Nationalism and Its Impact on Reservation Resource Development." *University of Colorado Law Review* 47 (1976): 617–626.

Jacobson, Cardell. "Internal Colonialism and Native Americans: Indian Labor in the United States from 1871 to World War II." *Social Science Quarterly* 65 (March 1984): 768–800.

John, Elizabeth A. Harper. "Nurturing the Peace: Spanish and Comanche Cooperation in the Early Nineteenth Century." *New Mexico Historical Review* 59 (1984): 346–366.

———. "Portrait of a Wichita Village, 1808." *Chronicles of Oklahoma* 60 (Winter 1982–1983): 412–437.

———. "The Taovayas Indians in Frontier Trade and Diplomacy, 1719–1768." *Chronicles of Oklahoma* 31 (Autumn 1953): 268–289.

———. "The Taovayas Indians in Frontier Trade and Diplomacy, 1769–1779." *Southwestern Historical Quarterly* 57 (October 1953): 181–201.

———. "The Taovayas Indians in Frontier Trade and Diplomacy, 1779–1835." *Panhandle-Plains Historical Review* 26 (1953): 40–72.

Johnson, Leroy, Jr., and Edward Jelks. "The Tawakoni-Yscani Village, 1760: A Study in Archaeological Site Identification." *Texas Journal of Science* 10 (December 1958): 405–422.

Johnson, N. B. "The National Congress of American Indians." *Chronicles of Oklahoma* 30 (Summer 1952): 140–148.

Jozhe, Benedict. "A Brief History of the Fort Sill Apache Tribe." *Chronicles of Oklahoma* 39 (Winter 1961–1962): 427–432.

Kavanaugh, Thomas. "Southern Plains Dance Tradition and Dynamics." In *Native American Dance: Ceremonies and Social Traditions*, ed. Charlotte Heth, pp. 105–123. Washington, D.C.: National Museum of the American Indian, Smithsonian Institution with Starwood Publishing, 1992.

Kelly, Lawrence. "The Indian Reorganization Act: Dream or Reality?" *Pacific Historical Review* 44 (1976): 291–312.

Kickingbird, Kirke. "The American Indian Policy Review Commission: A Prospect for Future Change in Federal Indian Policy." *American Indian Law Review* 3 (1975): 243–253.

Leonhardy, Frank. "Domebo: A Paleo-Indian Mammoth Kill Site in the Prairie Plains." *Contributions of the Museum of the Great Plains* no. 1 (Lawton, Okla.: 1966): 1–43.

Levine, Francis. "Economic Perspectives on the Comanchero Trade." In *Farmers, Hunters, and Colonists: Interaction between the Southwest and the Southern Plains*, ed. Katherine Spielmann, pp. 155–169. Tucson: University of Arizona Press, 1991.

McAlister, Gilbert. "Kiowa-Apache Social Organization." In *Social Anthropology of North American Tribes*, ed. F. Eggans, pp. 99–172. Chicago: University of Chicago Press, 1955.

Meredith, Howard. "Native Response: Rural Indian People in Oklahoma, 1900–1939." In *Rural Oklahoma*, ed. Donald Green, pp. 74–83. Oklahoma City: Oklahoma Historical Society, 1977.

Meredith, Howard, and Vynola Newkumet. "Melford Williams: Caddo Leadership Patterns in the Twentieth Century." *Journal of the West* 23 (July 1984): 64–69.

Momaday, N. Scott. "Native American Attitudes to the Environment." In *Seeing with a Native Eye: Essays on Native American Religion*, ed. Walter Capps, pp. 79–85. New York: Harper and Row, 1976.

Monahan, Forrest D. "Kiowa-Comanche Reservation in the 1890s." *Chronicles of Oklahoma* 45 (Winter 1967–1968): 451–463.

Mooney, James. "Passing of the Delaware Nation." *Proceedings of the Mississippi Valley Historical Association*, ed. B. F. Shambaugh, pp. 329–340. Cedar Rapids, Iowa: Torch Press, 1911.

Moore, John. "The Enduring Reservation of Oklahoma." *State and Reservation: New Perspectives on Federal Indian Policy*, ed. George Castille and Robert Bee, pp. 92–109. Tucson: University of Arizona Press, 1992.

Neighbours, Kenneth. "Robert S. Neighbors and the Founding of Texas Indian Reservations." *West Texas Historical Association Year Book* 31 (October 1955): 65–74.

Nelson, Michael, and Bradley Brooke. "The Winters Doctrine: Seventy Years of Application of 'Reserved' Water Rights to Indian Reservations." *Arid Lands Resource Information Paper* no. 9. Tucson: Center for Arid Land Studies, University of Arizona, 1977.

Opler, Morris, and Harry Hoijer. "The Raid and War-Path Language of the Chiricahua Apache." *American Anthropologist* 42 (October–December 1940): 617–634.

Parker, Patricia L. "Traditional Cultural Properties." *Cultural Resources Management* 16 (1993): 1–5.

Philip, Kenneth. "Termination: A Legacy of the Indian New Deal." *Western Historical Quarterly* 14 (April 1983): 165–180.

Prucha, Francis Paul. "American Indian Policy in the Twentieth Century." *Western Historical Quarterly* 15 (January 1984): 5–18.

"Revival for a Rare Art." *Life International*, March 16, 1959.

Rood, David. "Wichita Texts." In *Caddoan Texts*, ed. Douglas Parks, Native American Texts Series 2 (1977): 91–129.

Smith, Ralph. "Apache Plunder Trails Southward, 1831–1840." *New Mexico Historical Review* 37 (January 1972): 20–42.

———. "The Comanche Bridge between Oklahoma and Mexico, 1842–1844." *Chronicles of Oklahoma* 34 (Spring 1961): 54–69.

———. "The Tawehash in French, Spanish, English, and American Imperial Affairs." *West Texas Historical Association Yearbook* 28 (October 1952): 18–49.

Speth, John. "Some Unexplored Aspects of Mutualistic Plains-Pueblo Food Exchange." In *Farmers, Hunters, and Colonists: Interaction between the Southwest and the Southern Plains,* ed. Katherine Spielmann pp. 18–35. Tucson: University of Arizona Press, 1991.

Spielmann, Katherine. "Coercion or Cooperation? Plains-Pueblo Interaction in the Protohistoric Period." In *Farmers, Hunters, and Colonists: Interaction between the Southwest and the Southern Plains,* ed. Katherine Spielmann, pp. 36–50. Tucson: University of Arizona Press, 1991.

Spier, Leslie. "Wichita and Caddo Relationship Terms." *American Anthropologist* 26 (April–June 1924): 258–263.

Stahl, Robert. "Joe True: Convergent Needs and Assumed Identity." In *Being and Becoming Indian: Biographical Studies of North American Frontiers,* ed. James Clifton, pp. 276–289. Chicago: Dorsey Press, 1989.

Stuart, Paul H. "Financing Self-Determination: Federal Indian Expenditures, 1975–1988." *American Indian Culture and Research Journal* 14 (1990): 1–18.

Thoburn, Joseph. "The Prehistoric Cultures of Oklahoma." In *Archaeology of the Arkansas River Valley,* ed. Warren Moorehead et al. New Haven, Conn.: Yale University Press, 1931.

Voegelin, Erminie. "Kiowa-Crow Mythological Affiliations." *American Anthropologist* 35 (1933): 470–474.

Watt, Frank. "The Waco Indian Village and Its People." *Central Texas Archeologist* 9 (1968): 3–48.

Wedel, Mildred. "The Wichita Indians in the Arkansas River Basin." In *Plains Indian Studies: A Collection of Essays in Honor of John C. Ewers and Waldo R. Wedel,* ed. Douglas Ubelaker and Herman Viola, pp. 118–134. Washington, D.C.: Smithsonian Institution Press, 1982.

Wedel, Waldo. "Notes on Plains-Southwestern Contacts in the Light of Archeology." In *For the Dean: Essays in Anthropology,* ed. Erik Reed and Dale King, pp. 99–116. 1950.

———. "Further Notes on Puebloan–Central Plains Contacts in Light of Archaeology. "In *Pathways to Plains Prehistory: Anthropological Perspectives of Plains Natives and Their Pasts,* ed. Don Wyckoff and Jack Hofman, pp. 145–152. Oklahoma Anthropological Society *Memoir* 3 (1982).

Whiteman, Henrietta. "White Buffalo Woman." In *The American Indian and the Problem of History,* ed. Calvin Martin, pp. 162–170. New York: Oxford University Press, 1987.

Wilkinson, Charles, and Eric Biggs. "The Evolution of the Termination Policy." *American Indian Law Review* 5 (1980): 139–194.

Wyckoff, Don, and Timothy Baugh. "Early Historic Hasinai Elites: A Model for the Material of Governing Elites." *Mid-Continent Journal of Archeology* 6 (1980): 225–288.

DISSERTATIONS

Brant, Charles. "The Kiowa Apache Indians: A Study in Ethnology and Acculturation." Ph.D. dissertation, Cornell University, 1951.

Buller, Galen M. "Comanche Oral Narratives." Ph.D. dissertation, University of Nebraska, 1977.

Elam, Earl. "The History of the Wichita Confederacy to 1868." Ph.D. dissertation, Texas Tech University, 1971.

Holder, Preston. "The Role of Caddoan Horticulturists in the Cultural History of the Great Plains." Ph.D. dissertation, Columbia University, 1951.

Rood, David. "Wichita Grammar: A Generative Semantic Sketch." Ph.D. dissertation, University of California, Berkeley, 1969.

Trager, Edith. "The Kiowa Language: A Grammatical Study." Ph.D. dissertation, University of Pennsylvania, 1960.

Turcheneske, John Anthony. "The Apache Prisoners of War at Fort Sill, 1894–1914." Ph.D. dissertation, University of New Mexico, 1978.

INDEX

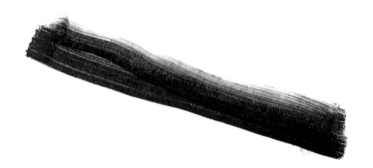

WITHDRAWN